that he stands high.
His pupils must
share in his own
eager search after
lovely harmonies and
melodies, and in his
success in finding
them. Personally, also,
he must be inspiring.
I wish him all
success in his under-
takings in the fields
of composition and
teaching.

Mrs. H. H. A. Beach

Detroit Monographs in Musicology/Studies in Music, No. 13

Editor
J. Bunker Clark
University of Kansas

Amy M. Beach

THE REMARKABLE MRS. BEACH, AMERICAN COMPOSER

A Biographical Account Based on Her Diaries, Letters,
Newspaper Clippings, and Personal Reminiscences

by

WALTER S. JENKINS

edited by

JOHN H. BARON

HARMONIE PARK PRESS   •   MICHIGAN   •   1994

Front endsheets:
Letter from Mrs. Beach to Walter Jenkins, 1935

Back endsheets:
Letter from Mrs. Beach to Walter Jenkins, 1937

Frontispiece:
Portrait of Mrs. Beach, ca. 1910
Courtesy Howard-Tilton Memorial Library, Tulane University

Printed and bound in the United States of America
Published by
Harmonie Park Press
23630 Pinewood
Warren, Michigan 48091

Editor, J. Bunker Clark
Book design, Elaine J. Gorzelski
Typographer, Colleen McRorie

Library of Congress Cataloging-in-Publication Data

Jenkins, Walter S., 1909-1990.
     The remarkable Mrs. Beach, American composer : a biographical
account based on her diaries, letters, newspaper clippings, and
personal reminiscences / by Walter S. Jenkins ; edited by John H.
Baron.
         p.   cm. — (Detroit monographs in musicology/Studies in music
; 13)
   Discography:
   Includes bibliographical references (p.) and indexes.
   ISBN 0-89990-069-0
    1. Beach, H. H. A., Mrs., 1867-1944.   2. Women composers—United
States—Biography.   I. Baron, John H.   II. Title.   III. Series.
ML410.B36J46   1994
780'.92—dc20
   [B]   94-21509

to

Ruth Jenkins, Judy and Joan

Contents

Illustrations   ix

Prologue: Walter S. Jenkins   xi

Preface   xiii

Acknowledgements   xv

Part 1: Amy Marcy Cheney, 1867-85

    Prelude   3
    Childhood   5
    Beginning of a Career in Music (1883-85) 7
    Romance (1885)   14

Part 2: Mrs. H. H. A. Beach, 1885-1911

    No. 28 Commonwealth Avenue (1885-90)   19
    Mass in E-Flat (1890-92)   23
    Chicago Columbian Exposition (1893-95)   30
    Gaelic Symphony (1896-99)   37
    Piano Concerto (1900-04)   48
    Piano Quintet (1905-09)   55
    The Deaths of Dr. Beach and Mrs. Cheney (1910-11) 66

Part 3: Amy Beach as Musician of the World, 1911-36

    First European Trip (1911-14)   71
    Return to America: The War Years (1914-21) 77
    MacDowell Colony (1921-26)   84

Second European Tour (1926-27) 89
Back in America (1927-28) 91
Third European Tour (1928-29) 95
Illness and Recovery (1929-30) 97
New York City as Winter Home (1930-31) 100
Canticle of the Sun (1931-32) 107
Cabildo (1932) 113
The Busy 1930s and the Beach Routine (1933-36) 118

Part 4: Mrs. Beach the Philanthropist, 1936-44

England and Illness (1936) 133
The Waning Years (1937-40) 136
The Last Years (1940-44) 149
Some Recollections of Mrs. H. H. A. Beach 169

Appendix

Analysis of the *Gaelic Symphony* by the Composer 173

Bibliography

Other Writings on Mrs. H. H. A. Beach 179
Recent Publications on Mrs. H. H. A. Beach 181
Recent Editions 182
Discography 183

Indices

Works by Mrs. Beach Cited in This Biography 189
Titles by Opus Number 195
Names, Places, and Things 199

Illustrations

Amy Cheney Beach, ca. 1890   *frontispiece*

Walter S. Jenkins, 1961   xii

Charles A. Cheney, Amy's father   4

Clara Imogene Marcy Cheney, Amy's mother   4

Amy Cheney as a child   6

Amy Cheney as teenager   11

Program of recital by Amy Cheney at Wellesley College   11

Dr. H. H. A. Beach   15

Residence of Dr. and Mrs. H. H. A. Beach   20

Mrs. H. H. A. Beach, probably 1890s   24

Program cover for the concert by the Handel and Haydn Society of Boston   27

Program of the premiere of Mrs. Beach's Mass   28

Mrs. Beach at the Steinway, outdoor concert at the Panama-California International Exposition   32

Excerpt from Mrs. Beach's *Gaelic Symphony*, signed by "Amy"   42

Mrs. H. H. A. Beach with friends, ca. 1912   73

Beach Club of Hillsboro, N.H., with the composer, late 1930s   110

Mrs. Beach, a photo owned by Ruth Shaffner, ca. 1935   134

Mable Pierce, Harriet Oldfield (standing), Mrs. Beach (sitting), Lillian Buxbaum, photographed by Mr. Bachrach in Centerville, 1938   143

Sculpture of Mrs. MacDowell by Bashka Paeff   148

Backside of postcard of Paeff's sculpture of Mrs. MacDowell, addressed to Jenkins and signed by Paeff   148

Mrs. Beach, Cape Cod, ca. 1938   152

Prologue: Walter S. Jenkins

Walter S. Jenkins was born in Manchester, New Hampshire in 1909 and graduated from the University of New Hampshire in 1931.[1] He received a master's degree from Harvard, and continued studies in New York City during the mid-1930s. He was music director of Bennett Junior College in Millbrook, New York, and at the Castleton, Vermont, Normal School. For a short time he was college organist at Brown University. In Claremont, New Hampshire, he organized the Claremont Community Orchestra and Chorus and, in 1939, conducted there the first performance outside New York City of Aaron Copland's opera *The Second Hurricane*. During World War II, from 1942 to 1945, he was in the United States Army. In 1946 he married Ruth Philbrick and subsequently had two daughters, Judy and Joan.

From 1946 to 1974 Jenkins was associate professor of music at Newcomb College of Tulane University, where he taught primarily music theory and composition. During this time he was active in the American Guild of Organists, served as music director and organist of several important churches in the New Orleans area, and was program annotator for the New Orleans Symphony. He was professor emeritus from 1974 until his death in 1990.

Jenkins's compositions include a Prelude and Passacaglia for orchestra, which was premiered by the New Orleans Symphony in 1947 with the composer as conductor, and *Ash Wednesday*, a cantata commissioned by the Louisiana State University Contemporary Music Festival in 1950. During the 1930s Jenkins conducted the National Symphony of Washington, D.C., in his *Four Pieces for Orchestra* (the concert was in Manchester, New Hampshire). He also composed chamber works such as Quintet for Clarinet and Strings (1936), *Violin Sonatina for Doris and Peter Hansen* (1962), *Canons for Violin and Viola* (1962), and Suite for French Horn and Oboe (1950). In addition he wrote songs, church music, and solo piano pieces.

---

[1] Biographical information on Jenkins has been kindly supplied by Ruth Jenkins. Some of it appeared in Jenkins's obituary in the *New Orleans Times-Picayune*, 5 August 1990, section B, p. 9, written by John Pope.

According to his own accounts, Jenkins first met Mrs. Beach in the 1930s when he first came to the MacDowell Colony as a composer. No doubt she was attracted by his youth, enthusiasm, charm, and flaming red hair, while he was awed by the famous lady whose birth-state they proudly shared. Over the next few years Jenkins was often with Mrs. Beach and asked her many questions about herself and her compositions. After Mrs. Beach's death at the end of 1944, Jenkins continued to frequent the Colony and to visit Mrs. MacDowell. Since he spent most summers in New Hampshire, he often went over to the Colony and worked on his biography in its archives before the Beach materials there were dispersed. He also kept close ties to the Beach Archive at the University of New Hampshire, where all his Beach papers have been deposited.

Photo courtesy of Jenkins/Beach Collection

Walter S. Jenkins, 1961

Preface

When Walter S. Jenkins met Mrs. H. H. A. Beach at the MacDowell Colony in 1935, he was immediately fascinated by the great lady, who along with Marian (Mrs. Edward) MacDowell was the dominant personality at the Colony. Over the next nine years he met her not only at the Colony but also in New York, and during this time he continually questioned her about her life and attitudes. When she died at the end of 1944, Walter took it upon himself to be her definitive biographer. Mrs. Beach's principal heir, Mrs. Lillian Buxbaum, entrusted him with Mrs. Beach's diaries, letters she had received from friends and associates, newspaper reviews she had collected of her concerts and compositions, and miscellaneous documents. Ruth Shaffner, Mrs. Beach's close confident during the 1930s and 1940s, sent him her vast collection of letters the composer had written to her. During the ensuing years he researched every aspect of her life, including family histories and the opinions and recollections of those who knew her. A 500-page book was completed by the mid-1960s, but it was not published owing to a number of reasons. Besides some faults in the manuscript, Mrs. Beach was a personality who was not of interest to any but a small coterie of musicologists at the time. She was a woman, she was American, and she was a romantic, and until the late 1970s those were ample grounds to dismiss her.

Walter Jenkins's dream of a fitting biography of Mrs. Beach, whose genius and generosity he unhesitatingly admired, was unfulfilled at the time of his death in 1990. But times have changed, and it seems now that such a book is of great interest to an ever widening audience of Beach admirers. Today she is regarded as one of the towering figures in American musical history. She was also a key player in the great improvement in the position of professional women in American arts. Her struggles for American women and American musicians need to be told to today's generation, which often forgets the terrible conditions under which American composers and American women composers in particular had to work just a few decades ago.

During the two decades that Walter and I were colleagues at Tulane University, I never saw his manuscript or the Beach materials at his home, though I knew that he was preparing something significant about Mrs. Beach. When I was entrusted with the manuscript with the aim of publishing it, I realized some of the many difficulties which faced Walter and which also faced a publisher. Walter was a fine musician and a sensitive gentleman, but he was not trained as a musicologist or as a writer. The manuscript needed to be revised and made accessible to the non-specialist as well as musical historian. There are many details in the manuscript which seem of minor importance in themselves and have been eliminated or relegated to footnotes; where relevant, I have summarized them. Walter's original manuscript, however, is available to scholars at the University of New Hampshire so that these details can be checked. I have also corrected some dates and rearranged some chronological data into topically related paragraphs. His appendices, which include family trees, wills, ASCAP receipts, lists of compositions, and other documents, have been left out here. On the other hand, Walter knew Mrs. Beach and considered it his duty to publish the facts of her life as he gleaned them from his various sources. Much of what he wrote had to be saved to reflect his intentions and personal knowledge of Mrs. Beach. Whenever Walter's personal recollections enter into the manuscript, these are indicated with the first person without quotation marks.

No attempt has been made to analyze any compositions by Mrs. Beach or to evaluate her position in the history of American or world music. Others started to do so already in Mrs. Beach's lifetime, and it will be the task of future scholars to continue to do so. This book, however, is the documentary biography of a great woman. I, for one, am indebted to Walter Jenkins for telling the story of her life, and I am honored to help him make that story available to others.

John H. Baron

Schawe Professor of Music
Newcomb College
Tulane University
New Orleans
January 1994

Acknowledgements

This book has been published with the generous assistance of the Newcomb College Foundation and the Tulane University Faculty of Liberal Arts and Sciences. We appreciate also the help of many librarians and archives, such as Wilbur Meneray (Tulane University Archives), Wayne D. Shirley (Library of Congress), the library of the University of New Hampshire, and the Public Library of Providence, Rhode Island. Special thanks are due to Mrs. Walter Jenkins, who has continually provided insight into her husband's work and has made all his materials available to this editor. Professor J. Bunker Clark's careful reading and criticism of the manuscript has been invaluable in bringing this biography to fruition.

Finally, Walter Jenkins owed a great debt to the many friends and acquaintances of Mrs. Beach who spoke to him, corresponded with him, and sent him materials. Their names appear frequently in the course of the biography.

Part 1: Amy Marcy Cheney, 1867-85

Prelude

Amy Marcy Cheney was born in Henniker in the Contoocook River Valley, New Hampshire, on Thursday, 5 September 1867, during an interlude of Indian summer. The climate of that early autumn day presaged much of Amy's life, pleasantly filled with the joys of accomplishment that ultimately carried her name to the far corners of the earth.

Amy was a product of her family and environment, both of which helped shape her character and career. Amy's parents, Charles Abbott Cheney (26 August 1844-26 July 1895) and Clara Imogene Marcy (4 May 1846-18 February 1911), were both descendants of hearty pioneer stock and had many distinguished relatives. Charles Cheney's father Moses Cheney, Jr. (Amy's paternal grandfather) was descended from John and Mary Cheney, who were in Newberry, Massachusetts, as early as 1635. Charles's mother Rebecca Rundlett (Amy's paternal grandmother) was a direct descendant of General Henry Dearborn, who marched all night from Exeter, New Hampshire, to fight for the colonists at the Battle of Bunker Hill the next day. He was Secretary of War during Thomas Jefferson's entire eight-year administration, and later United States Minister to Portugal. Henry himself was descended from Godfrey Dearborn, a native of Exeter, England, who helped found Exeter, New Hampshire, in 1639.

Amy's mother Clara, in turn, was a direct descendant of John Marcy, one of the thirteen original settlers of Woodstock, Connecticut, who went there from Roxbury, Massachusetts, in 1686. Among his descendants were Captain Nathaniel Marcy, who fought in the Revolution, and William Learned Marcy (born 1786 in Hillsboro, New Hampshire), who was Governor of New York, Secretary of War under President Polk, and Secretary of State under President Pierce.

Amy's immediate forebears on her father's side were in the paper business. Moses Cheney, Sr. (born 31 January 1793, in Thornton, New Hampshire) went to work in his uncle John Pattee's paper mills and later had his own mills, which flourished. Luther Roby, a Concord printer, printed a large family Bible on paper made by Cheney and his brother-in-law Abraham Morrison, which is known as the "Cheney Bible." Amy owned a copy of this Bible printed on her great-grandfather's paper.

**Charles A. Cheney,
Amy Beach's father**

**Clara Imogene Marcy Cheney,
Amy Beach's mother**

Photos courtesy of Special Collections,
University of New Hampshire Library

Moses Cheney, Jr., Amy's grandfather, moved to Henniker in 1864 and set up a paper manufacturing mill with his only son, Charles, Amy's father. Charles, who had a strong academic background at Phillips Academy in Exeter, was more motivated to business than college. When he married Clara, Amy's mother, in 1866, he moved with her near to the mill so that he could be on top of his duties as personnel manager. So enthusiastic was he with the potentialities of his father's business that in the months before the birth of his first and only child he was convincing himself that one day his first-born would quite naturally join the partnership he and his father had so recently established. Although Charles was somewhat disappointed that the child was a girl, Moses was thrilled and exhibited steadfast devotion toward Amy to the end of his life.

With Amy's heritage of such distinguished ancestors, there is little wonder that she demonstrated at an early age a rare ability to achieve success on her own. That ultimately she became a musician of the highest caliber and a composer of great distinction was no surprise. These were the years when many women in America and abroad were struggling for recognition of their accomplishments in many fields, and the hard struggle for professional equality made some women determined to succeed. Amy's success might be attributed not alone to purely musical assets, of which she possessed a great many, but also to her inherited Yankee will power and her exposure to the battles for women's rights in her own day. She possessed an inherent strength of character, and her indomitable will impelled her to be unswervingly faithful and devoted to all her tasks. With consummate integrity she lived up to the most noble personal and professional standards without ever seeking an easy way to fame and fortune, though sharing both in abundance.

Although she inherited a love for reading and collecting books and an ease with foreign languages from her father, Amy's specific propensity for music and her musical talent came largely from the Marcy side of her family. In later life she herself often recounted her grandfather Chester Marcy's fine clarinet playing and the unusually high soprano voice of her mother's mother, Amy Waterman. Her aunt, Mrs. L. H. Clement ("Auntie Franc"), possessed a much-admired contralto voice, while her own mother sang and played the piano with enough skill and refinement that she dared to appear occasionally in concerts. Amy also had some talent in art which, like music, came to her from the Marcys. Auntie Franc's daughter Ethel Clement inherited less the musical than the artistic talents of the Marcy family and went on to a distinguished career in art in America and in Paris.

Childhood

As a child Amy continually surprised her family and friends by her remarkable memory. Her bright, inquisitive nature was constantly alert for new information, which she rarely forgot. She knew the alphabet at seventeen months, and a few weeks later started repeating by memory nursery rhymes she had heard. By the time she was three, she could read her favorite story, Charles Dickens's *A Child's Dream of a Star*. The next year she appeared regularly at Sunday School concerts and recited psalms or poems, one of the latter lasting thirteen minutes.

When she applied this faculty to music, she learned rapidly the songs and tunes sung in her home. By the time she was one, she had memorized forty separate tunes and could sing them flawlessly. She had absolute pitch, and was able to improvise and sing an alto part to a given soprano melody before she was two years old. As reported years later,

> When two years old she was taken to a Boston photographer for a sitting, and when all was ready for the picture she suddenly paralyzed her audience by singing at the top of her voice "See the Conquering Hero Comes." The artist who had been practicing (as one of the chorus of the first Peace Jubilee) the celebrated chorus of Handel, exclaimed, "Why, that baby is really singing it. That is more wonderful than anything we shall see at the Jubilee." The picture was a success.[1]

Amy's mother encouraged her to relate melodies to the colors blue, pink, or purple, but before long Amy had a wider range of colors, which she associated with certain major keys. Thus C was white, F-sharp black, E yellow, G red, A green, A-flat blue, D-flat

---

[1] *San Francisco Dramatic Review*, 10 December 1905.

Amy Cheney as a child

violet or purple, and E-flat pink.   Until the end of her life she associated these colors with those keys.   She preferred the major tonalities since "Music in the minor keys made her sad and disconsolate."[2]   She was very sensitive to all sounds, even the sound of laughter or that of rain drops on the window ("she would beg her mother to 'wipe the tear'" off the window).

Beginning of a Career in Music (1883-85)

The Cheney family moved to Chelsea, a suburb of Boston, about 1871, and when she was six, Amy started piano lessons from her mother.[3]   Her progress must have been exceptional, for the following year, when she was seven, she "rendered a piano solo [at the Unitarian church] with a style and finish of execution worthy of a professional," even though her feet could not yet reach the pedals, and shortly afterwards played Chopin's Waltz in E-flat, op. 18, at a private soirée in Boston.[4]   Amy's exceptional ability on the piano was soon noted by local friends of the family and by distinguished visitors.   Louis Elson remembered one occasion when "the young miss (at a private gathering) transpose[d] a Bach fugue . . . by memory . . . at about the age of fourteen."[5]   The big debut, however, came on Wednesday evening, 24 October 1883, at 7:45.   Amy made her first formal public appearance by playing in Mr. A. P. Peck's Anniversary Concert at the Boston Music Hall. A grand orchestra was conducted by Mr. Adolf Neundorff, who volunteered his services. Soloists included Miss Clara Louise Kellogg (soprano), Miss Hope Glenn (contralto), Mr. Jules Jordan (tenor), Mr. Timothie Adamowski (violinist), Mr. Howard M. Dow (accompanist), and Miss Amy Marcy Cheney (pupil of Carl Baermann.[6])   Seated at the Chickering, Amy performed the Moscheles G-minor Concerto with the orchestra and Chopin's Rondo in E-flat by herself.   The ensuing reviews, in ten Boston newspapers and one New York paper, made it clear that the highlight of the evening's entertainment was the debut of Amy Cheney.   She was:

> a surprise and a delight.   A surprise that a young girl of sixteen should
> make her debut as a pianist in a grand concerto with orchestra, and
> a delight to find in that young girl a performer so far developed that

---

[2] Interview of Mrs. Beach by George Y. Loveridge, *Providence Journal*, 4 December 1937, 5.

[3] Not in Jenkins's account.   Cf. Adrienne Fried Block, "Beach," in *The New Grove Dictionary of American Music* (1986), 1:164.

[4] February 1875, from Jenkins papers.

[5] Louis C. Elson, "Mrs. Beach, American Composer," *Musician*, July 1905, 267.

[6] According to Block, Amy's first piano teacher was her mother, then Ernest Perabo, and finally Baermann.

she could hardly have done much more or much better had the figure of her years been written backward. She is plainly a pianist to the manner born and bred. Her technique is facile, even and brilliant. But fine as her technical qualities are, it is the correctness and precocity of her musical understanding that must, in the end, excite admiration. Her playing is wholly without affectation. A special charm was added to her performance by the freshness, the artless simplicity, and the thorough grasp of the composer's meaning that signalized them. It was not a mere imitative talent which was displayed; the nuances were given with such delicate finish, such attention to the ensemble, that it was evident that the artist was speaking of herself, and not merely reproducing the teacher's thought. Her playing gave evidence of scholarly comprehension and judicious discernment. Miss Cheney is evidently either a great talent, or a great genius; it is too early to declare which. . . . To have heard her without seeing her would have given the auditor no suggestion of her youth.[7]

The *New York Tribune* (October 1883) added:

She plays with the intelligence of a master, but her most remarkable and extraordinary gifts, such as "natural pitch" and her powers in composition, are really known only to her teachers, who prophesy for her a great future.

Amy's obvious success invoked fear in Mrs. Cheney lest her daughter incur the often destructive intrusions and distractions that come with fame. From this day in 1883 and until her marriage two years later, Mother Cheney held the reins of Amy's destiny with firm hands. From summer 1883 to January 1884 Amy spent hours perfecting her repertory for forthcoming solo recitals. The first such recital of the new year was an afternoon affair on January 9, and in accordance with long-standing custom the featured soloist was "accompanied by" (alternated with) Mrs. George Henschel (wife of the distinguished conductor) and Mr. Charles Martin Loeffler of the Boston Symphony Orchestra (who later became a distinguished composer). The program, in Chickering Hall, opened with the seventeenth Prelude and Fugue from one of the *Well-Tempered Clavier* by Bach, followed by Mendelssohn's Phantasie in F-sharp minor, op. 28. After some songs sung by Mrs. Henschel, Amy played Henselt's three Etudes, op. 5, Chopin's Nocturne in D-flat, op. 27, and Liszt's *Le Rossignol*. After another set of songs, Amy and Loeffler performed Beethoven's violin sonata, op. 12, no. 3. The reviews were just as ecstatic as after the symphony concert; the *Boston Advertiser* (10 January 1884) reported:

But much as her technique pleases, it is her musical sense and sentiment which charm; for these are the qualities which, however much teaching

---

[7] *Boston Daily Advertiser*, 25 October 1883.

may develop and refine them, must be innate and individual. The almost imperceptible poising over a note, and the almost imperceptible pausing upon it; the caressing touch in a melodious phrase, or the airy turn of an ornament; the sharpness or the softness of a trill; the justness of taste which keeps feeling from crossing the narrow line into exaggeration or pathos—these are the characteristics which, in their times and places, we recognize in Miss Cheney. . . .

And from the *Boston Transcript* (10 January 1884):

There is a certain artistic wisdom in all she does that is far beyond her years. Her musical feeling, although more cultivated and more sure in its instincts than that of most young girls, is still wholly of the sort that is natural in a young girl of her age; it has preserved its whole innocence, purity and candor; the bloom is still on it. Here lies her greatest charm. Her playing of Henselt, for instance, is simply delightful.

The program of January 9 was repeated at a concert in the Andover (Massachusetts) Town Hall on Tuesday, 19 February 1884, at 2:45 p.m., and at the Bradford Academy the following day. Since Mrs. Henschel did not assist Amy and Loeffler on these two occasions, Amy added a Berceuse by Fauré and a Canzonetta by Benjamin Godard to fill out the program. The *Boston Beacon* reviewed these events by noting:

Miss Cheney, the popular young pianist, gave recitals recently at Andover and Bradford, which were attended by large and fashionable audiences. This gifted little lady possesses real genius, and with it all rare modesty and grace which secure her an increased circle of friends and admirers wherever she appears.

Amy returned to Chickering Hall for a second recital on Wednesday, March 19, at 8 p.m. She was "assisted" by Miss Gertrude Franklin (soprano, accompanied by Leon Keach), and Mr. Wulf Fries (cellist). Her program consisted of an F-minor Suite by Handel, Beethoven's Six Variations, op. 34, an F-minor Sonata by Scarlatti, Rubinstein's Barcarolle in G minor, Chopin's Bolero, op. 19, a *Wiegenlied* by Henselt, and Liszt's *Valse impromptu*. Fries joined her for the Beethoven Sonata, op. 19, for violoncello and piano. Once again the newspapers extolled the precocious talent of the teenage girl, and they recognized that she played

not with the perfection of the best maturity, of course, but with a fulness and a truth which many mature players never reach in more than one or two of their pieces.[8]

---

[8] *Boston Advertiser*, 20 March 1884.

The success of Amy's appearance at Mr. Peck's Anniversary Concert only six months earlier led Peck to invite her to perform at his annual concert on Wednesday night, April 23, in the prestigious Boston Music Hall. Amy's contribution was Weber's *Polacca brilliante*, op. 72, in the von Bülow edition, on the first half of the program, and on the second half Rubinstein's Romance, op. 44, and *Valse-Caprice* in E-flat. This time she was "assisted" by a number of star singers (Marcella Sembrich[9] and S. Salchi of the Henry E. Abbey Italian Opera Company, among others), Signor Mattoli (violoncello), and the Beethoven Club (a string sextet). Although the press showed great respect for the singers, it did not ignore Miss Cheney. Nora Perry of the *Boston Post* (24 April 1884) wrote:

> I should not neglect to mention the child prodigy, Miss Cheney, who has been giving such extraordinary pianoforte performances here. In her short dress, with her long hair braided, she is a pretty, innocent sight—a girl such as one might meet any day on the Common going to school. But she begins to play: you shut your eyes for a moment and listen to the wonderful touch. You look again. Yes, it is a child who is sitting there, but it is a child of genius, such as Liszt was and Mendelssohn. Study, practice, long industry may do much, it has done much with this girl, but without the supreme gift of genius it would not have produced such results. What Miss Cheney will achieve as she grows older it is idle to prophesy, but from this beginning there should be a maturity of powers that would place her among the great geniuses of the world.

Although the season already had been a busy one for the young pianist, there was still one more concert. For her sixth and final concert of her first season as a professional performer, Amy gave a recital at the School of Music of Wellesley College, then directed by Charles H. Morse.[10] She performed pieces that had appeared on her earlier recitals by Handel, Beethoven, Scarlatti, Henselt, Chopin, Liszt, Rubinstein, and Weber. She was assisted by Morse accompanying Miss Clara E. Munger (soprano) of the Wellesley College music faculty.

The months following Amy's first concert season were filled mainly with work, for she was not one to rest after strenuous activity if she knew more was soon expected of her. She studied pieces to be added to her 1885 program, including two well-known piano concertos: that of Chopin in F minor and Mendelssohn in D minor. Meanwhile, in late summer or early fall 1884, while visiting her piano teacher Carl Baermann in his home

---

[9] See below for the warm friendship between Amy and Madam Sembrich, which began at this time.

[10] Morse later became head of the Music Department at Dartmouth College. Frank Morse, his brother, was a long-established vocal teacher in Boston. The brothers owned adjoining summer homes in New Boston, New Hampshire, overlooking the Weare Hills, and several miles from the summer home of Benjamin Lang (1837-1909), another musical Boston family whose daughter, Margaret Ruthven Lang (1867-1972), was a composer and colleague of Mrs. Beach. The Langs' property, on the banks of the Piscatisquog River, reached by a covered wooden bridge, lay some twenty miles from the old Cheney home in Henniker. See also the articles on these two Langs in *The New Grove Dictionary of American Music* (1986).

Homer & Co.   *53 Temple Place, Boston.*

**Amy Cheney as teenager,
about the time of her Boston debut**

**Program of recital by Amy Cheney at
Wellesley College, 12 May 1884**

"MUSIC IS WELL SAID TO BE THE SPEECH OF ANGELS." — *Carlyle.*

Wellesley College
✳ SCHOOL·OF·MUSIC ✳
Monday Evening, May 12th, 1884.

Piano Recital
(139th Concert. 9th Series.)

BY

MISS AMY MARCY CHENEY.

ASSISTED BY

MISS CLARA E. MUNGER, SOPRANO.

CHARLES H. MORSE, Professor of Music.

↝ PROGRAM ↝

1. SUITE — in F minor . . . . *Händel.*
   (Prelude — Fugue — Allemande — Courante — Gigue.)

2. SIX VARIATIONS. Op. 34 . . . . . . *Beethoven.*

3. SONATE — in F minor . . . . *Scarlatti.*

4. ARIA — Regnava nel silenzio (" Lucia ") . . . *Donizetti.*

5. *a.* ETUDE — in A major. Op. 5 . . . . . *Henselt.*
   b. NOCTURNE. Op. 27–2 . . . . . . *Chopin.*
   c. VALSE IMPROMPTU . . . . . . *Liszt.*

6. SONGS — *a.* Ich hatte einst ein schönes Vaterland . . *Lassen.*
   b. Du bist wie eine Blume . . . . *Rubinstein.*
   c. Er der Herrlichste von Allen . . . . *Schumann.*

7. *a.* BARCAROLLE — in G minor . . . . . *Rubinstein.*
   b. POLACCA BRILLANTE — Op. 72 (Bülow Edition) . *Weber.*

in Cambridge, Amy met and performed for William Mason, a member of a large and distinguished musical family. Mason recounts that he

> met at [Baermann's] house Miss Cheney whom I heard play and who certainly impressed me as being a young lady of remarkable talent and attainments. She has a strong, firm and at the same time elastic touch which evinces strength of character and at the same time she plays "musikalisch" as the Germans express it.[11]

It seems that earlier Mrs. Cheney had taken Amy to see Dr. Henry Harris Aubrey Beach of Boston, since the young girl had sustained a hand injury. Dr. Beach took an interest in Amy right away, and sent to his friend Mason both a copy of a review of one of her concerts and some composition of hers. Mason hesitatingly found that the composition "I think evinces talent."

The year 1885 saw five major performances, beginning with a pair of afternoon concerts in Andover (February 11) and Bradford (February 26). She performed the Prelude and Fugue no. 8 from one of the *Well-Tempered Clavier* by Bach, Beethoven's Variations, op. 34, a gigue by Graun, three études by her teacher Baermann, Rubinstein's *Valse-Caprice*, and Rheinberger's Toccata, op. 104. She was assisted by the violinist Leopold Lichtenberg in Beethoven's Romance in G, Joachim's arrangements of a Brahms *Hungarian Dance*, and Rubinstein's Sonata in A minor. Amy ended this season with another recital, held in the Brookline Lower Town Hall on Saturday afternoon, May 16. For the first time she played an entire recital without any "assistants." She performed music by Chopin, Rheinberger, Liszt, and Rubinstein from her earlier programs, to which she added another Bach Prelude and Fugue from one of the *Well-Tempered Clavier* (no. 13 in G major), Schumann's *Kreisleriana*, and a different group of études by Baermann.

The highlight of the 1885 season, however, was Amy's two appearances with major orchestras. On March 28, at the 24th and last concert of the fourth season of the Boston Symphony Orchestra under Wilhelm Gericke, Amy played the Chopin concerto upon which she had worked the previous fall. The concert was the talk of the town,[12] and the critics were full of praise:

> Where in this country could there be found a pianist capable of performing Chopin's great F minor Concerto, opus 21, better than Miss Amy Marcy Cheney, who played it at the last of the present series of symphony concerts, on Saturday evening,—except her master and counselor, Professor Baermann? She is still but a girl, not yet entered even into young womanhood, and it would be foolish to pretend that there are not artists who can surpass her in some elements of force and fire, of dash or of endurance; but there is none, so far as we know, who can unite so many of the requisites for a true rendering of the best literature of the piano. Within even a few months her technique has

---

[11] Letter from William Mason to Dr. H. H. A. Beach, Orange, New Jersey, 3 October 1884.

[12] *Boston Beacon*, 4 April 1885.

acquired that inexplicable *something* which distinguishes the artist from the accomplished amateur, from the proficient student, and even from the virtuoso, while her spirit has grown in perception and sympathy and emotional resource. She has now almost the full command of the instrument which is so remarkable in Professor Baermann, which artfully brings out all the reserve power of the strings, but stops just short of their harsh protest upon being forced, and which can yet touch them so delicately that, with a shade less pressure, their airy sounds would cease to be audible. . . . For tenderness of mood, never sinking into the vagueness of rhapsody, and never chilled by too precise statement, the larghetto was preeminent, and ought to be memorable as a standard of comparison hereafter.[13]

The success of this concert led to another a month later with Theodore Thomas and his own orchestra of seventy musicians. Thomas brought his ensemble to Boston for concerts on April 28 and 29, and at the second of these, a "Young People's Popular," modeled on those of the "Educational Series" which had proved so successful the previous season in New York, Amy performed the Mendelssohn D-minor Concerto. Of course, Thomas's orchestra and his leadership were extolled, but one reviewer stated that the bright star of the occasion was "Miss Cheney, who played the D minor *Concerto* by Mendelssohn with all that care and finish and refinement of feeling for which she is becoming noted."[14] For the first time, however, one critic found some fault in her playing:

At the risk of seeming hypercritical, we will say, however, that in parts of this [first] movement, notably in the second theme, the young artist seemed to obtain dynamic force somewhat at the expense of grace and buoyancy of phrasing—temptation of which pianists of slight physique are particularly exposed. But, barring this faint blemish, Miss Cheney's playing was so highly artistic, so soulful and marked by so much intelligence and good taste, that one cannot but find it worthy of the highest praise.[15]

To Gericke's great credit, he recognized that Amy's talent was so great that she deserved special attention. He therefore invited her to attend any and all rehearsals of the Boston Symphony Orchestra so that she might learn as much as possible by studying the musical sounds she heard and comparing them with the composers' scores. She took full advantage of every opportunity of learning both the art of orchestration and that of musical composition, and the result was her composition of such successful orchestral works as her *Gaelic Symphony*. Eventually the Boston Symphony Orchestra established a practice of admitting music students to one rehearsal weekly, and other orchestras soon copied an idea that proved so fruitful in Amy's case.

---

[13] *Boston Daily Advertiser*, 31 March 1885. Reviews also appeared in the *Boston Evening Transcript, Boston Herald, Boston Sunday Gazette, Boston Evening Traveler, Boston Beacon,* and *Boston Home Journal.*

[14] *Boston Courier.*

[15] *Boston Transcript.*

Romance (1885)

At a quiet family gathering on "the maid's day off," Thursday, 13 August 1885, Mr. and Mrs. Charles Abbott Cheney announced the engagement of their only daughter, Amy, not quite eighteen years old, to Dr. Henry Beach, M.D., of Boston. The wedding, likewise a quiet family affair, was scheduled for the afternoon of December 2 at Trinity Episcopal Church, Copley Square, Boston.

If this announcement came as a surprise to Amy's friends and many acquaintances, there is no indication that this was a sudden decision.[16] As mentioned already, Amy had visited Dr. Beach for treatment of a minor hand injury, and the physician had taken more than a professional interest in her by promoting her career with his friend William Mason. While Amy attended school and studied the piano in Boston, she was living at the Bellevue Hotel, not far from Henry's office. He, in turn, was an amateur musician and music lover[17] and together with his first wife, Alice C. Mandell,[18] subscribed to concerts, so that Amy Beach was an important musical figure in his eyes before she became something much more. Once they became acquainted in the doctor's office, their friendship quickly developed. As one of Amy's friends later recalled,

> Dr. Beach made a stained-glass window for her hotel bedroom when she was thirteen or so because she complained of looking out on a brick wall. Whether he painted the glass or just contrived something, I don't know. But it was probably his first tribute to her. She was, apparently, a pet and protege of both the doctor and his first wife.[19]

While Henry knew Amy, it seems unlikely that any romance was involved until after the death of the first Mrs. Beach in 1880, when Amy was thirteen. After all, Henry was eight months older than her father and not of the age of one who might assume to be her suitor, and he was the scion of one of the socially élite families of Boston who would not be inclined to scandal. But it was probably shortly thereafter that he fell in love with her, and she and her ever watchful mother undoubtedly were aware of the fact soon afterwards.

> When Dr. Beach first took her hand in his, he fell in love with her. Her hand was so soft and tiny, yet pliable and supple enough to reach the largest of musical chords.[20]

---

[16] It was never my good fortune to hear from Mrs. Beach's own lips the intimate details of these particular days of her girlhood, and without knowledge that this biography might one day develop, I listened to many of her recollections without prying beyond the spontaneous expositions she often gave of her earlier years.

[17] Mrs. Beach later stated, "Ever since he was a boy of ten, he turned to music and to singing for relaxation from his more serious work."

[18] Alice came from New Bedford, Massachusetts, and married Henry in 1871.

[19] According to Esther Willard Bates, one of the composer's long-time friends.

[20] According to Ella Lord Gilbert, a New Hampshire musician and loyal supporter of Mrs. Beach.

Dr. Beach was born in Middletown, Connecticut, on 18 December 1843.[21] During his childhood he moved with his family to Cambridge where he was educated in the public schools. Between 1864 and 1866 he served in an army hospital as a sergeant of ordinance. Later he was appointed surgical house officer at Massachusetts General Hospital while he pursued his M.D. degree at Harvard, which he obtained in 1868. For the next fifteen years he taught practical anatomy at Harvard Medical School and was associated with Professor Oliver Wendell Holmes, Sr. After 1879 he was visiting surgeon at Massachusetts General Hospital, and throughout his life remained one of the hospital's surgical consultants. By 1886, Dr. Beach spent most of his professional hours in private practice and in writing articles for medical journals and for learned societies.[22]

Dr. H. A. Beach

Photo courtesy of Special Collections,
University of New Hampshire Library

It should have been apparent by early 1885 that the relationship between Henry and Amy was rapidly maturing. Henry performed a new song by Amy, "Jeune fille, jeune fleur," at a student recital at 1616 Tremont Street on Friday, 16 January 1885, which she published two years later as part of her opus 1. Mrs. Cheney, who saw in Dr. Beach the perfect, devoted husband for her daughter, encouraged the romance.

With the marriage of Henry Beach and Amy Cheney, Amy passed out of her childhood and into the professional world as Mrs. H. H. A. Beach.

---

[21] During the period between Dr. Beach's accident on 25 April 1910 and his death the following June 28, Mrs. Beach probably wrote the brief, undated, unpublished essay in her own hand upon which the following account of Dr. Beach's life is based. See also the obituary of Dr. Beach in the *Barnstable Patriot*, Monday evening, 4 July 1910, under the Centerville heading.

[22] The similarity of Dr. H. H. A. Beach, Mrs. Beach's husband, to the fictional Dr. Beech in John P. Marquand's *The Late George Apley* was denied by the famous author, who claimed never to base characters of his novels on real people (letter from Marquand to Jenkins). Both Dr. Beach and Dr. Beech were ardent ornithologists, and everyone who lived in Boston in 1910, including Marquand, would have known of the real Dr. Beach.

Part **2**: Mrs. H. H. A. Beach, 1885-1911

No. 28 Commonwealth Avenue
(1885-90)

Dr. Henry H. A. Beach and Miss Amy Marcy Cheney were quietly married in Trinity Church last Wednesday afternoon at five o'clock, the Rev. Phillips Brooks officiating. The bride, who wore a white satin costume, with tulle veil fastened by sprays of orange flowers, entered the church with her father, Mr. Charles A. Cheney, and was received at the chancel by the bridegroom, according to the English custom. The services were simple and impressive, Mr. George W. Chadwick and Mr. Arthur Whiting playing the organ very beautifully, while Dr. Brooks performed the solemn marriage rite. The ushers were Dr. Otis K. Newell and Dr. H. C. Baldwin. Dr. and Mrs. Beach, who are passing their honeymoon in New York, will later receive the congratulations of their many friends.[23]

Upon completion of their wedding trip, the couple returned to Dr. Beach's fashionable red-brick townhouse on Commonwealth Avenue in which he had lived since 1879. The doctor's offices were on the first floor, and the couple occupied the upper floors. Mrs. Beach, completely untutored in the duties and responsibilities of a homemaker, created an enviable domicile, nonetheless, with the help of a staff of good servants. Henry, in turn, adjusted his busy medical practice so that, as much as possible, he was available to further his new wife's professional career.

When the couple returned to their home from New York, they plunged into the important preparations for Christmas. Dr. Beach was anxious to have his bride partake of all the season's gaiety and to present her to his many friends. Later she described her life as his wife as arduous and a tax on her utmost powers of social intercourse (according to Esther Bates, letter to Jenkins, 3 October 1957). Mrs. Cheney had not brought up her daughter to be a socialite, and the eighteen-year-old, pig-tailed genius of the piano had not yet had to deal with the Boston élite. But Dr. Beach was, by nature,

---

[23] Announcement in the Boston newspapers, early December 1885.

**Residence of Dr. and Mrs. H. H. A. Beach,
25 Commonwealth Avenue, Boston**

Photo by Professor Norman E. Vuilleumier, July 1959

a very out-going and genial man who, however appreciative he was of his wife's musical career, never liked to avoid the many social demands made upon them because of professional practices. This part of his personality was, no doubt, largely responsible for his professional success as well as that of his wife.

Immediately after the Christmas holidays of 1885, Mrs. Beach settled into a more accustomed routine of practice. She had been engaged by Wilhelm Gericke as soloist for the Boston Symphony Orchestra's nineteenth regular subscription concerts on 19 and 20 February 1886. For the first time she would appear as Mrs. H. H. A. Beach, and for the first time she transferred from a Chickering piano to a Steinway. She performed Mozart's D-minor Concerto with the Beethoven cadenzas:

> The piano-forte part was played by Mrs. H. H. A. Beach, and one could but feel from beginning to end how well the work and the player complemented each other. While Mrs. Beach was still occupied with the profession, from which selfishness may be pardoned for wishing she had not retired, she was eminent for the lucidity, the simplicity and the absolute truth of her readings, rather than for ardent urgency or powerful emphasis. The same characteristics were evident on this occasion, when she came out for an evening from the quiet of her home to gratify the public and to advantage a noble charity by the contribution to its treasury of honorarium formally due her as a soloist. The brilliant, but still soft and undazzling ease of the allegro, the smoothness tender, but unaffected, of that romance which it is easy to make lackadaisical, and the pearly precision of the rondo, were all new but not unexpected illustrations of the true artist, quick in native apprehension and patient in faithful study. Mrs. Beach was gladly welcomed and twice heartily recalled.[24]

---

[24] *Boston Advertiser.* Other reviews appeared in the *Boston Beacon, Boston Gazette, Boston Courier*, and *Boston Transcript.*

The critics, however, were alarmed that "so fine a musical endowment as hers should be withdrawn from a professional career."[25] To them it seemed unlikely that a married woman would continue a public career, even though Mrs. Beach, her husband, and her mother never gave any indication that her marriage would terminate her professional life. Rather, as we shall see, from this time Mrs. Beach began to show more interest in composition, which inevitably would take time away from concertizing.

For the moment, however, she gave a few recitals, often as benefits for some charity and usually associated with Dr. Beach's profession. For example, on Wednesday evening, 3 March 1886, Mrs. Beach joined Dr. Oliver Wendell Holmes[26] and the Honorable James Russell Lowell at an author's reading at the home of Mr. Robert Treat Paine, 6 Joy Street, to benefit a kindergarten for the blind.[27] She played Mendelssohn's Prelude and Fugue in F minor, Chopin's Etude in A-flat (op. 25), Nocturne in D-flat (op. 27), and *Valse in C-sharp minor*, and Liszt's *Rigoletto Fantasie*, while Lowell and Holmes read from their poetry. Again on March 31 she gave a solo recital to aid the Convalescent Home of the Children's Hospital at Association Hall. Added to her March 3 program were Raff's *Metamorphosen* and her teacher Baermann's *Klavier-Stücke in Waltzenform*. One review, in the *Boston Transcript*, continued to fear that Mrs. Beach would withdraw from public life.

> Music lovers may well congratulate themselves that, so long as deserving charities exist in Boston, there will be occasional chances of hearing Mrs. Beach play. . . . Her playing yesterday afternoon was delightful; her technique seems to have gained even in smoothness and clearness during the last year or two, fine as it was when she first came out. . . . Mrs. Beach's playing is so exquisite in its way that one cannot but indulge himself in the fairest hopes for her future development. . . . It remains with her alone to show that besetting sin of pianists of her sex—*superficiality*. This world groans under so many women pianists of excellent gifts and training, and of considerable renown, but to whom pianoforte playing seems to be a mere matter of sentiment and fingers! That brains and carefully acquired knowledge have anything to do with it seems never to have occurred to them. As yet Mrs. Beach certainly cannot be charged with superficiality; she evidently knows quite enough for her present purpose. But when that young peach-bloom begins to wear off, as in time it must, may she show herself to be "one woman picked out of ten thousand," and fill its place with that so rare virtue which is called thorough musicianship. If she does, the world is ready to be at her feet.

---

[25] *Boston Transcript.*

[26] Holmes was an admirer of Mrs. Beach. On 12 November 1886, he wrote to her "Many thanks for the piece of music of your composition which you have kindly sent me. I wish I were more adept in your divine art and I could thank you more fittingly, but not more warmly. Believe me, dear Mrs. Beach." In a postscript Holmes thanks Dr. Beach for flowers sent on his birthday (August 29): "*I hope* I thanked him soon after my birthday but there was so much to confuse my memory that I feel uncertain about it."

[27] *Boston Beacon.*

The following year Mrs. Beach performed only one recital. On 9 March 1887, at two o'clock, she played for the benefit of the Ladies' Aid Association of Children's Hospital. The concert took place in Christian Association Hall, Boylston and Berkley Streets, and the program consisted of five sonatas by Johann Christian Bach (C minor), Mozart (F major), Scarlatti (F minor), Beethoven (*Appassionata*), and Chopin (B minor).

> That sounds like Bülow or Rubinstein, but it is none the worse for awakening such associations, and we doubt if many of the audience found the program otherwise than enjoyable. . . . One does not have too many opportunities of hearing Mrs. Beach in public. . . . Would only that she might play somewhere else than in Association Hall, where the basso continuo of horse cars, and the frequent obbligati in locomotive bells and hand-organs furnish additional accompaniments never contemplated by the composers. Yet all this circumambient din could not conceal the fact that Mrs. Beach played very delightfully . . . one felt now and then that it is getting to be high time for her to be on guard against a tendency to over-sentimentalize. What is very true sentiment in childhood is often mere sentimentalism in advancing maturity. The Chopin *Sonata*, for instance, seemed to drag more than a little, and one longed for more of virile fire and impetuosity, beautifully as it was played. But, per contra, and this, too, where one would least have expected it, Mrs. Beach did some really great playing in the Andante of the Beethoven *Sonata*. The tempo struck us as a shade too slow, but the phrases were carried through with a security of emphasis, the movement was played with a sober thoughtfulness, a maturity of sentiment, wholly free from all sentimentalism, that left nothing to be desired. The audience was both large and enthusiastic.[28]

The partial withdrawal from the concert stage was largely the result of Mrs. Beach's increasing activities as a composer. She had studied the rudiments of theory with Junius Hill, Professor of Music at Wellesley College, and her copies of the treatises on orchestration by Berlioz and Gevaert in French were well thumb-worn by the time she was married. Now she slowly and carefully began to write songs, including two of opus 2 to texts by Dr. Beach, an ardent lover of songs. And she began to send them to singers beyond the Boston area, such as Olive Risley Lenard, who acknowledged receiving "your beautiful song" on 26 November 1887. The following spring she composed her own cadenza to Beethoven's C-minor Concerto (Beach's op. 3), which she performed on 21 April 1888, with the Boston Symphony Orchestra, again under Gericke.[29]

In the second of her two recitals in the 1889 season,[30] Mrs. Beach introduced her *Valse-Caprice*, which followed her performance of Brahms's Intermezzo (op. 76, no. 3) and which

---

[28] *Boston Transcript.*

[29] Howard Malcolm Ticknor describes her performance of the cadenza in the *Boston Globe*. It is also reviewed in the *Boston Post*.

[30] The first took place on January 24 to benefit the Society for the Prevention of Cruelty of Children. Both concerts were in Huntington Hall of the Institute of Technology, Boylston Street.

preceded her performance of Chopin's Ballade in G minor. Sandwiched in between these major works, the piece seemed to one critic "a charming and dainty bit of musical embroidery, bright in thought, musicianly in spirit, abundant in difficulties used with artistic taste and wholly pleasing and interesting in the hearing." Also on this program of March 21, which was a benefit for the Marine Biological Laboratory, was Bach's *Italian Concerto*, Mozart's Sonata in A minor, a gigue by Graun, Beethoven's Variations, op. 34, Moszkowski's *En automne*, and three transcriptions by Liszt.

Mass in E-Flat (1890-92)

Although she continued to give occasional recitals, Mrs. Beach became even more seriously involved with composition in 1890. She continued revisions of her Mass, op. 5, upon which she had been working since 1886, and completed the *Three Vocal Duets*, op. 10. During the summer the first of many music festivals at the Weirs, Lake Winnipesaukee, sponsored by the New Hampshire Music Teacher's Association (of which Mrs. Beach was a charter member), took place, and on the second day of the festival Mrs. Rose Carter Crafts of Nashua sang her songs "With Violets" and "The Four Brothers." On 19 and 27 February 1891, Mrs. Beach gave two recitals at Tremont Temple for the benefit of the Marine Biological Laboratory, and on the second of these she gave the world premiere of her Ballade, op. 6. While the first concert was devoted to the works of Chopin,[31] the second was a major change in emphasis in programming. Half of the concert was traditional: Bach's *Chromatic Fantasie and Fugue* in the von Bülow transcription, and Beethoven's *Les Adieux* piano sonata, but scattered among these European master-pieces were the compositions of American composers. Besides her own work, she performed John Knowles Paine's Nocturne, op. 45, Arthur Foote's *Capriccio* from the Suite, op. 15, MacDowell's *Etude de concert*, op. 36, and George W. Chadwick's Caprice in G minor. Mrs. Beach's piece received an important review by the most famous Boston critic, John Sullivan Dwight, who speaks of the Ballade as

> a composition of larger form than most of the preceding, and developed
> out of interesting subjects. Naturally a Ballad tells a story and is more
> or less dramatic. This one in the latter portion waxed to an emphatic
> and exciting climax, holding attention to the end.[32]

---

[31] The Chopin concert is reviewed in the *Boston Transcript*.

[32] *Boston Transcript*, 28 February 1891.

Metcalf

503 WASHINGTON STREET,
BOSTON, MASS.

Mrs. H. H. A. Beach, probably 1890s

The following month, on March 23, Mrs. Beach performed at a benefit for the late teacher-composer Calira Lavallee, whose family had been left destitute upon his death. She played two of Lavallee's compositions, *Souvenir de Toledo* and *Le Papillon*. Also on the program was the premiere of Mrs. Beach's song "Wilt Thou Be My Dearie?" (op. 12, no. 3) on a text by Robert Burns (dedicated to Dr. Beach). It was sung by Mrs. W. F. Whitney, a well-known Boston soprano, accompanied by Mrs. Beach. They also performed "The Blackbird," op. 11, no. 3, "Ariette," op. 1, no. 4, and "Dark Is the Night," op. 11, no. 1.

> Mrs. Beach's songs aroused genuine enthusiasm. . . . In response to unmistakable demands of the audience for more, Mrs. Whitney sang *The Thrush*, also by Mrs. Beach.[33]

Mrs. Beach's first church music was the Mass completed in 1891, but its premiere was postponed for another year. Meanwhile she wrote a much shorter work, a setting of the 117th Psalm, *O Praise the Lord, All Ye Nations*, op. 7, designed for the consecration service installing Rev. Phillips Brooks as Bishop of the Episcopal Diocese of Massachusetts. It was not a commissioned work but was composed by Mrs. Beach to honor the man who had performed her wedding.[34] Upon sending Brooks the work, he replied from his residence at 233 Clarendon Street that:

> It is indeed a great delight and pride to me that you should have given me the indulgence of your beautiful art and honored the beginning of my new life with what I know is noble music. I am sure you will believe that I am deeply touched by what you have done and shall always treasure it among my best recollections of the happy and honorable things which have come to me in life. The arrangements for the consecration service have not yet begun to be made, but I trust that when they take their shape, those who have them in charge may find a distinguished place for your anthem, which will then always keep an association in which I shall take great pleasure. Will you and Dr. Beach accept the assurance of my most sincere and kind regard. . . .

The consecration service actually occurred on 14 October 1891, at the same church where the Beachs were married. The psalm was performed at the Offertory by a choir of 52 voices under the direction of James Cutler Dunn Parker. According to one account, it leant "noble dignity" to that part of the service.

The momentum in composition and performances of Mrs. Beach's music, which had been increasing during the years 1890 to 1891, reached even greater proportions in 1892. At the same time she continued performing. The new conductor of the Boston Symphony

---

[33] *Boston Transcript.* "The Thrush" is op. 14, no. 4, on a text by E. R. Sill, dedicated to Mrs. Beach's cousin, Mrs. L. H. Clement (Auntie Franc).

[34] Brooks was not without interest in religious music. He is probably best remembered as the author of the Christmas hymn "O Little Town of Bethlehem."

Orchestra, the famous Arthur Nikisch, wrote to her and asked her to perform with the orchestra.[35]   As a result, on January 23 she performed the Chopin F-minor Concerto, which was warmly received.   "The final rondo was beautifully clear and even, and Mrs. Beach had a double recall."[36]

The highlight of the season, however, was the long-awaited first performance of Mrs. Beach's Mass. It took place on 7 February 1892, at 7:30 p.m., in the Boston Music Hall. Carl Zerrahn conducted the 681st concert by the Handel and Haydn Society accompanied by members of the Boston Symphony Orchestra and assisted by a solo quartet consisting of Mrs. Jennie Partrick Walker (soprano), Mrs. Carl Alves (contralto), Italio Companini (tenor), and Emil Fischer (bass). Benjamin J. Lang played the organ part. Also on the program was Beethoven's *Choral Fantasy*, with Mrs. Beach playing the piano part.

Composed from 1886 to 1891,[37] Mrs. Beach's Mass is the first such composition in concert form by any American woman composer. At no time had Mrs. Beach's career elicited such extensive journalistic coverage as now. Nathan Haskell Dole wrote that the occasion

> should be marked with a white stone in the musical history of Boston.
> A Mass written for solos, chorus, orchestra and organ, by a woman
> not out of her "teens" was performed . . . to the acceptance of an
> immense audience.[38]

To this Julia Ward Howe added (*Women's Journal*, 13 February 1892):

> The performance . . . gave great pleasure to the lovers of good music
> in this city. It did this, and much more. It made evident the capacity
> of a woman's brain to plan and execute a work combining great serious-
> ness with unquestionable beauty. Women have done noble work in
> pictorial and plastic art, and have often attained the highest merit in
> the interpretation of music. Mrs. Beach is, so far as we know, the first
> of her sex who has given to the world a musical composition of the
> first order as to scope and conception. One of the leading characteristics
> of this was an unmistakable fervor and feeling, which brought out,
> instead of concealing, the grandeur of the words which the music was
> intended to illustrate. Some of its passages were actually luminous with
> a brightness akin to that of faith and true sentiment.

---

[35] Letter from Mrs. Amelie Nikisch to Mrs. Beach, Brookline, Massachusetts, 23 April 1891.

[36] *Boston Beacon.*

[37] The program for the premiere stated that the work was composed in 1889, but Mrs. Beach told me that basically it was composed from 1886 to 1889, that it was completed for all general purposes in 1889, but that slight revisions continued to take place in the score into 1891.

[38] *Boston Musical Herald*, March 1892.

Program cover for the concert by the Handel and Haydn Society of Boston
at which Mrs. Beach's Mass was premiered, 7 February 1892 (note her company)

SEVENTY-SEVENTH SEASON

SIX HUNDRED AND EIGHTY-FIRST CONCERT

SUNDAY EVENING,

FEBRUARY 7, 1892

The

Beach Mass

FOLLOWED BY THE

Choral Fantasia of Beethoven

MRS. JENNIE PATRICK WALKER, SOPRANO

MRS. CARL ALVES, ALTO

MR. ITALO CAMPANINI, TENOR

MR. EMIL FISCHER, BASS

MRS. H. H. A. BEACH, PIANIST

MR. CARL ZERRAHN, CONDUCTOR

MR. B. J. LANG, ORGANIST

Miss PRISCILLA WHITE, soprano, and Col. I. F. KINGSBURY, tenor, members of the chorus, will complete the sextet in the Choral Fantasia.

Players from the Boston Symphony Orchestra

Mr. FRANZ KNEISEL, Principal

Program of the premiere of Mrs. Beach's Mass

Philip Hale, in the *Boston Journal* (8 February 1892), joined the chorus of approval:

> It is a work of long breath. It shows knowledge, skill and above all,
> application, patience and industry. She has not followed closely an
> illustrious predecessor; she has had fixed ideas of her own, and she
> has not hesitated to carry them out.

Not only the Boston reviewers noticed the new piece, but also those from New York.
According to the *New York Sun* (18 February 1892), "Mrs. Beach is the first woman in
America to compose a work of so much power and beauty. Music Hall was packed, and
the piece scored a grand success." Mrs. T. H. Garrison wrote in the *Woman's Journal*
(13 February 1892) that "the reposeful dignity of form, and the solemnity and fervor which
characterized the work, gave convincing evidence of the healthful vigor of the composer's
mind, and of her originality in construction and expression." The *Trade Paper Journal* of
New York took pride in noting that "the event of the season in musical circles" was a
piece by the daughter of one of its members, C. A. Cheney. Mrs. Beach was cheered
both in the Mass and in her playing of the Beethoven, where "she was greeted with
plaudits long and loud. . . . The floral tributes were profuse and elegant."

Several months later, on May 11 and 12, Mrs. Beach played for the first time her
Fireflies, op. 15, no. 4, at concerts of the Cecilia Society. During the summer (July 28),
at the annual Festival of the New Hampshire Music Teachers Association at the Weirs,
a mixed quartet from the First Congregational Church of Nashua, New Hampshire,
premiered "Peace I Leave with You," op. 8, no. 2. On November 9, Mrs. Beach played
her Ballade and introduced a new piece, *In Autumn*, op. 15, no. 1, in a concert at the New
England Conservatory of Music sponsored by the Beneficent Society. On November 29,
Miss Lillian Carllsmith, in a recital in Chickering Hall, sang Mrs. Beach's songs "Ecstasy"
and "Ariette," with the composer at the piano.[39] The program also included first Boston
performances of songs by Arthur Foote, S. C. Downs, and Margaret Ruthven Lang.
Mrs. Beach also played a group of her piano pieces, including the first performance of
Dreaming and repeat performances of *In Autumn* and *Fireflies*.

New York finally beckoned Mrs. Beach in the fall of 1892. At the end of November
Mrs. Carl Alves premiered, in her New York recital, Mrs. Beach's famous song "Ecstasy,"
op. 19, no. 2, dedicated to Mrs. Alves and with text by Mrs. Beach herself.[40] A few days
later, on December 1, Miss Hattie Bradley sang Mrs. Beach's songs "The Blackbird" and
"The Secret," presumably in their initial New York if not world premiere.[41] Then, on

---

[39] Not all the reviews were complimentary of Miss Carllsmith. Mr. C. L. Capen, *Boston Advertiser*, 30 November
1892, found "her phrasing has the serious fault of not discriminating between the final notes of masculine and
feminine rhythms, and she frequently renders the last note of a phrase with far more volume than is its due." He
also objected to the choice of language, which sometimes was German and French but also included English
translations.

[40] The *Chicago Mail*, 20 December 1892, describes Mrs. Alves as "the leading contralto singer of America" and
gives further information on her career.

[41] This took place as part of the guest lecture by Frederic Dean on the upcoming New York Symphony program
of the next two days.

December 2 and 3, Walter Damrosch led the New York Symphony Society in the world premiere of Beach's *Mary Stuart*, concert scena and aria, op. 18, words by Schiller, with Mrs. Alves as contralto soloist. It was the first time that that organization had performed the work of a woman composer. Frederic Dean, writing in the program for the concert, described the aria as depicting

> Mary's first release from prison, just before her meeting with Elizabeth. Behind her is her dungeon, about and above her the free open air, the beautiful foliage and the "wandering clouds," to which she entrusts messages of love to her native land.

In many later performances the work was renamed *Wandering Clouds*. A reviewer at the time called it

> a very talented work. As regards style, musical expression of the purport of the text, and particularly the treatment of the orchestra, the composition reminds one emphatically of the so-called "new German method," which is rooted in the soil of Berlioz, but whose trunk and boughs are filled with Lisztian and Wagnerian juices. Among the great qualities of the composition are perfect musical characteristics of situation, temperament and word. The sentimental expression of feeling of the unfortunate Scottish queen . . . , the longing sigh which the imprisoned one sends after the scurrying clouds, form in fact an enticing poetic example of production in musical form, and it cannot be denied that Mrs. Beach's music embodies perfectly the expression of that moving scene.[42]

Chicago Columbian Exposition (1893-95)

The opening of the Columbian Exhibition in Chicago had important consequences for music in general and for Mrs. Beach in particular. On Monday, 1 May 1893, the Woman's Building at the Fair officially opened with ceremonies of the Board of Lady Managers. Mrs. Beach was commissioned to write a *Festival Jubilate* for the occasion, which was performed immediately following an address by Mrs. Potter Palmer on the emancipation of women.[43]

---

[42] *New York Staats-Zeitung.*

[43] The suffrage movement was in high gear at this point. Susan B. Anthony had just been elected president of the National American Suffrage Association.

Theodore Thomas conducted three hundred voices of the Apollo Club and an orchestra in what was judged a very poor acoustical situation.[44] Nonetheless, the reviewer of the *Chicago Tribune* called the work "a masterpiece of musical composition," and "as was to be expected, [Mrs. Beach] has won new laurels for herself and her art." She was awarded a Columbian bronze medal and diploma with the citation

> For a valuable contribution of musical works, including songs, a mass, concerto and Jubilate for dedication of the Woman's building of the World's Columbian Exposition, for the great care and study shown in the conception and technical detail.

With this performance, Mrs. Beach's music began to be heard outside the northeast part of the United States and attracted world-wide attention.

Other new Beach titles appeared in the same year. Pianist Richard Hoffman performed "Phantoms," op. 15, no. 2, in a concert by the Piano Trio Club in New York on February 27, and pianist Mr. E. B. Strong repeated it the following May 11 on a recital at the Elms School in Springfield, Massachusetts. Strong also performed Beach's "Dreaming." In San Francisco, the Schumann Club directed by David W. Loring performed her chorus for female voices "Little Brown Bee" at its May 16 concert. Mrs. Alves continued to sing Mrs. Beach's songs at her recitals in New York, such as that on May 28 when she delighted a large audience with "Ecstasy" as part of Frank Damrosch's choral concert. Back in Chicago on July 5, Mrs. Beach attended a three-day session of the Woman's Branch of the Congress of Music of the World's Fair. On the opening day she played a group of her piano pieces "In Autumn," "Fireflies," and "Ballade," the last of which was dedicated to the famous Chicago pianist Fannie Bloomfield Zeisler. On July 6 she teamed up with Maud Powell, the finest violinist in America at the time, for the premiere of her "Romance" in A minor, op. 23, dedicated to Miss Powell. On the last day of this session, Jeanette Dutton sang Mrs. Beach's "Sweetheart, Sigh No More" for the first time in public.

The Chicago press was as enthusiastic about the new "Romance" as was the public. The audience "cheered to the echo when the number had been completed, and compelled its repetition."[45]

> Miss Maud Powell, violin in hand, stepped to the platform, followed by Mrs. H. H. A. Beach. Everyone looked expectant. Mrs. Beach took her seat at the piano, and the composer of *Romance* interpreted her own creation to the skillful obligato of Miss Powell. The selection was listened to in sympathetic silence, and at the close tears glistened in many eyes. Miss Powell was voted an artist of much merit.[46]

---

[44] *Chicago Herald*, 24 April 1893, and *Chicago Tribune*, 2 May 1893.

[45] *Chicago Times*, 7 July 1893.

[46] *Chicago Record*, 7 July 1893.

**Mrs. Beach at the Steinway, outdoor concert at the
Panama-California International Exposition, San Diego, May 1916**

A few months later, Miss Powell wrote to Mrs. Beach from her residence in New York City,

> The dainty, artistic edition of your charming *Romanza* was sent me
> yesterday. Please accept my gracious thanks. I am using the *Romanza*
> this winter and shall hope to have the pleasure of playing it in Boston
> some time during the season. Our meeting in Chicago and the pleasure
> of playing together made a most delightful episode in my summer's
> experience. I trust it may soon be repeated.[47]

Others continued to perform Beach's works. Lillian Nordica sang "Ecstasy" and
Jeannie M. Crocker introduced a new song, "For Me the Jasmine Buds Unfold," both in
separate recitals in Boston on October 16. On November 13, Kate Rolla introduced two
new songs, "Elle et moi" (text by Felix Boret) and "Extase" (poem by Victor Hugo), at
a recital for the New York Manuscript Society. Both songs were from op. 21, which is

---

[47] Letter from Maud Powell to Mrs. Beach, New York, 6 December 1893.

dedicated to the Baroness de Hegermann-Lindencrone, who "sang a group of Mrs. Beach's songs to the delight and acceptance of a large company of distinguished persons" in Stockholm, including the king, "who expressed deep interest in the songs and other compositions, especially the Mass in E flat."[48] Mrs. Agnes Thomson sang an arrangement of *Mary Stuart* for soprano and piano at a Wagner Club Concert in Chicago on December 6. Miss Carllsmith included "Ecstasy" in her second recital of the year on December 11, this time with Arthur Foote at the piano.[49] The following day, the New York Symphony Orchestra under Walter Damrosch played Mrs. Beach's *Bal masque*, originally written as a waltz for piano, op. 22. Mrs. Alves introduced "Ecstasy" to Cincinnati at an Apollo Club Concert there in December, and in Los Angeles the Students' Musical Club presented the *Gradual, Et incarnatus, Sanctus* and *Hosanna* from the Mass in a concert of compositions by women composers. Finally, Mrs. Beach had written a Christmas hymn "Bethlehem," which was performed twice on December 24 in Boston at the morning service of the First Church, Unitarian (Foote was the organist) and at an afternoon service of the First Baptist Church.

On November 27 Mrs. Beach gave a recital at Steinert Hall to benefit the West End Nursery and Infant's Hospital. She was assisted by Miss Crocker (soprano) and Mrs. Homer E. Sawyer (contralto). After various solo piano pieces and accompanied vocal solos, all three performed Beach's "The Night Sea" and "Canadian Boat Song," both vocal duets. Mrs. Beach ended the afternoon event with a group of Chopin works. Two days later the *Boston Transcript* noted the publication by Arthur P. Schmidt of *Lyric Fancies: Album of Songs for Soprano or Tenor, by American Composers*. Mrs. Beach's songs lie beside those by MacDowell, Chadwick, Foote, Lang, John Hyatt Brewer, Irene Hale, Frank Lynes, Helen Hood, H. H. Huss, Clayton Johns, B. Schlesinger, Wilson G. Smith, G. Templeton Strong, G. W. Marston, Charles Dennee, Jules Jordan, F. A. Porter, and Clara Kathleen Rogers. Thus began an association between Mrs. Beach and Schmidt that would last until her death.

Each succeeding year had seen an increase in Mrs. Beach's musical activities. Now the performances of her music outnumbered her concert engagements, and her music was heard in an ever-widening geographical area. In 1894 there were at least sixty-two concerts in which Beach either performed or on whose programs her music was played. The song "Ecstasy" was particularly popular with two dozen performances by such notable singers as Lillian Nordica, Lillian Blauvelt, Sigrud Lunde, and Clara Smart. Lillian Russell sang it in London and elsewhere in England. George J. Parker sang it to benefit the poor of the Mt. Vernon Church in Boston, and Mrs. Sawyer sang it at the Boston Music Hall for the benefit both of Emmanuel Church in Boston and of the Baptist Hospital. Another song, "Ariette," appeared on programs by Marsha C. Melchert and Emma Howe. Miss Wilson of New York City sang "The Blackbird" in June at the New York Music Teacher's Association convention in Buffalo. McLeod of the First Baptist Church repeated Mrs. Beach's "Christmas Hymn" on January 21. A certain Mrs. Bangs sang "Extase" at a concert of the Amateur Musicians Club in Chicago, while Priscilla White sang other songs from op. 2:

---

[48] *Boston Globe.*

[49] Years later Foote wrote to Mrs. Beach about "those golden days of the 90's and a little after!"

"Chanson d'amour" and "Elle et moi." "Little Brown Bee" was performed by the Treble Clef Club on March 19, by the Cecilia Club Chorus of Boston on May 3, and by the Cecilia Society of Brooklyn, conducted by John H. Brewer, on December 12. The songs "Spring," "My Star," and "Sea Song" were beginning to become popular. "Just for This" and "Jasmine Buds," too, appeared on various programs. On December 4, Katherine Bloodgood sang the premiere of "Vilanelle" at a concert of the New York Manuscript Society.

Although the songs were the works most often performed, Mrs. Beach's piano music was not neglected. Arthur Foote continued to champion Mrs. Beach's music by playing her "In Autumn" on his piano recitals in Longwood, Massachusetts, Boston, and Buffalo, and Mrs. Emil Paur, wife of the conductor and a distinguished pianist, performed "Menuet italien" on her Brooklyn recital on December 7. In addition to the piano music, an orchestral arrangement of *Bal masque* was played on January 2 by an ensemble in Boston under Mr. Lothian.

One highlight of the 1894 season was Mrs. Beach's performance in Chickering Hall in Boston on January 22 with the famed Kneisel String Quartet. Franz Kneisel and Mrs. Beach performed her violin "Romance," and she joined the entire quartet in Schumann's Piano Quintet. Warren Davenport wrote:

> Mr. Kneisel played the *Romanza* in that highly polished manner that we always expect from him in his artistic efforts. He imported also a sympathetic touch to his part that was in consonance with the charming manner in which Mrs. Beach gave the piano accompaniment. The Romanza is a credit to its composer, for it is a delightful piece not at all intricate but melodious withal, and effectively placed upon the instrument.[50]

Philip Hale called the work "a pleasing piece with a theme that at once interests an audience." The performance of the Schumann Quintet may have had further implications for Mrs. Beach, who not long after wrote her own, very successful Piano Quintet.

On March 13 Mrs. Beach gave a piano recital sponsored by the Harvard University Musical Club at the Harvard Annex. As was now her custom, she complemented her performance of the European masters (Bach, Beethoven, Brahms, and Chopin) with works by the American School (Paine and Beach). On May 7 she gave for the first time a recital devoted exclusively to her own works. The performance, arranged at Wellesley College by her former teacher Professor Junius Hill, included not only solo piano works but also the "Romance" played by Lillian Chandler and songs sung by Priscilla White (soprano, a former Wellesley student), Mrs. H. E. Sawyer (contralto), and Emma Howe (the voice teacher at Wellesley College):

---

[50] *Boston Traveler*, 23 January 1894. Other good reviews of the *Romance* appeared in the *Boston Globe* and *Boston Herald*. Reviews by Howard M. Ticknor in the *Courier*, in the *Boston Advertiser*, and the *Times* of 28 January 1894 were not so complimentary. The *Times* writer, for example, said "The thematic material of the new romanza did not strike us as particulary attractive or significant. . . ." Their reviews of her piano playing in the Schumann, however, were as glowing as ever.

Mrs. Beach was gowned in white satin. She quickly charmed her audience. At each frantic burst of applause she smiled as if she thought the Wellesley girls and their enthusiastic clapping a delightful joke. . . . Mrs. Sawyer has a melodious voice and interpreted Mrs. Beach's strains sympathetically. Miss Priscilla White, who has a pretty way of holding up her head and trilling like a bird, sang three little French songs, which Mrs. Beach has set to music. . . . Of Mrs. Beach's piano solos, probably the most notable was a ballard [sic] in D flat. Wellesley also had the honor of hearing two manuscript selections, "Menuet Italien" and "Danse des Fleurs," played for the first time.[51]

The success of the all-Beach concert at Wellesley prompted a repetition of the program on June 11 at the final concert of the season of the College Club of Boston. The only change was that Elise Fellows, not Chandler, played the "Romance." The affair was in honor of Mrs. Beach and, as one might expect, was as much a social one as a musical one. It was a huge success. Held at the Bellevue Hotel from 4 to 6 in the afternoon, it was worthy of coverage by the local newspaper.

Mrs. H. H. A. Beach, whose name heads the list of American women composers, gave several of her most admired compositions. Mrs. Beach is a short, plump woman with dark hair simply arranged and bright coloring. She was becomingly gowned in pale pink satin and fine black lace. . . . The president of the club, Mrs. Shannon Davis, was very handsomely gowned. . . . Miss McIntire and Miss Goodwin presided over the refreshment table, which was artistically set out with the club color-heliotrope. . . . A few of the guests present were: Dr. Beach, Mr. & Mrs. Vinton, Mr. & Mrs. Wm. Lloyd Garrison, Mr. & Mrs. Frank Garrison, Miss Munger, Mr. & Mrs. Paur, Mr. Kneisel, Hon. Roger Wolcott, Mrs. Ira M. Morse, Mr. and Mrs. N. H. Dole, Dr. Parten, Mr. & Mrs. G. W. Chadwick, Rev. J. Ward, Mr. & Mrs. Ferrar Cobb, Mr. & Mrs. H. M. Ticknor, Mr. & Mrs. Fennoilosa, Mr. & Mrs. Arthur Foote, Mrs. B. S. Colege, president of the Wednesday Morning Club, Gen. Dalton, Gen. Champlin and Col. Barrett.[52]

One notable performance in 1895 was Mrs. Beach's appearance on February 16 in the Saint-Saëns Second Piano Concerto with the Boston Symphony Orchestra under Emil Paur. Louis Elson wrote:

It is a pleasure to state that the pianist who gave such great promise in her childhood has not retrograded. In the first movement her shading ran to extremes, and there seemed to be but few gradations between

[51] *Wellesley Examiner*, 12 May 1894. A nearly identical review appeared in the *Boston Globe*, 8 May 1894.

[52] *Boston Advertiser*. The *Trade Paper Journal* again took note of a memorable occasion on which the daughter of its member, Charles A. Cheney, was honored.

piano and forte, but some of this fault must be placed upon the composer rather than upon the executant, and the ensemble was generally excellent. Mrs. Beach made a great success in the second movement, a dainty scherzo, in which her crisp, demi-staccato style suited the composition admirably, and the scalework was as clear as crystal. . . . In the final saltarello there was also some commendable playing, both by soloist and orchestra. The difficult chord skips were made with absolute surety and there was some fine octave work in the solo part. Several recalls and a large floral tribute rewarded the artist at the conclusion of the Concerto.[53]

1895 also saw the first performance of several new compositions, including Mrs. Beach's songs "Across the World" (premiered by Katherine Bloodgood in New York on January 29), "Just for This" and "Wouldn't That Be Queer" (premiered by Gretchen Schofield at the Zethus Orchestra Concert in Boston, January 30),[54] "Sleep, Little Darling" (premiered by Margaret Goetz in Chicago on November 15), and "Within Thy Heart" (premiered by Mrs. Carl Alves in Newark on December 18).[55] The cantata for women's voices, *Rose of Avontown*, op. 30, on a text by Caroline Mischka, was first heard at a concert of music by women composers of the New York Manuscript Society on December 18; the Lenox Society Chorus was under Maude Morgan.[56] And on April 27, Kurt Paur performed for the first time, on a school concert, the solo piano piece "Harlequin."

Meanwhile, Mrs. Beach's older compositions gained an ever wider audience. There was a growing interest in her music in Europe. Mme. Stone-Barton sang "Elle et moi" in London at Mrs. Vanderveer Green's April Musicale, and Baroness de Hegermann-Lindercrone performed the piano piece "Fireflies" in Stockholm. In addition, her music was now regularly performed throughout the United States. Edith E. Torrey sang "Chanson d'amour" on November 11 in Chicago; Allen Spencer played "Menuet italien" at Northwestern University in Evanston, Illinois, in January, and in Chicago in October, while Miss Wetzler played *Phantoms* in Chicago in November. Arthur Foote continued to feature Mrs. Beach's music in his many concerts not confined to the East Coast. *Jubilate* was heard in Louisville on May 1.

But Boston continued to be the main location where Beach music thrived. Priscilla White sang "Chanson d'amour" on January 23 at the Boston Music Hall, which featured the great Belgian violinist Eugène Ysaÿe; Elene Eaton sang "Ariette" in Boston on February 18; "Menuet italien" was on Madame Paur's Music Hall recital on March 11 and on her Boston Art Club recital on May 2; Clara Munger sang Beach's "Aria" (= "Arietta"?) at a Chickering

---

[53] *Boston Advertiser*, 18 February 1895. Warren Davenport, in the *Boston Traveler*, was just as impressed. Other reviews were in the *Globe*, *Gazette*, *Transcript*, *Post*, and *Beacon*.

[54] The same two songs, as well as "Sleep, Little Darling," were sung by Miss Howe on a program of the Wellesley College Germania Orchestra on December 2.

[55] She also included "Sleep, Little Darling" on the program.

[56] A review appeared in the *Boston Post*. A later performance was reviewed in the *Boston Transcript*.

Hall recital on March 23; and on May 2 Mrs. Beach accompanied the singers Priscilla White and Mrs. Homer E. Sawyer in an all-Beach concert at Abbot Academy in the November Club House in Boston. *Bal masque*, in its orchestral arrangement, was played by the Boston Pops on June 13 under the direction of Signor A. de Novellis. The list of works performed in 1895 extends much further and demonstrates concretely that by this time, before her thirtieth birthday, Mrs. Beach was regarded as one of America's most famous, prolific, and popular composers.

The year 1895 also brought some changes in the Beach's personal lives. On July 26, Charles Cheney, then fifty, died of blood poisoning brought on by post-surgical infection. He was buried in Forrest Hills Cemetery, Jamaica Plain, Massachusetts, on July 30. The following October, Eliza Waterman Marcy, Mrs. Beach's grandmother, also died. Mrs. Beach's mother, Mrs. Cheney, was now all alone in New Hampshire, so at the urging of Mrs. Beach and her husband, she moved into their Commonwealth Avenue home. The fact that the Beaches were childless and that Mrs. Cheney had kept a close watch over her daughter's musical career even after her marriage made the arrangement especially congenial. Dr. Beach himself welcomed the move since Mrs. Cheney took over many of the household chores which were a burden to Mrs. Beach and freed his wife for those most important tasks of composing music. She never had to shop, even for the little but necessary things of life, and she did not concern herself over the servants who were instructed to wait on her. When, fifteen years later, Mrs. Beach experienced herself the loss of both husband and mother within a short space of time, she realized not only how valuable those two had been for the development of her career but also how much the arrangement had helped her mother cope with her personal tragedy.

Gaelic Symphony (1896-99)

The following year witnessed even greater triumphs for Mrs. Beach. Although she had achieved much success with her miniature compositions and had written a number of sizeable works, it was the premiere of her *Gaelic Symphony* by the Boston Symphony Orchestra under Emil Paur on 30-31 October 1896 that established her as a major American composer. This work enjoyed the greatest success of any American symphony by any composer of Mrs. Beach's generation.[57] The newspaper reports exceed in length the reviews of any previous works of hers and attest to the impact that it made on the audiences in Boston. The critic of the *Boston Courier* wrote:

---

[57] Mrs. Beach wrote her own analysis of the symphony, a copy of which is with Jenkins's manuscript at the University of New Hampshire. Cf. Appendix A.

The simple fact that Mr. Paur has put at the head of his third programme a manuscript symphony hitherto unheard, by Mrs. H. H. A. Beach, was in itself a guarantee that this new composition, the *Gaelic Symphony*, had the worth which entitled it to such an honorable place in the repertoire of the season. . . . From the single hearing that we could have of this symphony we derived great pleasure and content, and we are ready to award to it a great meed of praise.

Mrs. Beach entitled her symphony *Gaelic*. Just why does not openly appear. Perhaps because some melody comes to its close with the peculiar drop which is accepted as significant of Celtic music, although it is found elsewhere. But, probably, as we would guess, rather because its moods are significant of those which history and poetry have roused in the composer's mind and heart, and are intended to hint to the hearer the windy waste, the gloomy world, the strange sadness, the scarcely less strange gayety and the restless combative spirit of the land and life of the ideal Gael.

A marked characteristic of the symphony is its decisiveness; almost every movement begins with measures of chords which are as a command to listen and obey. The first sets out with a great chromatic rush as of unimpeded blasts, across which strikes in a sonority of trumpets the primary theme, as if Ossianic heroes were gathering in spite of whirlwind and storm. And so in many other instances the thought is almost imperative and spoken without any hesitancy or concession. What is to be said is said clearly and frankly; no theme is of meager size or vague shape, and each stamps itself on the mind as well as on the ear. While these themes blend as they are in duty bound to do, they preserve their characteristic, identity, and none seeks to hide itself behind some other, —they are fellows and equals.

Perhaps the one thing which will chiefly impress in regard to the symphony is its robustness. By this we do not mean noise; although the scoring is constantly full, large and powerful, but certainty and tension of grasp. One does not feel that there is any danger of the score pulling apart, so to speak, or that the orchestra rushing on in their several ways will escape the controlling hand only to be brought together at the last in a confused heap, like a team of runaway horses. There is purpose and plan in all the stress and speed, and when the exigency of the moment is passed, ease and relief come, and the convenient episode conducts naturally to the next trial. It is often dense, but we never found it cloudy. Also there is fine consideration for individual character. The symphony was heard with close attention, and there was long and warm applause after each movement. Of this the orchestra were entitled to a share, for they played with great care and an almost affectionate enthusiasm.

Philip Hale particularly liked the last two movements. "The Scherzo," he reported in the *Boston Journal* (4 November 1896), is thoroughly admirable, a delight to the amateur and the musician. And in the last movement, there are passages which proclaim loudly a breadth of conception, a skill in carrying out a grand design, a master of climax, that are not always found in modern symphonies. Themes that arrest the attention are treated in heoric spirit. The climax is sure, irresistible.

Mrs. Beach is a musician of genuine talent, who by the imagination, technical skill and sense of orchestration displayed in this symphony has brought honor to herself and the city which is her dwelling place.

Three days later Hale returned to the symphony and stated that "Mrs. H. H. A. Beach may quite justly be regarded as an epoch maker who has broken through old boundaries and presented an enrichment and extension of woman's sphere in art such as has not been surpassed or even equalled by any contemporary of her sex."

Among the others who reviewed the *Gaelic Symphony* was Percy Goetschius, who found that Mrs. Beach had "demonstrated the loftiness of her aims and her complete command of the broader music forms."[58] George Whitefield Chadwick wrote to her to congratulate her on a work "full of fine things, melodically, harmonically and orchestrally, and mighty well built besides." He counted her now "one of the boys" among American composers, but hastened to add "Oh, why wasn't I born a woman!"[59] The *Boston Globe* (1 November 1896) described her as "very modest and pretty as she came out to acknowledge the plaudits following the playing of her compositions."

The symphony was heard again on 4-5 February 1897 in Buffalo, conducted by John Land. The performance was heralded by Charlotte Mulligan in the *Buffalo Courier* (5 February 1897) as noteworthy because of the fact that the composer was a woman under 30 years, though she stressed that the sex of the composer is unimportant in judging its quality:

Taking the testimony of the musicians who have studied this symphony, it abounds with orchestral beauties, where great value becomes apparent as the forms are more perfectly brought out in outline by the various instruments. . . . Mrs. Beach possesses a discerning grasp of symphonic forms. . . . The verdict after both performances was unanimous, namely that it was a beautiful and dignified work.

The New York City premiere took place in Brooklyn on March 27 by the Boston Symphony under Emil Paur. The *Brooklyn Daily Eagle* reported on March 28:

Mrs. Beach's work is . . . remarkable, for she is not yet 30 years of age, and is of American education as well as Yankee in birth. It would not

[58] Percy Goetschius, *Mrs. H. H. A. Beach* (Boston/New York/Leipzig: Arthur P. Schmidt, 1906), 13.

[59] Letter by Chadwick to Mrs. Beach, 2 November 1896.

be in the least surprising after a publication of this example of her writings, should she develop as marked a gift for orchestral composition as that of Raff or St. Saens. In fact, it is those identical writers that she most often suggests, though it is obviously through accident, and not intention. Her symphony is called *Gaelic* because of its Gaelic rhythms, and the use of a melodic figure that is like the opening of *The Campbells Are Coming*. This figure is played upon in the symphonic fashion, its best use being in the Siciliana. There is not a little strong writing, manful, one might call it, in which the instruments are handled with confidence and authority, if not always with the fullest knowledge of their possibilities. She is fond of the string tremolo, and many sustaining chords are broken in this fashion, with novel effect. Occasionally the working out of themes is crude and the combinations are, at frequent intervals, hard, noise resulting where force is intended; but in the main the effects are legitimate and the orchestration scholarly. In the *Siciliana* the melody has absolute charm, while the lento has sentiment. As in three symphonies out of four the closing movement is almost perfunctory and least engaging, the author usually having written himself out before he reaches it. We may pride ourselves on being the only nation that has a woman composer of symphonies, at this writing, and as she has youth and enthusiasm, we may expect to hear yet more admirable works from her pen.

Most other critics were enthusiastic about the symphony,[60] but Henry Krehbiel of the *New York Tribune* noted that

two numbers were put into the [program] for the obvious purpose of irritating curious attention. One was a concert overture by E. C. Phelps, a citizen of Brooklyn, and the other a symphony in E minor by Mrs. H. H. A. Beach of Boston. Mr. Paur does strange and inexplicable things when compiling his programmes, and in this instance he associated the new works with such trivialities from the pens of standard composers, that no apology, not even the one implied by the announcement that the overture was dedicated to the memory of the founder of the [Brooklyn Institute of Arts and Sciences], and the symphony was the composition of an American woman who was expected to be on hand to hear it, was necessary to justify the scheme. . . . Possibly Mr. Paur had a kindly purpose in selecting these pieces, wishing to save the music of Mr. Phelps and Mrs. Beach from comparison with the masterworks of classical and modern writers which are the staples of our concert programmes, but he need not have done it. The listeners were not many and their attitude toward the music was conventional. Mr. Phelps was in the room and heard his music, but that circumstance

---

[60] For example, *Brooklyn Standard*, 29 March 1897, and *Brooklyn Citizen*.

did not seem to concern anybody, nor was there apparent any curiosity touching the personality of the composer of the symphony, though Mrs. Beach's music was received with the greater amount of enthusiasm. Such a reception was deserved, for in scholarship, in idea, in variety and ingeniuty of treatment and in orchestration, the symphony is far and away the better work of the two. . . . Though [Mrs. Beach] did not venture far away from the symphonic path, she made many a pretty excursion into the romantic wildwood through which it runs, and always came back with a dainty and fragrant trophy of one kind or another. If the themes of her work were held as interesting in themselves as her treatment of them, especially the instrumentation with which she has clothed them, the symphony would merit taking out of the category of works which have chiefly an interest of curiosity and performing for its own sake. She has called it "Gaelic" and justified the epithet by the use of some melodies with Irish rhythms and turns, but the task of stamping the whole work with a spirit which would be recognized as characteristically Gaelic seem to have been beyond her powers.

Krehbiel continued by hoping that the leading French woman composer of the time, Cécile Chaminade, would come to America.

Paur was obviously proud of the symphony, so he scheduled other performances of it the following season, both in Boston and in New York. Once again all the Boston critics hailed the work as the best of its kind by any American, save perhaps Edward MacDowell,[61] while the New Yorkers only grudgingly accepted it.[62] The *New York Times* reviewer expressed a common view that

Mrs. Beach's *Gaelic* symphony . . . [shows] that composition is not beyond the grasp of the feminine mind. This symphony is not a profound work, and it makes no attempt at an exploration of the classic methods of development. But as a series of tone pictures, it has considerable charm. The first and last movements are somewhat turgid in style and uncertain in form, but they have a good deal of vigor and are rich in color. The two middle movements which are built on melodies of Celtic character and ingeniously treated with solo passages, are engaging by their simple and fluent melody.

---

[61] Reviews in *Boston Courier*, 13 February 1898, *Boston Herald, Boston Transcript, Boston Beacon*, 12 February 1898, *Time and the Hour*, February 1898. Philip Hale of the *Boston Journal* is the only one to express some reservations, especially "the third movement [which] is long-winded, laboriously contrived, and at times downright dull."

[62] The most scathing review appeared in the *New York Staats-Zeitung*, 18 February 1898. Generally Dr. Beach did not let his wife read such adverse criticism, but in this case, that Mrs. Beach knew this criticism well, is attested by the fact that she herself wrote out a translation into English from the original German.

Excerpt from Mrs. Beach's *Gaelic Symphony*, signed by "Amy"

On the same program Paur included Charles Martin Loeffler's *Fantastic Concerto* for cello and orchestra; Loeffler, a distinguished composer and violinist who sat next to Kneisel on the first violin stand of the Boston Symphony Orchestra, never felt a rivalry with Mrs. Beach, whom he highly respected.

This second year of the *Gaelic Symphony* also found performances in other regions of the country. It was performed in Kansas City on March 5 under John Behr. The *Kansas City Times* of March 8 called it a remarkable composition, which makes unusual demands upon every instrument. It may justly be ranked as one of the best examples of the symphony which has ever been given here.

Austin Latchett was more concerned with the sex of the composer in his review in the *Kansas City Journal*:

> There may be no logical reason why women should not write as good music as men; but it is a fact that they have not written so brilliantly, so profoundly nor so prolifically as men have. They are almost unknown in the symphonic world. Presented anonymously, there would probably be no one to suspect that yesterday's symphony was the work of a woman; but knowing it to be such, it is but natural that some of its most distinctive beauties should be directly associated with its feminine origin.[63]

Theodore Thomas conducted the symphony in Chicago on April 8-9, and while it was apparently well received by most,[64] at least one critic was most unsympathetic.[65] Finally, in November, Fritz School conducted the work in San Francisco.

Mrs. Beach's other works, meanwhile, were not being ignored in 1896 and 1897. The song "Ecstasy," the violin "Romance," and the *Rose of Avontown* (a ballad for women's voices) remained particularly popular. The violinist Florence Heine performed "Romance" in San Francisco and Pasadena on 6 and 8 July 1897, respectively, and Marian Carpenter did the same thing in Peoria and Chicago on October 11 and December 15. William Chapman conducted the "Ballade" at the Rubinstein Club in New York in January, Benjamin Lang did the same with the Cecilia Society in Boston on February 3-4 and 16, and other performances took place in Minneapolis (February 24), St. Paul (March 24), and Los Angeles (June 17). Several other choral pieces were performed in Boston on Easter[66] and Christmas.[67] The *Three Flower Songs*, op. 31, introduced the previous year, were sung in Detroit and Philadelphia and were quickly becoming favorites with women's choral societies throughout the country. A new set of choruses for women's voices entitled *Three Shakespeare Songs*, op. 39, was introduced by Professor C. B. Stevens on December 8 with the Detroit Madrigal Club.

On Monday evening, 4 January 1897, the Kneisel Quartet presented the fourth concert of its twelfth season in Association Hall, with works by Beethoven (op. 59, no. 2), Mozart (E-flat), and Beach (Sonata for Piano and Violin in A minor, op. 34, performed

---

[63] This is part of a lengthy review of the piece. Cf. also the *Kansas City World*.

[64] As reported in the *Boston Beacon*.

[65] [Jenkins does not cite his source here.]

[66] "Alleluia, Christ Is Risen," op. 27, at Old South Church.

[67] "Bethlehem" at Boston's First Baptist Church, as well as at the Jefferson Avenue Presbyterian Church in Detroit and the Plymouth Church in Minneapolis.

by Mrs. Beach and Franz Kneisel). The sonata was a new piece, "an eminently sincere, spontaneous and able work, and one that bears the stamp of originality, as well as scholarship of surpassing merit."[68] The piece was played again in Buffalo on February 25 by Mr. and Mrs. Davidson at a string quartet concert, and it was repeated in Boston by Mrs. Beach and Kneisel at a recital tendered the students of the New England Conservatory of Music. Two new violin works (*La Captive* and *Berceuse*, op. 40) were introduced in Chicago by Rudolph Berliner, accompanied by Amy Major, on December 9; both enjoyed great popularity as salon pieces throughout the composer's lifetime.

The next year, 1898, witnessed frequent performances of Mrs. Beach's works. Especially important was another performance of the *Rose of Avontown* on September 28 at the Worcester (Massachusetts) Festival, conducted by Chadwick. Philip Hale reported in the *Boston Journal* that

> all these pieces [on the program] were performed for the first time at a Worcester Festival Concert, but I am told that Mrs. Beach's cantata, with piano accompaniment, was sung here last Spring by an amateur organization, the Home Music Club of this city. Mrs. Beach's cantata was sung in Boston by the Cecilia and therefore no criticism of its inexorable sweetness is now necessary. The orchestral accompaniment, written by the composer especially for this Festival, is appropriately sweet. The cantata was sung in appropriately lady-like manner.[69]

There were also two all-Beach programs that year. One, in which the composer participated, was on March 31 at Association Hall, Boston, in aid of the Elizabeth Peabody House, the kindergarten settlement. The concert included thirteen songs, five quartets, two duets, and four pieces for violin and piano. Such a varied program called upon the services of several well-known Boston musicians. On May 11 in Beloit, Wisconsin, the Schubert Club, assisted by Eleanor Bliss of Madison, presented a concert whose program was just as varied as the earlier one in Boston. The reviewer in the *Beloit Daily Free Press* concluded that "the general impression of the evening was in the highest degree complimentary to Mrs. Beach, as composer, and to the performers who so successfully made us acquainted with her music."

On June 1 Theodore Thomas conducted an orchestra and chorus of 400 voices in the world premiere of Mrs. Beach's "A Song of Welcome," op. 42, written especially for the opening of the Trans-Mississippi Exposition in Omaha, Nebraska. Five days later Miss Edmands sang Mrs. Beach's "The Thrush" on board the ship *Etruria* in mid-Atlantic to raise money for the Maine Monument Fund.

The Sonata for Violin and Piano was one of the most popular of Beach's pieces during the next season, that of 1899. The performance of it on March 14 at Sanders Theater, Harvard University, during a Kneisel Quartet concert featured Mrs. Beach playing on

---

[68] Mr. C. L. Capen, in the *Morning Journal*, 5 January 1897. Cf. reviews also in the *Daily Globe* and the *Boston Courier*, 10 January 1897.

[69] Other reviews in the *Boston Herald* and *Boston Record*.

a Steinertone piano, an invention by Morris Steinert of the Boston piano company, whereby the volume of the piano was increased as needed for large-hall performance. Two weeks later Kneisel and Mrs. Beach repeated the sonata in Mendelssohn Hall, 119 West 40th Street, in New York City.

> True to their record, the Boston artists, in addition to the pleasure which everyone of their listeners knew their performance of familiar music would give, provided an additional delight in introducing a novel feature calculated to make for the advancement of musical culture in America.[70]

Despite admiration for Mrs. Beach, however, the reviewer continued with disparaging remarks ("her sonata is woefully immature and one-sided . . . both instruments are treated monotonously . . . in the matter of development or ornamentation its work amounts to nothing"). The following fall Professor Carl Halir of the Halir Quartet, accompanied by the famous Venezuelan pianist Theresa Carreño, introduced the Violin Sonata to German audiences, which were much more sophisticated than American ones. The concert in Berlin on October 28 was reviewed in the *Allgemeine Musik-Zeitung* on November 3:

> It is a wild, passionate piece, which, especially in the part of the piano, falls completely out of the chamber music style and presents itself as virtuoso music. It is not at all uninteresting thematically, and it is by no means poorly worked out; there is, indeed, a tendency toward artistic contrapuntal structure, but the impression made by the whole is more of a bombastic and bedecked salon-piece than a ripe work of art.

Another review, after discussing a new string quartet on the program by Stephen Krehl, noted

> a second novelty, a pianoforte and violin sonata by Mrs. Beach of Boston, splendidly played by no less a pianist than Teresa Carreño and Prof. Halir, [which] contains some good ideas and much brilliancy in both parts.[71]

The *Berlin Volkszeitung* reported

> It has fallen to the lot of Mrs. Beach, composer of the Sonata for violin and piano, to create new fantasies and on this ground her work can certainly be considered an enrichment of the literature of music, worthy of wider dissemination. Her principal themes are at times coy, as in

---

[70] *New York Daily Tribune.* The *New York Times* review is much more favorable.

[71] *Monthly Musical Record*, December 1899.

the Scherzo molto vivace; contemplative, as in the first movement; affecting, as in the *Largo con dolores*, which is somewhat too long-drawnout; blossoming into gay, sweet-scented luxuriance in the *Finale, Allegro con fuoco*. In style, she is not individual; her dependence upon Schumann and Brahms is unmistakable, which is a weakness, for which the feminine character furnishes ground and excuse.

The sonata is sonorous and grateful in both violin and piano parts, though the latter in the last movement somewhat oversteps the allotted bounds of chamber music. There was almost too much pomp and bravura under the hands of the fiery Spaniard (Carreño). One could see and hear how warmly she felt toward the new work, and Herr Halir also gave to it the very soul of his art as a violinist. So we made the acquaintance of a beautiful work by means of a most beautiful rendering, and have not delayed the expression of our acknowledgement in the liveliest manner.[72]

On 17 December 1899 Mme. Carreño wrote to Mrs. Beach:

You certainly owe me no thanks, my dearest Mrs. Beach, and I assure you that I have never had a greater pleasure in my life than the one I had in working at your beautiful Sonata and having the good luck to bring it before the Berlin public. I consider it a great privilege and I assure you I know how to *appreciate* it for you have no greater admirer of your *great* talent, than I am. I am most eagerly looking forward to the new Concerto and let me again express to you my innermost thanks for the dedication of it. It will indeed be a work of love to learn it. When shall I get it? I hope that it will be very soon!

As you had friends at the concert here (as you tell me) it is not necessary for me to enter into detailed accounts of how your beautiful sonata was received by the public, but perhaps, it will please you to know from an experienced old artist as I am, that it really met with a *decided success*, and this is said to the credit of the public. I think that you should have been pleased with the success and perhaps also, with the interpretation, especially that of Professor Halir who played it most beautifully and felt and expressed the greatest admiration for you, as is only natural he should. We both longed to have had you here with us!

During 1899 *Rose of Avontown* continued to please audiences all across America and was Mrs. Beach's most often performed work. It was sung in Birmingham, Alabama, on January 12, by the Treble Clef Club under Mrs. Guckenberg, and was reviewed by the local press as

---

[72] 30 October 1899. The translation is that of Mrs. Beach herself.

really the great work of the evening. . . . No woman has ever written a vocal composition equal to this, and as for the matter, very few of the master composers have ever done anything better in the same line. In it the club was at its best. Indeed, it surpassed itself. In musical feeling, tenderness of expression, nothing could have been finer.

On February 23 Charles B. Stevens conducted the cantata in Detroit's Philharmonic Hall on an all-Beach concert, and remarked that Mrs. Beach is "the greatest female composer on earth, excelling Chaminade both as a composer and piano virtuoso, and is an American."[73] Stevens conducted it again on May 9 in Port Huron, Michigan, with the Michigan Madrigal Club. Three more performances occurred in March in San Francisco under Mrs. Marriner-Campbell, in Duluth, Minnesota, by the Cecilia Society, and in Concord, New Hampshire, under Mrs. Louise Gage. Such was the popularity of this work that in March 1899 the East Stroudsburg, Pennsylvania, choral society was officially named the *Beach Choral Society*, and subsequently a number of other choral organizations and music clubs were named in honor of Mrs. Beach.

On May 11, an all-Beach recital of songs was given by the faculty of the Conservatory of Musical Art in New York City. Singing teachers were laying great stress on the practical worth of Mrs. Beach's songs, which now were being assigned to voice students and presented at their recitals. She continued to write new songs during 1899, which joined her already established songs on the concert programs of singers throughout America. On May 23 Katherine M. Ricker introduced "The Year's at the Spring" at a meeting of the Boston Browning Society, which had commissioned this and two other songs ("Ah, Love but a Day" and "I Send My Heart up to Thee"). "The Year's at the Spring" soon became one of Mrs. Beach's most well-liked works. She also wrote a set of five songs on texts by Robert Burns, op. 43: "Dearie," "Scottish Cradle Song," "O Were My Love Yon Lilac Fair," "Far Awa'," and "My Lassie."

Mrs. Beach's piano music continued to be performed, especially by Arthur Foote. On numerous occasions she expressed her appreciation to him for including one or more compositions of hers on the programs of his many recitals. Her "Menuet italien" had been very successful that year as played by Foote, and after she had written to him of her pleasure at hearing one of his recitals, he replied to her:

> I thank you for your very kind note. I did not play your piece to suit myself, so that I hope sometime to play it to you more as it deserves. I like it very much the more I play it—I was fascinated by it the first time I heard it, by you.

The principal piano composition by her that year, however, was the Piano Concerto, the premiere of which took place the following year.

---

[73] Reviews, all favorable, appeared on 24 February 1899, in the *Detroit Journal* and the *Detroit Tribune*.

Piano Concerto (1900-04)

The premiere performances of Mrs. Beach's four-movement Piano Concerto in C-sharp minor, op. 45, dedicated to Teresa Carreño, took place on 6-7 April 1900 in Boston's Music Hall with the composer at the piano and Emil Paur conducting the Boston Symphony Orchestra. For the concert the soloist performed once again on the Steinertone piano. Now, unlike on previous occasions when she was adulated by the Boston critics, Mrs. Beach experienced some of the most deleterious reviews of her life. Philip Hale wrote in the *Boston Journal*:

> It is now a week since the concerto was played, with Mrs. Beach herself as the pianist, and the disappointment of the first night is only deeper today. The concerto was a disappointment in nearly every way. The structure was large, pretentious; there was an overabundance of outside ornamentation, but the interior was bare and commonplace, and there is a well-defined suspicion that the foundations and walls were not substantial. The themes were not distinguished; the development was too often vague and rambling; the moods, when there were moods, were those of other composers; thus the mood of the opening [part] of the slow movement was palpably Wagnerian. The first movement was long drawn out, and when there was the thought of the end, there was a curiously unexpected and meaningless appendix. The scherzo was harmonically monotonous, and the finale—not one measure now remains in the memory. The orchestration was crude and necessarily ineffective.

Hale goes on to suggest that Mrs. Beach's training was faulty and incomplete and that her knowledge of musical art was not equal to her ambitions. "There were notes, notes, notes; and where there were so many notes there was inevitably a few pretty passages; but there was little or no display of vital musical thought, proportion, skill in structure, or taste or brilliance in orchestral expression."

Other Boston reviewers were equally negative. Louis C. Elson, writing in the *Boston Daily Advertiser* (9 April 1900), found that "the orchestration swallows up the piano in many passages . . . the whole first movement seemed rather indefinite . . . Mrs. Beach's concerto [has] little melody." The *Boston Herald* of April 8 reported the concerto to be

> weak in ideas, and, on the whole, crabbed and uninteresting. There is but little of the flowing melody in it, with scarcely a moment of reposeful cantilena, the solo part being, for the most part, little else than difficult, and not always clear passage work.
>
> The orchestration is steadily thick and noisy, and too frequently so massive that the solo instrument does not and cannot loom through

it . . . the concerto is monotonously void of contrasts. There are fire enough and passion enough in the work, but they did not appear to lead to anything that was coherent or comprehensible.

The critic of the *Boston Transcript* (undated clipping) suggested that Mrs. Beach would have been better off writing shorter, less pretentious works in order to gain more skill in writing for orchestra and more maturity in dealing with larger composition. He continued:

No doubt there is much beauty in the work, no little genuineness of feeling, a considerable fertility of invention. But there is too much going on at the same time; that is, too much until the work has been so rescored as to make its complexity intelligible to the ear. For one thing, however, she plays it wonderfully, with consummate technique and great beauty of expression. She was enthusiastically received, as well she deserved to be.

W. D. Quint gave the work a back-handed compliment when he stated in the *Boston Traveller* (9 April 1900) that "the most marked thing about Mrs. Beach's new work is its masculinity, strength and largeness looming in every direction." Only Howard M. Ticknor of the *Boston Courier* (8 April 1900) granted the concerto a favorable review.

Later that year, Mrs. Beach received an invitation to attend a performance of another concerto by a lady composer-pianist in Boston. Madame Helen Hopekirk, who had recently joined the faculty of the New England Conservatory, wrote a piano concerto which was to be premiered by the Boston Symphony Orchestra on one of its Cambridge, Massachusetts, concerts. Just prior to the premiere, Madame Hopekirk desired the valued presence of Mrs. Beach at a reading of the concerto at the Conservatory, and Mrs. Beach accepted the invitation. There is no indication of her opinion of the Hopekirk concerto, but there was no hesitation in showing interest in the music of a kindred soul: a struggling woman composer in Boston.

As in the past few years, Mrs. Beach's music was now widely performed. The Violin Sonata had performances on 2 March 1900 in Louisville, Kentucky, by John Surman (violinist) and Hattie Bishop (pianist), and in April at the Salle Playel in Paris by Ysaÿe and the pianist Raoul Pugno. There were four all-Beach concerts: in Limestone College, Guffney, South Carolina, on March 6; in Buffalo, New York, by the Cecilia Club later in March; in Evanston, Illinois, by the Women's Club on April 10; and in Steinert Hall in Boston on November 20. This last presented Beach's piano works on a pianola or player piano. The *Rose of Avontown* was presented by the Thursday Morning Club of Boston on January 18, and the Cecilia Club of Pittsfield, Massachusetts, repeated it in July. The Euterpeans of Milwaukee gave a performance of the *Rose* at a convention there, also in July. Various singers, such as Mrs. Marshall Pease of the Detroit Treble Clef Club and C. B. Stevens of Detroit, included Beach songs on their programs. Lillian Nordica, who performed "Ecstasy" and "Spring" in Rochester, New York, and elsewhere that year, received copies of songs from Mrs. Beach and acknowledged them in a letter in which she stated that she hoped to see Mrs. Beach in Boston and sing the songs for her personally.[74] Mrs. Beach also gave a solo recital on the Sanders Theater chamber music series at Harvard University on February 13, which included four of her own piano works.

The trend continued in 1901. Again both the cantata *Rose of Avontown* and the Violin Sonata had worldwide acclaim. The former was performed in New York City and in Birmingham, Alabama. After a performance of the sonata in London by the violinist Sigmund Beel, the *London Graphic* stated:

> A good, new sonata for violin and piano is something of a rarity, and Mr. Sigmund Beel is to be congratulated most heartily on having produced one at this concert at St. James Hall on Wednesday evening. It is the work of Mrs. H. H. A. Beach, and it is both pleasing and original. The first movement is a fine, broad piece of writing, founded on good melodies, the second theme being particularly charming. The slow movement, too, is very beautiful, and full of very real feeling, forming an admirable contrast to the vivacious scherzo which precedes it. The work is one which might very well be added to the repertoire of violinists, for it is certainly worth playing. The performance which Mr. Beel and Mr. Henry Bird gave of it was excellent in every way, and the violinist's fine tone and real musicianship have never been displayed to better advantage.[75]

Arthur Foote congratulated Mrs. Beach on the London performance of the sonata in the same letter in which he thanked her for praising his own new violin piece; despite her busy schedule and successful career, she never failed to have time to study the works of her contemporary American composers and to praise them.[76] Mrs. Beach, herself, and the violinist Max Bendix performed her sonata at Steinert Hall in Boston on March 20 at a concert by the Bendix Quartet. Rather than Schumann and Brahms, Wagner and Grieg seemed to be the influences on the piece according to William F. Apthorp, who was purplexed by the structure of the work but recognized that it had musical merit and, as with any new work, needed time to be fully appreciated. Even the highly critical Philip Hale found the sonata "among the most spontaneous and genial of her works,"[77] and Louis Elson called the sonata "a work of thorough worth."[78] Mrs. Beach once again performed the sonata with the Kneisel Quartet, this time in Philadelphia on December 16 and in New York on December 17.

---

[74] Letter, London, 10 September 1900.

[75] 29 November 1901. The *London Times*, on the same date, concurred.

[76] Letter from Foote at St. Botolph Club, 2 Newbury Street, Boston.

[77] *Boston Journal.*

[78] *Boston Advertiser.* Other reviews appeared in the *Boston Courier* by Howard Malcolm Ticknor, and in the *Anzeiger*, 23 March 1901, the only German-language newspaper in Boston at that time. Mrs. Beach herself made an English translation of the last review.

All-Beach concerts continued in Boston and in Chillicothe, Ohio. Songs were sung in Philadelphia, Boston, Detroit, and England. A section from the Mass (*Gradual*: "Thou Glory of Jerusalem") and an aria ("Wandering Clouds," the *Mary Stuart* aria) were performed at a concert of music by women composers given by the Baltimore Symphony Orchestra under Ross Jungnickel on March 14. Maud Powell continued her championship of Beach's music by including the Mazurka on a May 8 concert in Brooklyn.

Mrs. Beach appeared several other times in 1901 as pianist. For example, she performed a group of miscellaneous pieces for the MacDowell Club of Boston on January 20. So busy were these seasons that we may wonder how she managed to continue both performing and writing. According to her own notes, in 1901 she composed six piano duets ("Katydid," "Robin Waltz," "Good Night," "Evening Hymn," "Tarantelle," and "March"), the cantata *Sylvania*, the songs "Good Morning" and "Good Night," an aria "La Fille de Jephte" with orchestral accompaniment, simplified accompaniments to the songs "Sweetheart" and "La Secret," and a new piano accompaniment and a violin obligato to the "Hymn of Trust."

Although *Sylvania* was not premiered publicly until 1905, Mrs. Beach played the piano score at one of the Wednesday afternoon musicales in her home at 28 Commonwealth Avenue for invited guests. Among the honored listeners was John Knowles Paine of Harvard, who wrote to her a few days later:

> I did not half express my delight in hearing your beautiful cantata, so beautifully played by the composer. I have been haunted ever since by the memory of your music. Among modern works of this class it will have a very high place I am sure. Only it is so hard to make our American music known. I hope you will live long enough to enjoy the full recognition of your great gifts as a composer. I am proud of you as an American composer. Art knows no sex. Why should not a woman achieve as much in creative music, as in literature? George Sand, George Eliot etc. are not to have the field to themselves in the future. I will not add George Washington, as he did not even play the flute, as did his contemporary, Frederick the Great. With this episodical ending (quite in the form of a Strauss Symphonic poem) I thank you again for the memorable afternoon. When we meet again, I will tell you something quite to the point.
>
> Meanwhile I will end mystically,
>
> > Yours sincerely,
> > [signed John Knowles Paine]

On March 2 the following year, Paine wrote to Mrs. Beach again, this time in reference to his own composition *The Birds*, based on Aristophanes' play. He was scheduled to perform the piece a few days later for the Apollo Club, and apparently he had shown the score to Mrs. Beach, who wrote to him of her approval. Paine responded "I am glad that the 'Birds' sing to you, and I am pleased that you will be present at the Apollo Concert."

During the year 1902 Mrs. Beach was busy with many recitals. There was the Chickering Hall concert of Miss Terry's series on March 6, which marked the first public performance of the songs "Canzonette," "Good-Night," "Good-Morning," and "Come, Ah, Come," and the piano transcription of Richard Strauss's *Serenade*. Mrs. Beach accompanied the contralto Gertrude Edmands and the violinist Olive Mead.

> This was a pleasant concert of a restful nature. . . . Mrs. Beach and Miss Mead played the opening number, the *Kreutzer Sonata*, with simplicity and straightforwardness of style. . . . The ensemble was excellent, neither player overshadowing the other, and it is a satisfaction to add, the cover of the pianoforte was left open. The sonata was much applauded. . . . Miss Edmands sang two groups. . . . The three new [songs in this group by Beach], by the way, show skill in invention and careful workmanship, but on a first hearing they seem to lack the passion of "Ecstacy" and the tender simplicity of "Sweetheart and I" which Mme. Blauvelt sang yesterday.[79]

> Just now [Mrs. Beach] is giving her attention mainly to writing songs, in which grace and melody prevail. Womanly love of detail and a conscientious understanding of the copybook precept anent doing well whatever one does, are obvious features in Mrs. Beach's character, therefore one always feels absolute confidence that anything she considers ready for public production is quite worthy of public appreciation. . . . Mrs. Beach is always gifted with a keen discernment when it comes to choosing words for her songs.[80]

> Having accomplished some great things, such as her mass and her instrumental pieces of classical form, Mrs. Beach is paying more attention to writings which, although minor in extent, are yet large enough to contain perfected ideas of beauty, and in which melody and grace prevail. All the new songs were attractive and free-spirited, but we enjoyed most the *Good-Night* and *Good-Morning*, which, like that favorite, *The Thrush*, were instinct with quiet cheer and gentle joy. As pianist, she gave a Brahms *Caprice*, a Chopin study, and a delicately fine original transcription of a serenade by R. Strauss, all with more impetus and enthusiasm than she has always found for salon music, to which she has often given a rather too academic and serious treatment.[81]

Philip Hale preferred "Canzonetta" as "the most spontaneous and pleasing" song.

For two days in March, the 18th and 19th, Mrs. Beach was active on behalf of the Brooklyn Institute, founded in 1823. She performed a benefit recital on the first night, and the following evening she participated in a Department of Music dinner. The aim

---

[79] *Boston Transcript.*

[80] *Boston Home Journal.*

[81] *Commercial Advertiser.*

was to raise $1,300,000 for the building and endowment of a music hall. She played works by Bach, Beethoven, Brahms, Mendelssohn, Schubert, Liszt, and Chopin, as well as by herself:

> The artist proved that she is a fine interpreter of all these composers, a feat to be commented on, because many musical writers insist, in their performances, upon infusing their individuality throughout the performance. It were needless to say that Mrs. Beach's technical work was of a high order; it was refined and yet strong and she was justified in her confidence and self possession. Indeed, accuracy and a certain grace were among the main characteristics of her style. Were one inclined to be very critical it might be said that her trills were uneven in brilliancy, being sometimes crisp and at other times muffled. Her sentences and phrasing were always admirable and her fluency remarkable. . . .
>
> Mrs. Beach's contribution from her own compositions was a "ballade" in D flat, starting with a pretty theme. . . . It was warmly applauded. . . . It would almost seem that Brahms was a favorite writer with the artist so sympathetically were the numbers [by Brahms] played by her. . . . The poetry of Chopin's style so captivated the audience that Mrs. Beach was applauded until she consented to give an encore as half of the people were getting up to leave. The audience numbered many more than Mrs. Beach's recital in Manhattan.[82]

At the dinner the following evening, the toastmaster, Edmund D. Fisher, thanked Mrs. Beach for her concert, and she responded by playing three compositions of her own: "Fireflies," "Danse des fleurs," and "Dreaming." On the printed souvenir menu Fisher thanked her again by dedicating a poem to her:

> We love the music of the woods and streams,
>   And peace and calm contentment doth it bring;
> We love the rhythm of the ocean surge,
>   Whose voice in every hollow shell doth ring.
>
> The magic of the Great Composer's mind
>   Transmutes the songs of nature's heavenly choir,
> And symphonies in harmony divine,
>   With golden sound a listening world inspire.

Besides the Strauss transcription and the song "Canzonetta," op. 48, no. 4, Mrs. Beach completed several other songs in 1902 ("Wir Drei," "Ich sagte nicht," and "Junitage"), which would ultimately become part of op. 51. In addition she set the anthem "America" for mixed chorus and wrote an orchestral score for "Song of Welcome."

---

[82] *Brooklyn Eagle*, 19 March 1902.

Early the next year, after Mrs. Beach had congratulated Horatio Parker, then director of the School of Music at Yale University, on the success of his organ concerto in a concert in Chicago, he responded to her that "the approval of our fellow-composers is the reward best worth striving for in our kind of work and I appreciate it from you." Once again, she was ever ready to aid and encourage American composers.

In March 1903 there was another all-Beach concert in Boston, this time for the benefit of the Nursery for Blind Babies. Soprano Kileski-Bradbury, contralto Mrs. Homer E. Sawyer, and tenor George J. Parker sang to the accompaniment of Mrs. Beach. The reviewer for the *Boston Herald* repeated a lament that had first been heard the year following Mrs. Beach's marriage to Dr. Beach, namely that she performed in public only when there was a special benefit and otherwise deprived the public of her extraordinary pianistic gifts. More than ever, however, Mrs. Beach valued her home first and composition a narrow second, and she placed no great value on touring as a concert virtuoso. That she could be such a pianist, however, became evident later when necessity demanded it.

Another all-Beach concert took place in Chelsea, a suburb of Boston, on April 13. Madame Kileski and Olive Mead assisted the composer in a program that included, among other works, the Sonata for Violin and Piano and three Browning songs. Mrs. Beach played four solo piano pieces, two from manuscript, and when she finished,

> Mrs. Beach was met by the president [of the Chelsea Woman's Club], Mrs. Endicott, who presented her with an immense laurel wreath to which was fastened a bunch of pink roses tied with a club pink ribbon. The applause was so great it was some time before Mrs. Endicott could say that as a part of Mrs. Beach's earlier life was spent in our city, the Woman's Club as an organization of representative women wished to show their deep appreciation of the high reputation she had won in the musical world, to which the dainty little lady could only bow her thanks.[83]

Mrs. Beach treasured the laurel, which remained in a prominent place in her home until her death.[84]

As in the previous year, during 1903 Mrs. Beach's compositions were unpretentious. They included mostly arrangements and orchestrations. But meanwhile the composer's reputation was spreading, this time to Italy. The Boston soprano Marcella Craft, singing in Italy as Signorina Marcella Cratti, sang Mrs. Beach's "A Song of Love" and "My Sweetheart and I" in Italian translations; they were received by the Milanese public with "genuine pleasure."[85] The following year Emma Eames Story wrote to Mrs. Beach from Paris that

---

[83] *Chelsea Gazette.*

[84] The last time I saw the laurel wreath, presented to Mrs. Beach at this concert, it still hung on a wall in the music room of the composer's Centerville, Massachusetts, home, now occupied by its inheritor, Mrs. Lillian Buxbaum, a singer for whom Mrs. Beach wrote several of her later songs.

[85] *Musical Courier* and *Boston Herald*, 17 May 1903.

I have sung a great deal in the last two years your setting of Browning's words "The Year's at the Spring." It was first given to me by my mother. It has never failed to carry by storm any audience to which I have sung it.[86]

The son of the poet who lives in Florence is a great personal friend of ours, in fact more like a member of my husband's *family* than a mere friend. The other day in Florence I took the occasion to sing the song to him. He was intensely moved by it and said the music and the words seemed to form one thing so that one could hardly call it a "setting." He said that one could not imagine anything more perfectly "married" than his father's words to your music. I thought it would be a gratification to you to know this as the present Mr. Browning is a devoted lover of music having devoted a great deal of his time also to the study of it.

The only notable concert in 1904 took place on March 3 in Potter Hall in Boston, when as part of the Hoffman Quartet concert Mrs. Beach and Mr. Hoffman performed the Violin-Piano Sonata.[87] The compositions of this year, once again, were minor and mostly sketches or arrangements.

Piano Quintet (1905-09)

While the years 1901-04 were relatively quiet for Mrs. Beach, the activities of 1905 reached a new peak with three triumphant concerts in February, April, and December. The list of finished compositions for this year include *Balkan Variations*, the cantata *Sea Fairies*, the songs "The Years at the Spring" and "When Soul Is Joined to Soul," a *Te Deum*, a *Benedictus*, and the duet for soprano and tenor "Give Me Not Love." It also saw the premiere of her cantata *Sylvania*, which had been written in 1901. In addition, she performed in several concerts.

The *Balkan Variations* were played for the first time at Mrs. Beach's recital sponsored by the Faelton Pianoforte School at Huntington Chambers Hall, Boston, on February 8:

This recital proved most enjoyable to the large audience present, many of them students. The novelty of the program was Mrs. Beach's variations, heard for the first time. These Balkan themes, four in

---

[86] Letter dated 14 September 1904.

[87] Reviews in *Boston Journal* and *Daily Advertiser*, both 4 March 1904.

number, are of the folk song type. There are seven variations, in which a funeral march, valse lento, a bit of canon, and other devices are used most effectively. The set of variations shows Mrs. Beach at her best as a creative musician.[88]

These themes, from folk songs of that long-harassed borderland between Christian and Moslem Europe, are in general of a melancholy character, and from them Mrs. Beach has developed a series of compositions marked by deep feeling, and great variety and richness. At the conclusion of the programme, the artist obligingly responded to the applause by a sparkling little composition of her own, entitled "Fireflies."[89]

Philip Hale, who had been critical of some of Mrs. Beach's works in the past, returned to her list of great admirers with a glowing review in the *Boston Herald*:

Mrs. Beach is ranked high among American composers, and she is one of the few that has a foreign reputation based on knowledge of some of her works. Many women have composed and found publishers; very few have shown such diversified talent. She has won success with symphony and concerto and chamber music as well as with less pretentious pieces; with mass, jubilate, cantata, as well as with songs. Her songs have far more than a local reputation; they are found on the programmes of singers throughout the land. It is enough to say of her variations, played last night for the first time, that they show a sure acquaintance with the technic of composition; they are something more than an exercise, well planned and carried out; the musical contents are interesting without regard to the technical display; and the work will undoubtedly be ranked among her best.[90]

On April 7 the cantata *Sylvania* was first performed in Boston's Chickering Hall:

It is certainly a musical event of the first class that can attract an audience of 600 to 700 of the most cultured and enthusiastic patrons of the art in Boston, headed by such masters as Mr. Gericke, conductor of the Symphony orchestra, and Prof. J. K. Paine of Harvard university, to say nothing of other composers. . . .

This gifted woman, who is acknowledged as standing at the very head of American composers of her sex, deserved the distinguished tribute thus paid her, for not only her cantata, but the various other

---

[88] *Boston Journal*, 9 February 1905.

[89] R. C. DeWitte in the *Boston Transcript*, 9 February 1905.

[90] 9 February 1905. Other reviews appeared in the *Musical Times*, 11 February 1905, and the *Chicago Musical Leader and Concertgoer*.

selections from her works, of which there were an even dozen, were thoroughly charming, and kept her audience keyed up to a high pitch of esthetic delight and of enthusiasm all the evening.

The work, which is in text, a translation from the German, is well named "Sylvania," for it is illustrative of a sylvan wedding, and both the lines and music are redolent throughout of the whisperings of the forest, the carolling of birds and songs of elves and fairies. Like a "Midsummer Night's Dream," it carries the auditor away into an age where all the world is young and innocent and beautiful.

The work was rendered with rarest excellence by a chorus of about 50 highly-trained and youthful voices, about evenly divided as to sex, and conducted by E. Cutter Jr. director of the Amphion Club of Melrose, which formed the male part of the chorus. The solo roles were mainly rendered, and with fine effect, by Mme Caroline Gardner Clarke. Mrs. Beach herself furnished piano accompaniment which was surprisingly effective for so large a singing body, and Mr. Cutter achieved a notable triumph in the masterly manner in which he handled the whole performance.

The cantata was preceded by [. . .] song selections, which were rendered by Mme Clarke, George J. Parker, Miss Rebecca W. Cutter and Miss Grace Lowell Bradbury. Miss Cutter revealed a soprano voice of rare sweetness and beauty, singing a couple of love songs with a delicacy and tenderness and purity of tone that won for her a positive ovation. Miss Bradbury, in a duet with Mr. Parker, met with no less appreciation, showing the possession of a pure, flexible and powerful voice under perfect control and conspicuously marked by dramatic brilliancy.

Mr. Parker won notable favor by his tenor solos, and Jacques Hoffman rendered one of Mrs. Beach's "Romances" with exquisite sweetness and feeling on the violin.

At the close of the concert about half the brilliant audience crowded about the stage, and Mrs. Beach was obliged to hold an impromptu reception at which she was showered with congratulations.[91]

A few days later Mrs. Beach received letters from Paine and Chadwick congratulating her on the premiere of *Sylvania*. Paine extolled the event:

What a triumph you achieved at the concert! It was a great success in every way. I was delighted to hear the cantata given so well. I knew beforehand that it would be recognized by everybody as one of the finest works you have created. All honor to your genius![92]

With his usual charm, Paine concluded that "your mother sat behind me, no doubt she had her eye on me." Chadwick was equally thrilled by the concert:

---

[91] *Boston Globe*, 8 April 1905. Another review appeared in the *Boston Record*.

[92] Letter from Paine to Mrs. Beach, dated Harvard University, Cambridge, Mass., 11 April 1905.

> I heard the concert of your compositions on Friday night with greatest
> pleasure and pride. I say pleasure because your music is in every way
> so sympathetic to me, and pride because an American and a woman
> can produce such strong and musical ideas and express them with such
> thorough mastery, and how fresh, new and beautiful it all sounds after
> some of these unhealthy new concoctions, painfully grubbed out of the
> scale of whole tones! I congratulate you with all my heart and look
> forward to more of the same kind.[93]

After the triumphs of February and April, Mrs. Beach and her husband spent the
summer in Centerville on the southern tip of Cape Cod. There, just before departing for
Boston, she received a letter from Emil Paur, who had become the new conductor of the
Pittsburgh Orchestra. He invited her to perform the Saint-Saëns Piano Concerto, and he
and the orchestra would also do her *Gaelic Symphony*.[94] The eighth pair of regular sub-
scription concerts, featuring Mrs. Beach as both composer and performer, took place on
Friday and Saturday, December 29 and 30, in Pittsburgh's Carnegie Music Hall. Jennie Irene
Mix, a reporter from the *Pittsburgh Post*, interviewed the composer several days before.

> Desiring to meet the only woman who has ever composed a symphony
> that has been played by the great orchestras of this country, a repre-
> sentative of *The Post* called on Mrs. H. H. A. Beach yesterday afternoon
> in her rooms at the Hotel Schenley.
>   The caller found in the famous composer a woman of charming
> personality. There is nothing striking in her appearance. If one were
> to pass her on the street she would not be pointed out as "a genius,"
> there is no trace of oddity about her, for at first glance she seems no
> different from those women who cannot compose symphonies. But
> it is not long after beginning to talk with her that the listener realizes
> that a remarkable woman is speaking.
>   Mrs. Beach's face shows culture, force and sweetness in every line
> and her eyes are like twin stars so full are they of light. It is in her eyes
> and forehead that her intellect shows the most while the mouth and
> the chin are distinctly feminine and lovable. The caller fully intended
> to notice how Mrs. Beach was dressed but the truth is that as soon as
> she began to speak she so charmed her listener that no thought of
> clothes came to the mind and it takes a wonderful woman to do that.
>   Mrs. Beach is wholly lacking in conceit and preferred to tell of how
> interesting she found this great center of industry in the middle West
> to talking [about] herself. She is accompanied here by her husband,
> Dr. H. H. A. Beach, a prominent physician of Boston. The two had
> just returned from a drive through Highland park. "It is beautiful,"
> exclaimed Mrs. Beach with enthusiasm and Dr. Beach asserted it was
> worth coming to Pittsburgh to see.

---

[93] Letter from Chadwick to Mrs. Beach, dated New England Conservatory of Music, 12 April 1905.

[94] Letter from Emil Paur to Mrs. Beach, dated Vienna, 8 September 1905.

But they have come to the city for other reasons than to drive through the parks, for Mrs. Beach will be the soloist at the concerts of the Pittsburgh orchestra this week and her *Gaelic Symphony* will be played at the same concerts. She has composed a large number of works for the voice, the piano, the violin and some for chorus and orchestra, the most prominent among the latter being a mass, but even all these works do not represent the unusual degree of achievement attained in composing a symphony, which has been played by the great orchestras in the country under the greatest conductors. When the conversation was finally turned to the work of this woman who as a composer stands alone, she showed in every sentence the enthusiasm of one who loves her work.

She is not only a composer but a concert-pianist, and will play the Saint-Saëns concerto with the orchestra. Her hand is that of one of the favored musical ones, for it is a natural hand for the piano, of average size and wonderfully flexible.

Because of this flexibility its possessor has never been obliged to drudge over technique as have some.

The presence of Mrs. Beach in Pittsburgh is something of unusual interest, for in music at least there is none other like her, while her appearance indicates that she may transcend the majority of her sex in other lines than that of her art.[95]

Mix's review of the first concert was generally positive, but she seemed a little baffled by the fury and lack of repose in the symphony.[96] She reviewed the second concert with more enthusiasm for the concerto:

Mrs. Beach of Boston was the soloist and played Saint-Saëns['s] familiar piano concerto with fine power. Her playing is that of a broad-minded, experienced musician, who knows the whole gamut of musical expression, and the means employed to obtain all shades of effects. To an adequate technique and strength is joined the trained mind of the composer, used to the intricacy of all modern scores; the mental grasp, that lays before the listener the main lines of a composition undimmed by mass of detail, the power of subjecting self to the composer; the skill to interest the listener so that technical proficiency seems simply a means to an end—all these things are Mrs. Beach's to an unusual degree. One could dwell on the beauty of tone, the firmness and surety in chord work, the brilliancy of the octave work, were one so inclined, but the greater satisfaction was surely derived from the fact that the audience recognized a master mind subjecting itself to another master mind in the serious art-spirit that always commands admiration.[97]

---

[95] *Pittsburgh Post*, 27 December 1905.

[96] *Pittsburgh Post*, 30 December 1905.

[97] *Pittsburgh Post*, 31 December 1905.

But Mix did admit that the "symphony . . . seemed, on a single hearing a thing of beauty."

Mrs. Beach's efforts were also reviewed in the *Pittsburgh Times*, whose reporter briefly interviewed her during intermission. "Pittsburgh is greatly to be congratulated on having Mr. Paur as conductor of the Pittsburgh Orchestra—watch carefully that you don't lose him, for such men are scarce in the musical world, and he will be wanted everywhere." She continued "with sparkling earnestness":

> Your orchestra is deserving of the highest praise. I have listened carefully, with well-paid attention, and I find that every man plays with the individuality of a soloist and an artist; under the master hand of Mr. Paur they respond with the unity of a many-keyed organ under the slightest touch of an intelligent hand. The men seem enwrapped in Mr. Paur and give the closest attention—they seem to understand his very thoughts and respond instantly; going in the direction and giving the coloring he desires. While every man seems to apply himself individually, they are a very united whole.
>
> As to numbers, I do not believe your orchestra could be improved upon. Of course, a great spacious hall would require a greater number of pieces, but under normal circumstances and for the average hall, I should not improve upon the number of men. I think there is a limit to the size of an orchestra in attaining the best result; too many pieces become unwieldy, much the same as an exceptionally large chorus.
>
> To say that I am pleased with Pittsburgh audiences is but faintly conveying my delight at my reception here and the enjoyment I have found in the recitals. So completely attentive—why this very afternoon while I was playing the concerto which is very soft at times, one could hear a pin drop in any portion of the hall. I also noticed that when applause is given that it does not come from any one particular direction, but is general. It shows that appreciation is general and that Pittsburgh audiences yearn for the highest type of music. This appreciation has been clearly demonstrated by the responses during the recitals which I have attended.

She concluded the interview by repeating her esteem for Paur and hoping that he would be able to bring the Pittsburgh Orchestra to Boston later that season.[98]

Upon her return to Boston just after the New Year, Mrs. Beach immediately started preparing for her piano recital sponsored by the Faelton Pianoforte School. The recital took place on Wednesday evening, February 21, at 8 p.m., in the Arlington Chambers Hall. The occasion was rare in that Mrs. Beach did not play any of her own works.

---

[98] The *Pittsburgh Dispatch* also interviewed Mrs. Beach, where she repeated what she had already said in the other interviews.

But if she did not program her compositions here, others continued performing her music extensively throughout the country. Most popular in 1906 was the song "The Years at the Spring," which Johanna Gadski, Marcella Sembrich, Emma Eames, Lillian Nordica, and others included in their recitals. At Gadski's recital in Denver on February 15 at Trinity Church, the wintry air was transformed into a beautiful spring:

> The vital, vivid moment of the concert came, however, when as one of the English songs, Gadski sang that paean of affirmation which Browning penned and Mrs. Beach set to music, *The Year's at the Spring*. Gadski, robed in a frock of shimmering green gauze, had come on the stage wearing a heavy fur boa as a shield against the drafts of the house, and immediately swung out into the inspiring optimism of the music and sang. . . . That one song by Gadski was worth a year's deprivations in other directions.

Nine days later the same soprano sang the same song in San Francisco.

> In the second part of the program the group of modern songs was greeted with eager delight. Again the artist was kind, singing "The Year's at the Spring" and the "Spring Song" twice. . . . She was nothing short of superb. . . . The enthusiasm was such as is seldom seen here. . . .[99]

Later that year Gadski made a triumphant return to New York, proving that she was the leading Wagnerian soprano of the time. In a recital in Carnegie Hall, she bested her San Francisco recital by singing Mrs. Beach's song three times as an encore.[100] Then on to Boston in December she sang the song as an encore, which the young Boston critic Olin Downes considered "a real pleasure."[101] According to the *Boston Transcript*, this song was sung in Boston on nine programs in seven days.

> Yet so many repetitions, and of very varying understanding and expression, seemed in no way to stale it. At the ninth quite as much as at the first the listener was ready to believe that in its kind it is a very admirable song. The verses . . . are a perfect lyric, concentrated, rapturous, simple, springing even on the printed page into song. Idea and mood, word and rhythm melt into a single glowing whole. . . . It sounds inevitable; like the one more exalted speech that the verse could endure.[102]

---

[99] *San Francisco Bulletin*, 25 February 1906.

[100] *New York Sun*.

[101] *Boston Post*.

[102] *Boston Transcript*, 21 December 1906. H. T. Parker reviewed Sembrich's and Eames's performances in Boston.

Nordica sang "The Year's at the Spring" in New York, where it was called "one of the best songs produced on this side of the Atlantic."[103]   The popularity of the song was so great that it was arranged for chorus so that the many women's choral clubs in the country could sing it. In such an arrangement it was sung at a meeting of the Massachusetts Federation of Women's Clubs meeting in Springfield on 19 May 1906.

Other works by Mrs. Beach were also performed. Olga Samaroff, one-time wife of Leopold Stokowski and a pianist-teacher of great reknown, began programming Mrs. Beach's "Gavotte fantastique," op. 54, no. 2, in recitals with the tenor Van Norden, who was including "The Year's at the Spring" in his programs. On June 27 Samaroff wrote to Mrs. Beach:

> I had much success in St. Paul with your "Gavotte Fantastique" which is beautiful! The audience insisted on a repetition which however I could not give as my group (it was a miscellaneous program) was strictly limited. I intend to play it a great deal next season, and most certainly shall in Boston.
>
> I would be much interested to know the new Variations and it would be most kind of you to send them to me. . . . Hoping that I may have the pleasure of meeting you sometime in Boston. . . .[104]

Apparently Mrs. Beach sent her music to various artists to interest them in performing it. In March 1906, Rudolph Ganz, already residing in Chicago, acknowledged receipt of her piano concerto "which is new to me, but which will certainly soon become a friend."

Among the compositions Mrs. Beach finished in 1906 is an orchestral version of *Balkana* (the theme and two variations, one of which was new). She also published her *Service in A* (on January 16) and sketched out *Hibernia*, a suite for piano in three movements.

The annual piano recitals by Mrs. Beach for the Faelton School of Pianoforte continued in 1907 and 1908. The first took place on 6 February 1907, in Steinert Hall, Boston. Once again the composer played her *Balkan Variations*, op. 60, which was the only piece by her on the program. For the rest of the concert she played MacDowell's "Dans le hammac," "Danse andalouse," "To a Water Lily," and "Will o' the Wisp" (the first two from *Les Orientales*, op. 37, the last two from *Woodland Sketches*, op. 51). Carl Faelton joined Mrs. Beach in Busoni's arrangement of Liszt's *Rhapsodie espagnole*. The 1908 concert took place on February 12 in the same hall. Mrs. Beach played works by MacDowell, Brahms, Bach, and herself (*Suite française*, and *Les Rêves de Columbine*), and Carl Faelton joined her with Saint-Saëns's *Variations on a Theme by Beethoven*, op. 35.

For many persons the public concerts were supplemented by the private concerts that Mrs. Beach continued to perform at her home on Commonwealth Avenue for invited guests. Once a week, unless the composer-pianist was out of town, these musicales took place regularly. For the uninvited music lover, however, only the rare public performances

---

[103] *New York Sun.*

[104] Letter from Olga Samaroff to Mrs. Beach, 27 June 1906.

were a chance to recognize the greatness of Boston's leading pianist. A Boston visitor in 1907, Marion Dwight, was fortunate enough to hear a concert that may have been one of the private ones, and wrote a letter to the *Boston Beacon* (9 March 1907) in which she praises the city for its many attractions.

> After hearing all the great pianists who have visited here this season, I wish to say, if it is not too personal, that you have right here a rare and lovely artist in Mrs. H. H. A. Beach. Her interpretation of Bach, Chopin and Brahms is nothing short of wonderful. In her composition she shows a broad sense and beauty of imagination, which, though appreciated now by the truly musical, will be much more so in the coming years. Her modesty and quiet womanly dignity, combined with the rarest generosity of nature, make of her a figure which cannot be too highly thought of, and my privilege of having met her and heard her play will ever remain one of my dearest memories of delightful Boston.

Mrs. Beach's new compositions for these two years include *Suite française* and *Eskimos* for piano, the cantata *The Chambered Nautilus*, the songs "After," "Baby," "Mamma Dear," and "Hush, Baby Dear," and a major new chamber work, the Piano Quintet in F-sharp minor, op. 67. The premiere of the quintet took place at the third concert of the Hoffman Quartet on 27 February 1908, in Potter Hall, 187 Huntington Avenue, Boston, with Mrs. Beach joining the quartet, and the same artists repeated the work on April 24 at Tufts University. The program also included Schumann's F-major String Quartet and Debussy's Quartet. According to Louis Elson:

> The chief interest of the concert centred [*sic*] in a new piano Quintette by the greatest American woman composer, Mrs. H. H. A. Beach, and this interest was increased by having the composer herself at the piano. As a pianist, and particularly as a chamber-musician, Mrs. Beach has won a secure position. She has a keen insight into the ensemble effects and her piano-playing generally becomes a real support and not a disturbance; but last night, with the lid of the instrument raised, the piano often became too loud for the best results.
>
> In composition this eminent lady is not retrograding, as witness her recent powerful variations on Balkan Themes. The piano quintette of last night may not disturb the supremacy of the Schumann, the Cesar Franck, or the Brahms piano quintettes, but it is a fine composition nevertheless. It holds well to form and we are glad to see that Mrs. Beach does not bow down before the fetich [*sic*] of incomprehensibility and ugliness, which rules so much modern music. She still writes melodies and develops their figures in true classical manner.
>
> The introduction was rather odd; the soft, stationary tone of the violin and the "ff" preluding of the piano did not mingle at all, but at least the strange union aroused the attention of the auditor at the outset. There was an effective contrast in the first two themes, and some of the strong effects of the first movement came back in the finale.

Both in the first movement and in the Finale, Mrs. Beach worked up strong climaxes. Of the three movements the first seemed the most powerful at a first hearing.

The slow movement, with its muted beginning was rhapsodical in a large degree. Possibly its chief fault lay in the fact that it was fragmentary and too often tended towards accompanied solo; yet there was beauty in this also, and the whole composition was a worthy one. The composer was greatly applauded, recalled, and received a floral tribute.

There was an especially large audience present, Potter Hall being better filled than we have seen it at recent chamber concerts.[105]

The other premiere of 1908 was of *The Chambered Nautilus*, on April 25, at the Thursday Morning Club Concert in Jordan Hall.[106] The cantata

is of dramatic and romantic cast, and shines particularly by the uniform effectiveness of its vocal writing. The various moods of the poem are fittingly embodied in the musical setting. Especially in the last section, a stately ensemble, in which the soprano soloist and the organ have part, a high degree of impressiveness was attained.

Mrs. Beach was at the piano, and was the object of cordial manifestations on the part of the very large audience. Mr. Arthur Hyde conducted with fine efficiency. Miss Josephine Martin's splendid contralto voice was heard to advantage in the dramatic descriptive passages assigned her; and Mrs. Kileski-Bradbury's powerful and rich soprano dominated with telling power in the finale. Altogether, the performance may well have given great satisfaction to the club and to the composer.[107]

The previous December, Percy Goetschius had a chance to glance over the score, and he wrote to Mrs. Beach

I have just spent a most delightful hour with your truly exquisite *Chambered Nautilus*, and wish to tell you, warm from my first glowing impression, how keenly I have enjoyed it. It is not only exquisite, but scholarly in the fullest and most truthful sense of the word. What commends it to me as a work of singular value and significance, is the moderation and classic dignity you display—singularly valuable traits in the work of a composer of established reputation in this [era] of the dreadful Disease which, without being personal, one might call the DeBussy-disease—or Strauss or Max Reger-disease, for their writings exhibit a diseased condition which fills me with abhorrence as well

---

[105] *Boston Advertiser*, 28 February 1908. Other reviews appeared in the *Boston Herald, Boston Post, Boston Journal,* and *Boston Transcript* (this last a verbose report by H. T. Parker).

[106] According to a *New York Times* file, the work was heard first not in Boston but in New York City, at a private concert of the St. Cecilia Club in the Waldorf-Astoria Hotel on January 21, conducted by Victor Harris.

[107] *Boston Times*, 25 April 1908.

as sorrow. I am so glad that we have at least one *American composer* who is not affected by the plague! God bless you!

The pianoforte accompaniment is of course a bit difficult, but not unreasonably so; and in this day of universal technical facility, one scarcely thinks of difficulty any more. Besides, it is, alone by itself, alike a Chopin etude, a never-ending source of delight to him who studies it. I can hardly find words to voice my admiration of this, your latest achievement.[108]

In March 1908 there was another all-Beach concert in Lansing, Michigan, sung by Helen Rogers Smith.[109] The program was in honor of Mrs. Beach's aunt, Mrs. L. H. Clement, and her daughter. "By the assistance of Mrs. Clement and her daughter, Miss Smith gave each number as the composer intended it, having a full, beautiful, dramatic soprano voice to aid her in interpreting the most intense feeling as the range is wide in Mrs. Beach's songs."

The following February, Mrs. Beach returned again to Steinert Hall for her annual recital. On 17 February 1909, she and Carl Faelton played her piano concerto, with the latter as the "orchestra":

> Mrs. Beach's audiences are so largely composed of friends that her recitals appear like social receptions where nearly all are acquainted, and last night when she emerged, as it were, from her "musical shell" of retirement, Steinert Hall was well filled with interested auditors to greet the artist.[110]

Besides her concerto, Mrs. Beach also played Gottschalk's "Berceuse."

> Mrs. Beach is to be thanked for having the courage to play Gottschalk's "Berceuse." It is the fashion to sneer at this composer-pianist of genuine talent, but there are pieces signed by him that may still be heard with enjoyment.[111]

The only major musical event of the year 1909 for Mrs. Beach was the recital on November 9 of Marcella Sembrich in Boston. She included Beach's "Elle et moi," sung in French, at the end of her program. Sembrich was called the "queen of song recitalists, if not of grand opera" and the concert was considered "an artistic triumph of the first magnitude."[112]

---

[108] Letter from Goetschius to Mrs. Beach dated New York City, 15 December 1907.

[109] *Lansing Journal*, 3 March 1908.

[110] *Boston Globe*, 18 February 1909.

[111] *Boston Herald*, 18 February 1909.

[112] *Boston Journal*, 9 November 1909. Mrs. Beach had received two brief letters from Sembrich, the first in 1899 and the second dated 13 January 1909. Both referred to songs, which she was too busy at the time to study.

The compositions for the year 1909 include a two-piano suite in four movements and a song, "A Prelude." In addition Mrs. Beach orchestrated *The Chambered Nautilus*, made another choral arrangement of "The Year's at the Spring," and sketched the anthem "Thou Knowest, Lord."

The Deaths of Dr. Beach and Mrs. Cheney
(1910-11)

In the early hours of 25 April 1910, while making a house call upon a regular patient, a dowager whose anxieties exceeded her medical needs, Dr. Beach met with an accident from which he never recovered. Stepping unawares unto a steep flight of back stairs used primarily by the house servants, the doctor plunged to the bottom and was badly injured. His obesity and the severity of his bruises prevented an easy recovery; instead, he lingered in his bed at home over a period of nine weeks, and there, on June 28, at the age of sixty-six years, he died.[113]

The esteem with which Dr. Beach was held in Boston did much to ease his widow's grief, but it could not remove the anxiety which the loss created. The forty-three-year-old composer leaned heavily on her mother, who had long been a member of the Beach household and whose pragmatism had guided her daughter so well before her marriage. All engagements were cancelled or postponed indefinitely from the day of "that horrible anniversary," as Mrs. Beach later referred to April 25, the date of the accident.

Funeral services for Dr. Beach were held on Thursday morning, June 30, at Emmanuel Episcopal Church on Newbury Street, almost directly behind the Beach home on Commonwealth Avenue. The Reverend Dr. Elwood Worcester, rector of the church, officiated at the very simple services which attracted a church-full of distinguished representatives of the medical and musical professions of Boston. Immediately after the church services, Dr. Beach's body was taken to the crematory in Forest Hills Cemetery, and following cremation his ashes were disposed in an urn embedded in the Beach lot, 3988 Dahlia Path, where, at the back side of this lot, the bodies of Dr. Beach's mother, father, and father-in-law already lay.

Among the hundreds of letters Mrs. Beach received upon the death of her husband was one from Margaret Ruthven Lang, a Boston colleague now traveling in Europe.[114] Lang was an aspiring composer whose career had been totally eclipsed by that of Mrs.

---

[113] The most extensive newspaper obituary appeared in the *Barnstable Patriot*, Monday evening, 4 July 1910, under the Centerville heading.

[114] From Lang to Mrs. Beach, dated Geneva, 8 August 1910.

Beach, but nonetheless she remained a true and sincere friend and never showed any jealousy. Mrs. Beach always cherished this letter, which pointed out that Dr. Beach's death cannot be considered a loss "for such love and sympathy and trust [which shone from your husband's eyes] are the great enduring proof of immortality, and one feels this assurance most when one's loneliness is greatest."

After Dr. Beach's funeral, Mrs. Beach, with her mother, sought refuge at her Centerville home from the throngs of Boston friends who would console and advise her. There on Cape Cod, in deeper seclusion than she could maintain in Boston, Mrs. Beach found comfort in reading and in meditation. Until now she had been extremely protected by her mother and husband from all responsibilities of living, except as they related to her professional activities as composer and pianist. She had never known any matters involving management of a home or finances and had taken no part in her husband's business affairs. Her dependence now upon her elderly mother was almost more than Mrs. Cheney could bear, but Mrs. Cheney realized the urgency of preparing her daughter for the practical world and started to do so.

While not an unreligious person, Mrs. Beach had never affiliated with any particular church. During her childhood the Cheneys went to whatever Protestant church was convenient, and although she married an Episcopalian in an Episcopalian church, she had never submitted to the formal acts required by church law for active affiliation and participation in the Episcopal church. Upon her return to Boston that fall, Mrs. Beach accepted the ministrations of Dr. Worcester, whose consolations now took on a greater meaning for the widowed composer. She found comfort and strength in the theology and philosophy, which Dr. Worcester outlined to her in his frequent talks and in the readings he suggested. For the first time since April 25, Mrs. Beach now began to have a sense of self-control and a faith which was giving her the courage she so desperately needed to exist, not to mention the career which she had so suddenly abandoned after her husand's accident. As a confirmation of her renewed faith and of her desire now to exercise a more active life with a specific church affiliation, she received baptism at a private service, which Dr. Worcester performed on Friday, 4 November 1910, in Emmanuel Church, Boston.

Shortly after this, Mrs. Cheney suddenly collapsed, partly from the emotional strain she had endured and partly as the result of pneumonia. She died on 18 February 1911 and was buried in Forest Hills Cemetery on Tuesday afternoon, February 21. Her death took from Mrs. Beach her only close relative, but the spiritual strength and forebearance which had been growing within her during the past several months had, by the time of her mother's death, reached sufficient proportions to sustain her in this final blow. Instead of being crushed, as she had been the previous June, Mrs. Beach accepted her mother's death with a philosophy that surprised her closest friends. She immediately joined the confirmation class Dr. Worcester was beginning for the spring, and on Passion Sunday, 2 April 1911, the Right Reverend William Lawrence, Bishop of the Diocese of Massachusetts, confirmed her at Emmanuel Church in the precepts of the Protestant Episcopal Church.

Whether Mrs. Beach could have realized the greatness she had attained in her chosen career without the guidance and support of her mother and husband is a mute point, since until now they had given her no choice and she had sought nothing else. Now she had to stand alone, and without her newly found faith her career might never have reblossomed. Henceforth, the brief prayer from the second Office of Instruction, found in the *Book of Common Prayer* (p. 294), was her daily manna:

> Grant, O Lord, that they who shall renew the promises and vows of their Baptism, and be confirmed by the Bishop, may receive such a measure of Thy Holy Spirit, that they may grow in grace unto their life's end; through Jesus Christ our Lord. Amen.

With her new-found strength of will, Mrs. Beach was determined to learn how to attend to her affairs in their minutest detail. Although friends offered to assist her, she refused so that she could do for herself what her late husband and mother had previously considered their prerogative.

Part **3**: Amy Beach as Musician of the World, 1911-36

First European Trip (1911-14)

After the death of her husband, Mrs. Beach busied herself with plans for the future of her musical career. Her mother, who in the past had been such a dominant force behind her professional life, resumed her active role in these plans. For the first time Mrs. Cheney saw her daughter free from the incumbrances of marriage, able to project her activities without concern of geography which heretofore, as the devoted wife of a surgeon, she would not do. In the past, Mrs. Beach always accepted invitations to appear away from Boston only at the convenience of her physician husband. Dr. Beach had been inclined toward keeping his wife a "Boston" composer-musician, and to this end he used his professional and social influence to maintain an exhaustive calling list for his wife's salons. The world's great musicians rarely turned down the doctor's invitations to be a guest in the Beach music room, while local society and "persons of distinction" used all manner of means to be included in the guest list for the weekly musicales. The doctor did not want his wife to be in direct competition with those pianists who were influenced by the remunerative aspect of their tours and who were subject to adverse, sometimes brutal, criticism.[115] Now, despite the comforts of Cape Cod and New Hampshire that mother and daughter enjoyed, they planned a new career for Mrs. Beach that would expose her to the very world the doctor had shut out. With the sudden death of her mother in early 1911, Mrs. Beach now was compelled to follow the initial phases of this new career: her first trip to Europe.

Accompanied by her long-time Boston friend Amy Brigham, Mrs. Beach went to Munich in the fall of 1911 and began to arrange for recitals. Already her name as a composer was familiar to European audiences. Because she had always avoided the competitive field of a concert pianist, this seemed the wrong time to begin such

---

[115] Eventually, when Mrs. Beach reviewed and brought up to date the scrapbooks of her career during the lifetime of her husband, she inserted all criticisms, regardless of their tenor, and she often wrote in her reactions to them.

competition. Instead, she remained chiefly the interpreter of her own music which, by now, had become sufficiently voluminous to provide variety and contrast for programs. Her first success, however, was not on the concert stage. On 27 September 1911, Mrs. Beach was invited to submit several of her compositions for display in an exhibition sponsored by the German Lyceum Club of Berlin.[116]

After spending the winter in Munich, where she devoted her time to study, composition, and practicing, Mrs. Beach went to Rome and other Italian cities to visit some friends.[117] One of the highlights of this trip was a meeting with the Italian composer and pianist Giovanni Sgambati, for whom she played. Later Sgambati said that he never before really heard his own music until Mrs. Beach had played it. According to her cousin Ethel Clement, who apparently was present,

> This one can readily appreciate, as in addition to a brilliant and facile technique, and an astonishing capacity for a ringing tone production, Mrs. Beach's composer's understanding of the music under her agile fingers enables her to transform what in other hands, however skilled technically, might be a colorless combination of tones, into a brilliant weave of many distinct yet intricately woven voices, presenting a rich and wonderfully colorful tapestry of sound.

Mrs. Beach also spent some time at the villa of the widow of the novelist Marion Crawford, whose sentimental tales were the rage during the early years of the century. The Crawfords and the Beaches had long been close friends.

Upon return to Munich, Mrs. Beach's career began to move ahead. On 25 September 1912, the California singer Marcella Craft, prima donna of the Royal Opera Company of Munich, held a reception in honor of L. E. Dehmyer, a Pacific Coast manager from Los Angeles. Guests included Leopold Stokowski, conductor of the Philadelphia Orchestra; Olga Samaroff, his wife; Gracia Ricardo, Craft's accompanist; Arthur Rosenstein, another accompanist; Geraldine Farrar; Mrs. Beach, and others. Craft entertained by singing, among other works, some songs by Mrs. Beach. Mrs. Beach's apartment, with a large music studio, was in the same building in which Craft lived, and even before, when she used the alias Signora Cratti, she had included Mrs. Beach's songs in her recitals. She had first met the composer when, as a student in the New England Conservatory, she had enjoyed the generous encouragement of Mrs. Beach.

On Monday evening, October 28, Mrs. Beach served as guest accompanist for the violinist Dr. Wolfgang Bulau in a recital in Dresden's Palmengarten. They performed Jules Conus's Violin Concerto in E major, a Siciliano by John Adam Birckenstock, Mozart's Adagio in E minor and Gavotte, Saint-Saëns's *Introduction and Rondo Capriccioso*, and the program began with Mrs. Beach's own Violin Sonata, op. 34:

---

[116] Letter to Mrs. Beach from Adele aus der Ohe.

[117] Information given by Ethel Clement, Mrs. Beach's cousin.

Mrs. H. H. A. Beach with friends, ca. 1912

[The sonata] in four movements showed that Mrs. Beach's reputation
as a composer is well founded. The first movement particularly is
very effective; fine romantic feeling worked out in clear, readily
understandable form. This American composer proved at the same
time to be a splendid pianist.[118]

Mrs. Beach also introduced to the audience a *Waltz Fantasie* on Bavarian folksongs, which
still was in manuscript.

When the composer arrived in Berlin in November, a huge reception was given
in her honor at the American Woman's Club. Florence Easton-Maclennan of the Berlin
Royal Opera

---

[118] *Dresden Journal*, 29 October 1912.

sang a group of the songs which caused the heart of every American woman to swell with pride at the thought of feminine achievement. "June," "Ecstacy," and "[My] Sweetheart and I," led up by gradual climax to that splendid burst of optimism "The Year's at the Spring," which by unanimous verdict was given an incomparable interpretation by Mme. Maclennan. The bright fresh quality of her voice furnished an ideal medium for this sunshiny, spontaneous music, and the listeners were caught up into a seventh heaven of delight. Mrs. Beach also played numbers from her "Suite Française," and the day will be long remembered in the history of the American Woman's Club.[119]

In addition, the German Lyceum club, under the directorship of Adele aus der Ohe, arranged a musical soirée at which Mrs. Beach was the honored guest, and she was similarly honored at many social occasions, including a dinner at the home of Mr. and Mrs. Francis Maclennan.[120]

In mid-January 1913, Mrs. Beach's first large concert took place in Munich:

The American composer, Mrs. Amy Beach, gave a concert last week at the Bavarian Hotel, and in the very large audience, the Anglo-American colony was well represented. The program consisted largely of Mrs. Beach's compositions, and in the interpretation of them she had the cooperation of Marianne Rheinfeld, soprano, and Richard Rettich, violinist. That they were received with great enthusiasm goes without saying. Instead of expressing my opinion of Mrs. Beach's works, which could not help being influenced by both patriotic and personal considerations, I shall afford you an opportunity to learn a critical valuation of them by a German critic, who, as is suggested in the beginning of this letter, has in a very short time secured an influential position among the musical journalists of Bavaria. Freely translated Dr. Berrsche says: "Her violin sonata, Op. 34, is an earnest, respect-demanding work revealing genuine ability, and in a sympathetic way an intimate knowledge of Brahms. The first movement, and particularly the joyously-rhythmic *scherzo* with the trio over the organ-point of the violin, are its best parts. It is difficult to understand why in her songs the composer should forget her lofty purpose and descend into the sphere of Hildach and Meter-Halmund. That is the domain of shallow sentimentalism, of which one encounters in the violin sonata only infrequent and quite endurable traces. Elevated decidedly over this *niveau* is the song *I Dreamt I Loved a Star*. Mrs. Beach herself played the piano part of her works and also pieces by Bach, Beethoven and Brahms. Her pianistic faculty has not been trained to the same extent

---

[119] *Musical Leader*, 28 November 1912.

[120] *Boston Herald*.

as her capacity for composing. Her technique is not always reliable, and there is a great deal lacking in her touch, but in phrasing and in rhythm she always shows the good musician and therefore one listens to her with interest."[121]

Another concert in Munich followed in March in which she again appeared as pianist and composer.[122] During a concert of the Munich String Quartet, she joined the musicians to introduce her Piano Quintet in F-sharp minor:

> The sure, clear structure of the [quintet] and the natural flow of the diction is admirable. The speach of the composer is natural and works well artistically: it is real aestheticism.[123]

> In the Quintet Mrs. Beach shows her best side as a composer. It is the work of a musician of great ability and knowledge.[124]

Meanwhile, on February 14, the soprano Elisabet Christian and Mrs. Beach gave a recital in Breslau at the Grosser Saal der neuen Borse, which was well received.[125] Mrs. Beach performed her suite *Les Rêves de Columbine*, op. 65, "Scottish Legend," and "Fireflies," and the two together performed "Ein Tag nur Verschied" ("Ah, Love"), "Jeune fille, jeune fleur," and "Juni." The few days before in Berlin, the well-known singing teacher Romeo Frick and Mme. Karola Frick

> commenced a series of Sunday afternoon studio recitals, the first of which took place this week, being devoted to American song writers. Sixteen composers were presented on the program. . . . The climax of the group sung by Mme. Karola Frick was Mrs. H. H. A. Beach's splendid burst of optimism "The Year's at the Spring" a song which always sends people away with laughter in their hearts.[126]

During several weeks of June and July 1913, Mrs. Beach, traveling with her niece Miss Elizabeth Stone, visited the Scandinavian countries. "The party with which Mrs. Beach traveled was away from the railroad for over a month, using carriages and small steamers or walking, just as time and circumstances dictated."[127] In August announcements began

---

[121] Jacques Mayer, in *Musical America*, 15 February 1913. Other reviews appeared in the *Musical Courier* (reprinted from the *Breslauer Zeitung*, 15 February 1913), and the *Münchener Zeitung*, 21 January 1913.

[122] *Musical Leader*, 13 March 1913.

[123] *Münchener Zeitung*.

[124] *Münchener Neueste Nachrichten*.

[125] Reviewed in the *Breslau Zeitung*.

[126] *Musical Leader*, 13 February 1913.

[127] *American Music*. Also reported briefly in *Musical America*, 22 August 1913.

to appear for a concert of Mrs. Beach's Symphony and Piano Concerto, arranged by the American violinist and conductor Theodore Spiering, who had just been appointed director of the Berlin Freie Volksbühne.[128] The concerts were to take place in Berlin on December 18 and also in Leipzig and Hamburg:

> The occasion of the second symphony concert [December 18] with the augmented [Berlin] Philharmonie Orchestra, conducted by Theodore Spiering at the Philharmonie, . . . was a red-letter day for American creative . . . art. It was a day of triumph for the American composer, the American orchestra conductor, the American interpretive artist, on the world's greatest musical show-grounds. It was a day, in other words, upon which the ability of the American musician to compete successfully with his contemporaries of the older European countries, was eloquently and forcibly manifested.[129]
>
> When more of the quality of American art, like that exhibited at these concerts, and less of that produced by quaking, immature talents, is brought to the notice of audiences in European music-centres, the day—which in any event is bound to come,—when America will be universally recognized as a vital power in the realm of music cannot, it would seem, remain very far off.
>
> As a builder of novel programs for his orchestral concerts, Spiering has already gained considerable renown. His choice of novelties for the second program was particularly happy, including as it did the Concerto in C sharp minor, Op. 45, by his gifted countrywoman, Mrs. H. H. A. Beach, who introduced herself to the Berlin public on this occasion in the double role of composer and pianist.
>
> Those who have the privilege of knowing Mrs. Beach in private life are at once struck by her essential femininity and are then quite naturally surprised to find her creative work characterized by such a broad masculine tone. She has, in a word, the heart of a woman, but the head of a man, with splendid constructive faculty.
>
> This work, presented by the resourceful composer with admirable pianistic finish and verve, is not only a piano Concerto, but a pianist's Concerto, that is extremely grateful to the executive artist without losing its balance and descending to the level of a mere show-piece of virtuosity. . . .
>
> Although abounding in lively musical thought and clever invention, the work never once approaches the commonplace. Here also, as in her songs, Mrs. Beach reveals a marked faculty for giving the phrase a felicitous inflection. The chief tenet of her musical creed is Euphony, and she does not as do many composers, conceive the ugly to be original.[130]

---

[128] *Musical America*, 22 August 1913.

[129] Caroline V. Kerr, in the *Musical Leader*, 8 January 1914.

[130] Ibid. Reviews of the Leipzig concert were translated and summarized in the *Musical Courier*, 4 February 1914.

The symphony received equally warm praise in the Berlin press, just as the newspapers in Leipzig had extolled both the concerto and symphony when they were heard there the previous November.[131]

Return to America: The War Years
(1914-21)

The tensions developing in Europe, and which would explode into World War I at the end of June 1914, were having little effect upon Mrs. Beach and upon other wealthy Americans living luxuriously on the continent. It is not surprising, therefore, that we find Mrs. Beach still in Germany almost until the very moment of open hostilities. Many of her friends tried to alert her to the dangers of being detained abroad, but their fears caused her no anxiety, and in a casual manner she was able to arrange for her return to the United States on one of the last boats for America. Later, Mrs. Beach remarked as to her good fortune in getting home safely.

Back in Boston and comfortably ensconced once more in her Commonwealth Avenue home, she was able to reflect upon the success of her first European sojourn. She felt considerable elation at the reception her music had received abroad during the two and a half years she was there. And although she was not unknown in Europe as a composer before she went to Munich in 1911, she was considerably better known throughout Europe at the time of her departure. She did not write much music while there; she had not yet returned to her stride as a composer since her traumas of 1910-11. But her travels and professional successes in Europe, based on her piano playing and her older compositions, aroused in her a drive to renew her career and to do so with an enthusiasm greater than she had experienced at any time in her life.

As a result, not long after her return from Europe, Mrs. Beach began extensive engagements across America, often to benefit the victims of the war. Unlike her pre-war concerts in America, before select audiences and arranged by her mother, her husband, or friends, her new concerts were planned by herself; she now became her own agent and manager. She did not play before exclusive audiences in the largest musical centers, but went out to play for the people. Perhaps she would have earned a much greater professional reputation if she had sought big-league performances,[132]

---

[131] Reviews in the *Musical Courier*, January 1914, *Leipziger Tagblatt*, 24 November 1913, *Leipziger Neuesten Nachrichten*, 23 November 1913, *Leipziger Abendzeitung*, 24 November 1913, *Leipziger Zeitung*, 24 November 1913, and *Neue Zeitschrift für Musik*, 4 December 1913.

[132] Ernest Hutcheson thought Mrs. Beach and Mrs. Edward MacDowell were remarkably good concert pianists who had succumbed to the tragic mistake of playing mainly to second-string audiences instead of aiming only

but she did not really consider herself a concert pianist. She looked upon herself increasingly as a composer who played her own music and occasionally some of the standard repertory.

The first concert with which she was associated was at the MacDowell Club in Boston, where she "brought out two groups of her new songs composed while in Europe."[133] "An audience of some 700 people rose *en masse* as she stepped upon the platform, and after an address, Mrs. Beach was showered with flowers. . . ." Her first recital was in Kansas City, with Marcella Craft as assisting artist. In December she appeared in Boston with Mme. Karola Frick and the Hoffman Quartet, who played her Piano Quintet. A January 1915 recital in Portland, Maine, with Mrs. Lafayette Goodbar, vocalist, and a February recital in Detroit with Myrna Sharlow of the Boston Opera Company were devoted entirely to her own compositions. She also appeared in Columbus, Ohio, with Craft.

During the 1914-15 season Mrs. Beach took part in four New York concerts. A concert devoted solely to Beach works took place at Carnegie Hall given by the Granberry Pianoforte School. Then she joined George Sheffield, tenor, Theodore Spiering, conductor of the Berlin Philharmonic Orchestra, and the Olive Mead Quartet in a recital in Aeolian Hall. Once again she teamed up with Marcella Craft, this time at the Colony Club. Finally she performed for the New York MacDowell Club with George Hamlin, Eurica Dillon, and Spiering. One New York reviewer wrote:

> Wherever Mrs. Beach appears in concert it is a signal for a series of private entertainments to afford the opportunity of meeting this delightful woman whose personality is as rare as her gifts—and New York proved no exception. Receptions were given for her during the season of 1914-15 by Miss Emilie Frances Bauer, sister of the well-known song writer [Marion Bauer], Mrs. Ban Haggin, Miss Rebecca Crawford and Miss Emma Thursby.

In February Mrs. Beach's Symphony was performed by the Philadelphia Orchestra to rave reviews; most gratifying to the composer was its reception by the critics who valued it above other new symphonies by Frederick Stock, Guy Ropartz, and Paderewski performed by the same orchestra that year:

> The symphony that began the program before the usual large audience of the Academy yesterday made a profound impression. Mrs. Beach's writings are familiar to those who have followed the Boston Symphony

---

for the more discriminating concert and recital audiences, like those who clamor for the best seats at Town Hall, Carnegie Hall, and the other great concert halls of the country. He believed that Mrs. MacDowell would have done more for the cause of the MacDowell Colony in a few ten-thousand-dollar concerts than she did in quantities of hundred-dollar concerts, and that Mrs. Beach would have gained much greater professional respect had she sought and limited herself to the best audiences.

[133] According to Mrs. Beach's cousin Ethel Clement, the artist, who was living with her mother in San Francisco in 1914. Mrs. Beach became very close to Ethel and her mother, Mrs. Lyman H. Clement (Emma Frances Marcy Clement), over the next ten years.

Programs. She is the most eminent woman composer America has produced, and this symphony holds its own in the distinguished company of the few fine modern compositions in that form. The cordial reception of the work was due to its own patent merits. It was not known to the audience that Mrs. Beach was in the house until Mr. Stokowski turned toward the second-floor procenium box where she was seated and joined in the applause. Several times she was compelled to bow her acknowledgments of the spontaneous tribute to her genius as manifested in one of the most remarkable achievements set down to the credit of American womanhood.

In synthetic ability, in breadth and dignity of concept and architecture, in genuineness of feeling and authentic inspiration the symphony needs no critical allowance on the basis of sex. It leaves the Paderewski symphony or that of Mr. Stock, lately played, so far behind that there is no just comparison. . . . The solo violin of Witzemann and the beautiful notes of Sanby's cello suited the long sweeping curves of [the Lento] melody, with the strong infusion of the Scotch temperament, and came occasionally to the fore in ditties of the inimitable Gaelic flavor.[134]

During the spring of 1915, Mrs. Beach travelled to California,

where she was the recipient of many honors. . . . During the Musical Festival at Los Angeles she had the unique distinction of having her compositions on three programs—her quintet for strings and piano, and her Balkan Themes having been chosen for rendering by the performers themselves, while she herself was invited to give her concerto for piano and orchestra with the Los Angeles Symphony Orchestra. That season, as well as the year following she was honored by having a day named for her by the San Diego Exposition, when her compositions were given both out of doors at the great organ—and in the rooms of the California Building preceding a reception in her honor. At San Francisco on Women Composer's Day, she again rendered her concerto for piano and orchestra with the Exposition Orchestra under Richard Hagemann, when the Festival Hall was filled to overflowing.

At Easter, her Year's at the Spring was sung at the famous Easter Sunrise Service on Mt. Rubidoux at Riverside, Calif., when it stirred to the depths the hearts of the multitude assembled there, as, in the stillness of dawn on the mountain top, its glad cry arose—so appropriate to the occasion. . . . The following spring the same song was sung across the continent by telephone from San Francisco, seated at the banquet table with discs at their ears, having the unique experience of hearing the applause it called forth three thousand miles away.[135]

---

[134] Public Ledger, 27 February 1915. Other reviews in Philadelphia Press, Evening Bulletin, and Philadelphia Record, all on the same date.

[135] According to Ethel Clement.

In October 1915 Mrs. Beach inaugurated her second concert season with a recital in Salt Lake City. Fernanda Pratt also sang on the program. Then she returned to California for a performance of her Piano Quintet with the San Francisco Quartet Club, for whom she later wrote her Variations for Flute and Strings.[136]   After a series of concerts in southern California (Riverside and San Diego) with the baritone Jack Hellman, Mrs. Beach played a solo recital of her piano works in Stockton.

Her eastern concerts opened in December 1915 with a recital in Pittsburgh with Marcella Craft, and the two women followed with another recital in Sewickley, Pennsylvania. In Philadelphia she appeared next with Cecil Fanning. Her New York performances included a recital at the Musicians Club with Lucy Gates and a Mr. Harrison, tenor, and two appearances with the St. Cecilia Club, where her *Chambered Nautilus*, "Dolladine," and "Candy Lion" were given. Carl Busch conducted the *Gaelic Symphony* in Kansas City, and Mrs. Beach joined Frederick Stock for a performance of her Piano Concerto with the Chicago Symphony Orchestra.

After a spring tour of southern California, Mrs. Beach spent the summer of 1916 in San Francisco, where she concentrated on composition. While at the Exposition in San Diego, Dr. George Wharton James had brought to Mrs. Beach's attention a poem, "Meadowlarks," by Mrs. Ina Coolbrith, who had collaborated with Mark Twain and Bret Hart. Mrs. Beach now set the poem dramatically for high soprano and dedicated it to Mrs. Carrie Slone Freeman, in whose rose-bowered home in southern California Mrs. Beach had heard larks singing.[137]   About the same time she also wrote "In Blossom Time," "Night Song at Amalfi," "I," and "Wind o' the Westland."

> The poem, *Wind o' the Westland*, is by Dana Burnett, and came to Mrs. Beach's attention recently while she was staying in the midst of a wonderful orange-grove at Riverside, California. Every morning before dawn she was wakened by the tender plaint of innumerable mourning doves, and lay listening with dreamy enjoyment of their melting tones. Subconsciously the words of Mr. Burnett's beautiful poem seemed to fit in against the background of sound, and when the composer had completed her song, she was surprised to see that she had unwittingly used the plaintive call of the mourning dove as a figure in the accompaniment.[138]

The following season, 1916-17, was a very busy one. Mrs. Beach appeared with the Kneisel Quartet in her Piano Quintet in Chicago, Boston, Philadelphia, Brooklyn, and Princeton, New Jersey. A Chicago critic wrote:

> Mrs. Beach enjoyed a distinctive success, first for her work, then for her beautiful playing. Impossible is it to avoid reference to the personal

---

[136] The Quartet Club was reorganized under the name Chamber Music Society of San Francisco.

[137] According to Ethel Clement.

[138] A musical magazine.

impression Mrs. Beach creates on an audience, which is quite apart from her composition or her own playing. There is an atmosphere of something so great, wholesome and sensible about her, and with them are grace and dignity of bearing rarely seen on the concert stage or off. She is so natural that, watching the unstudied composure of the entire group, one had the sensation of being an onlooker at a private concert in some salon.[139]

In addition to appearing with the Kneisel Quartet, Mrs. Beach gave recitals with various assisting artists in Godfrey, Peoria, Rockford, and Chicago, Illinois; Boston, Attleboro, and West Newton, Massachusetts; Milwaukee; Toronto; and Lancaster, Pennsylvania. The Boston concert continued a tradition, since it was for the Faelton Pianoforte School. Besides recitals, Mrs. Beach performed her Piano Concerto in St. Louis and, on 2 March 1917, with the Boston Symphony Orchestra. The review of the former was again a rave:

> Yesterday's Symphony Orchestra concert at the Odeon was one of those rare events which exact the use of superlatives. The heroine of the triumph was Mrs. H. H. A. Beach, considered the most notable woman composer in musical history, who proved herself not only one of the great virtuoso pianists of the day, but a composer of brilliant genius irrespective of sex. The audience was in size one of the largest, and in enthusiasm the most warmly responsive of the year. As the performance of the concerto's first movement began to rush past, one's first impression was that there was one of the most amazing bravura displays ever conceived. There appeared to be an incessant blaze of fireworks, both in orchestra and piano. But soon it was borne in upon the mind that every one of those dazzling notes had its meritable place and meaning; that not one of them was introduced for mere ornament or parade; and then came the discovery that Mrs. Beach is a modern American, not only by birth, but in genius, that what seemed pyrotechnics was merely speed, and that in these days of motor cars and telephone, her masterpiece does not saunter along on foot, but travels with velocity of a Twentieth Century Express.
>
> Her inspiration had not only blinding speed, but also unflagging vitality, another American trait. One marvelled at the inexhaustible forms of energy from which poured forth this racing torrent of ideas. The proof of abounding life lay in the total absence of any sign of effort, any symptom of strain. Despite its prevailing chromatic hues, harmony and counterpoint, the concerto abounded in clearly discernible tunes. The consequence is, that although the work is technically most difficult, only a pianist and orchestra of the utmost expertness could perform it, there is also a fascinating popular appeal.[140]

---

[139] *Chicago Musical Leader.*

[140] *St. Louis Post Dispatch.*

Mrs. Beach performed the concerto again the following season, 1917-18, both in Chicago and in Minneapolis. After the Chicago performance Karleton Hackett wrote:

> Mrs. Beach is most at home when she can reduce the orchestra to the lowest point, or dispense with it altogether, as she frequently does. The piano is her instrument, she understands how to write for it, and how to play it, while the orchestra is evidently a considerable problem.
>
> As music, the concerto lacks a certain structural strength. It was not apparently conceived as an organic whole in which the piano formed but one of the essential elements, but it took form rather as a series of soli for the piano about which the orchestra was written. This gave it a somewhat disjointed effect, with the orchestra appearing and disappearing in a rather confusing manner. But the thematic foundation was strong, good, solid melodies that one could tie to, and Mrs. Beach made no attempt to stretch her powers beyond their limits. The music sounded sincere, as tho she felt it deeply, and she played it with a straightforward whole-heartedness that made it most agreeable to hear.
>
> There has been a vast amount of talk about "women in music" and the "wrongs of the downtrodden American composer," but, without knowing anything about the matter, I should judge that Mrs. Beach would not wish to be considered under either aspect. Her music and her playing stand by themselves without taking account of race, sex, or any other extraneous matters. Music is music because of the vigor of the creative impulse and the skill in the setting forth, and Mrs. Beach's concerto was very well worth hearing for its own sake without indulging in Fourth of July platitudes. Not epoch-making, but deserving a place on such a program for its own strength, even tho Mrs. Beach happened to be born in this land. She was most cordially received and warmly applauded by the audience.

The concerts with the Minneapolis Symphony Orchestra took place in the St. Paul Auditorium on December 13 and in the Minneapolis Auditorium the following night. Besides the concerto, the orchestra performed Beach's *Gaelic Symphony* and Chadwick's dramatic overture *Melpomene*.

Back in Boston, Mrs. Beach's *Four Children's Songs*, op. 75, were to be performed in concert. Typical of her thoughtfulness, she invited the author of the texts, Abbie Farwell Brown, to join her at the performance.[141] The songs were written from 1913 to 1915 and had been sung from manuscript in California and elsewhere before the Boston premiere.

Another song, "Song of Liberty," which was written back in 1902, suddenly became popular for its reflections of American sentiment at the end of World War I. Arrangements appeared for solo voice, men's voices, and women's voices, and at one point the Cleveland, Ohio, Board of Education ordered 500 copies for use in its schools. E. O. Edmunds of

---

[141] Letter from Abbie Farwell Brown to Mrs. Beach, dated 41 West Decar Street, Boston, 10 June [1918], in which she acknowledges Mrs. Beach's invitation.

Benton Harbor, Michigan, later called it "one of the best all around patriotic solos I have ever heard,"[142] and A. Walter Kramer, managing editor of *Musical America*, referred to it as "the only patriotic song that has been written since we entered the war that has real value as musical art."[143] The composer's patriotism was not limited to the writing of patriotic songs, nor was it an expression of some vague feeling of love for her country. Instead, the composer's greater concern was for those persons, regardless of country, who had suffered the terrible ravages of the war. To this end, her publisher advertised the sale of some of her original manuscripts "to the highest bidders for benefit of War Charities." Listed were "The Year's at the Spring," "I Send My Heart up to Thee," "My Star," *Scottish Legend*, and others. The notice appeared in *Musical America* and other music magazines on 1 June 1918, where the advertisement added, "In offering these MSS for sale, Mrs. Beach is supplementing the work she is doing for the Red Cross and other charities."

The season following the end of the war, 1918-19, was highlighted by two important performances of the *Gaelic Symphony*. Ossip Gabrilowitsch conducted it in December in Detroit, where it met with a "fine success."[144] A few weeks later Stokowski did it in Philadelphia, where "at both performances the Symphony had an unusually warm reception from the audience."[145]

The major concerts in which Mrs. Beach was involved as composer or performer or both were only a small portion of her appearances during the war. She was occupied largely with touring the United States in concerts of her own music, often for war charities, often for women's clubs, often for Federated Music Clubs, and often for small audiences arranged by friends. At this time, her closest relatives were either in California (her aunt and cousin Emma and Ethel Clement) or in New Hampshire and in the Boston suburbs. Much of her leisure time, when she was not giving recitals and concerts, was spent in Hillsboro, New Hampshire. There she rented rooms in the home of Jessie Parker on Church Street and adopted this as her legal residence, which it remained for the rest of her life.[146] She greatly admired the Parker family because of its serious, scholarly nature, and she spent many hours with them in the kitchen over freshly brewed coffee. She took her meals with Clara Belle Taylor Miller, who lived across Church Street from the Parkers. Like Mrs. Beach, Mrs. Miller, too, had a love for the woods and fields, and she and Mrs. Beach spent many hours wandering along the river bank. Often, on a moon-lit night, these two women would wend their way together to a location behind the Methodist Church to watch moon patterns on the usually smooth surface of the quiet stream. Clara Miller's next-door neighbor later recalled (letter from Florence[?] K. Favor to Jenkins, 8 July 1959):

---

[142] 23 December 1920.

[143] Letter from A. Walter Kramer to Arthur P. Schmidt, Mrs. Beach's publisher, dated 4 June 1918. Cf. also Kramer's review of the song in *Musical America*.

[144] Letter from Gabrilowitsch to Mrs. Beach, dated Detroit, 31 December 1918, in which he regrets that Mrs. Beach could not attend the performance.

[145] Letter from Stokowski to Mrs. Beach, dated Philadelphia, 25 January 1919; Mrs. Beach did not attend. Reviews in *Philadelphia Public Ledger*, *Philadelphia Inquirer*, *Evening Bulletin*, *North American*, and *Philadelphia Record*.

[146] Eventually the Clements moved to Hillsboro, into the Parker home.

> the people in town showed [Mrs. Beach] great honor, and she, in return, was very gracious to all. She remembered us all with gifts from abroad.

Mrs. Beach's Commonwealth Avenue home in Boston had been rented to physicians much of the time since she left it in 1911, and she never returned there to live; she sold it in 1924.[147] Her cottage on the knoll in Phinney's Lane, Centerville, Cape Cod, continued to be her summer home for the remainder of her life.[148]

After her return from Europe in 1914, Mrs. Beach had also busied herself with activities of the National Federation of Music Clubs and the Music Teachers National Association. She was among the early members of the New Hampshire Music Teachers Association, which was dedicated to performing music by native and contemporary composers.

MacDowell Colony (1921-26)

While Mrs. Beach was enjoying fame and success as a composer-pianist at the turn of the century, her closest rival was Edward A. MacDowell. Unlike Mrs. Beach, MacDowell, six years her senior, had returned to this country to settle in Boston only after years of European study and success as a concert pianist and composer. He moved to Boston in 1888, three years after Amy Cheney's marriage to Dr. Beach. Although there is no evidence that they were close personal friends, they knew each other's work and admired it. In later years, Mrs. MacDowell frequently spoke of the personal and professional admiration her husband had for Mrs. Beach.

After MacDowell's death in 1908, and especially after Mrs. Beach's return to America from her first European trip in 1914, the two widows became devoted personal friends.[149] Both continued to speak of the other as Mrs. H. H. A. Beach or Mrs. Edward MacDowell,

---

[147] According to the Suffolk County Registry of Deeds, Book 1449, p. 62, Amy M. Beach sold this valuable property for $30,000, the same price for which Dr. Beach had bought it in February 1879. It was not until October 1937 that she finally disposed of her household furnishings from this home, which had been stored in a Boston warehouse for thirteen years; some items she gave to her friend Mrs. Lillian Buxbaum; a truckload of other items went to her home in Centerville; the rest was not saved. In 1938 she disposed of her chinaware and other small articles which had long been in storage; she gave David McK. Williams a Beethoven deathmask and Ruth Shaffner a gold spoon and three glass dishes.

[148] On 6 July 1943, Mrs. Beach wrote a codicil to her will that gave the Centerville property to Mrs. Lillian Buxbaum in return for Mrs. Buxbaum's supervision of the property and its owner throughout the owner's lifetime.

[149] On 2 January 1938, Mrs. MacDowell wrote to Mrs. Beach:

> One of the first things I am thankful for in this New Year is my blessed friend, you. How good, how dear you have been.

rather than by their first names.[150] This reflects their mutual understanding of what was "proper." Years after Dr. Beach's death, his widow was sometimes asked why, as a professional woman, she had always used "Mrs." in connection with her name, especially her professional name. Her only answer was that it was "proper" for all "proper" married Bostonian women to be known as "Mrs. so-and-so." When further pressed why she would not want to be known as Amy Beach, her answer was that this simply "was not done." She emphasized that *nice* married women just did not go by the name of "Miss so-and-so." She scorned those acquaintances of hers who were married but preferred to be known to the world at large by the appellative "Miss." The widow of Edward MacDowell and the widow of Dr. Beach each experienced a great sense of respectable comfort, as they called each other "Mrs." throughout their long association. To only her closest, most intimate friends was Mrs. Beach "Amy," and she would have been displeased if she heard the rest of us call her by her first name.

Until MacDowell's death, Marian Nevins MacDowell remained quietly behind the scenes of her composer-husband's life. Following his death, she rose to a stature of great distinction through her determination to carry out a dream of his. She established the MacDowell Colony in Peterborough, New Hampshire, in 1908, and devoted the rest of her life to making it a permanent, self-perpetuating corporation. To this end, eventually, Mrs. Beach had an important part.

From the inception of the Colony, Mrs. Beach had shown great interest and an understanding of the tremendous problems Mrs. MacDowell faced, but it was not until 1921 that she began taking an active part in the Colony "family." In that summer, during the Colony season of June through September, Mrs. Beach was personally invited by Mrs. MacDowell to sample the life of a colonist. The purpose of the colony was to provide the ambiance and conditions under which the guest could create; the dream of MacDowell had been to establish a haven for work, where one could organize his or her ideas from the abstract to the concrete, undistracted by the routines of ordinary living. As a creative colonist, with other creative colonists, the guest would be stimulated by the knowledge that he or she is part of a pool of creative activity and that he or she could be inspired in his or her own work by his or her association with other artist-members of the Colony family. To this end MacDowell envisioned the family to be made up of representatives of the verbal, the tonal, and the visual arts. In music this meant composers who might or might not be performers, but not performers who were not composers. In carrying out MacDowell's vision, it was to this environment that his widow persuaded Mrs. Beach to go, even reluctantly. As Colony director, Mrs. MacDowell often had to coax skeptical but eligible friends to experience the merits of her project. She knew the importance of the influence of a *convinced* colonist upon the future life of the MacDowell Colony.

---

[150] To the end of Mrs. MacDowell's life (1956), I never heard her refer to Mrs. Beach by her first name Amy, so formal was their intimacy. The composer's letters to Mrs. MacDowell are always addressed to "My Dear Mrs. MacDowell" and signed "Amy M. Beach"; Mrs. MacDowell always addressed her friend as "Dear Mrs. Beach" and signed her letters "Marian MacDowell" or "M. MacDowell."

Mrs. Beach had never been skeptical of the Colony's value, but unlike some less fortunate creative artists, she experienced to a lesser degree the struggle with distractions that Edward MacDowell envisioned for others and experienced himself. Because of her reputation by 1921, she had already enjoyed the personal acquaintanceship of many of the world's well-known creative artists in fields other than music. Mrs. MacDowell's insistent invitation had no especial inducement for Mrs. Beach, who did not want to offend by refusal, although she frankly did not look forward to her stay at the Colony with an anticipation of significant accomplishment there. To be at the Colony meant leaving her Hillsboro rooms or her Cape Cod house. At both places the composer had an established routine for composing. Yet to her astonishment, as soon as she settled into the routine of the Colony day, her musical ideas gushed forth in an almost uncontrollable manner. The freedom and clarity with which these ideas formed in the composer's mind caused her to enjoy a sense of accomplishment that she rarely found in more familiar surroundings. The experience was, therefore, the first of annual pilgrimages that continued nearly to the end of her life and from which came the original sketches of nearly all subsequent compositions.[151]

The room that Mrs. Beach occupied that first summer in the two-hundred-year-old Eaves Residence Hall has become known as "The Beach Room."[152] Eventually the composer aided in the refurnishing of this sunny bedroom. Originally it faced the entrance gate, which then stood at the end of MacDowell Road, leading up a long slope from the center of the town of Peterborough. The gate was subsequently moved around the corner and parallel with the side of the Eaves. Today MacDowell Road passes the graves of MacDowell and his wife in the little private cemetery where they alone rest in front of a granite boulder. The plot is surrounded by a granite wall, edged with a garden of perennials, the original seeds of which MacDowell brought from Europe. In 1921, the flower beds by the Eaves porch contained plants also grown from some of these seeds.

Beginning in 1922 Mrs. Beach occupied a studio a short walk from the Eaves.[153] The studio contains one large room, entered from a wide stone open porch. A huge fireplace opposite the entrance appears to be in an alcove, because each of the back corners of the room have been partitioned off to accommodate a lavatory at the left and a large closet at the right. Like all the Colony studios, Mrs. Beach's studio—known as the Regina Watson Studio—is simply furnished with a piano for composers, a large table for writing, a couple of comfortable chairs, a few straight chairs, a bookcase, and many logs for the fireplace. There are a few scatter rugs to break the coldness of the hardwood floor. The wall is plastered but left unpainted. Casement windows are on all four sides.

The gravel roadway, which winds around in back of the Eaves through a splendid hay field, forms a fork a short distance from the studio. One branch goes to the Sprague Studio made famous by David Diamond who, as a young composer, insisted he had once

---

[151] A guest whose experiences paralleled Mrs. Beach's was Edward Arlington Robinson, who, once he was persuaded into going to the Colony, became a perennial resident who could not wait until the next June to return to the studio assigned to him, which peeked through the trees to Monadnock Mountain.

[152] The room was in "The Eaves" or, because it was a residence hall for female colonists, "The Eves."

[153] The Watson Studio was occupied each year by two or three other creative artists during the months when Mrs. Beach was not at the Colony.

seen the ghost of Elinor Wylie there when he occupied it. The other branch of the road passes closely to the side of the Watson Studio. The road accommodates only these two studios and is used mainly at mid-day when lunch and mail are delivered. A large granite boulder causes the road to veer rather sharply away from the porch. A clump of white birch trees stands by the corner of the porch. Many pines and a few rock maple trees surround the studio on a slight knoll. There is no extensive view from the Watson Studio, as is the case from some other studios, but the comfort and convenience of the Watson has made it a studio greatly appreciated by its occupants.

From Mrs. Beach's first days at the Colony, all her composing was done outdoors, except in inclement weather. Sometimes she went indoors and transcribed the newly-conceived musical ideas at the desk, after which the music was played over on the piano. Often, however, the desk work was not concerned with the same ideas germinating outdoors; according to many entries in her diaries, she would frequently work at her desk in the studio on ideas from previous visits to the Colony or conjured up at other places. Likewise, many ideas sketched outdoors were then transformed into finished compositions away from the Colony.

Both Mrs. Beach and Mrs. MacDowell were happy at the outcome of the new arrangement. It was the beginning of an association much deeper than their previous friendship, for Mrs. MacDowell soon learned to depend upon Mrs. Beach for strength in the difficult task of keeping the Colony open during many troublesome times. In 1934 Mrs. Beach was elected first vice president of the Edward MacDowell Association. Mrs. MacDowell often asked Mrs. Beach to represent her at meetings to honor the name of MacDowell and, at the same time, to raise even a few dollars toward the mountanous annual expenses of the Colony's operations. On one such occasion Mrs. Beach represented Mrs. MacDowell at a MacDowell dinner at Derry, New Hampshire, when the music club of that town had taken upon itself the responsibility of furnishing the Pine Studio at the MacDowell Colony. The club's president, Mrs. Ella Lord Gilbert, later described the event:

> We put on a MacDowell Dinner, with nine tables seating 10 each—all tables decorated to represent a MacDowell composition, and the ten tickets for each table hand-painted to match the decorations. [Mrs. Beach] never quite got over the beauty of that dining room. Mrs. MacDowell was to have come, but was in a hospital in New York after the auto accident which laid her up for two years—so Mrs. Beach came in her place. Even though it was back in 1923, we charged $2.00 a ticket—sold every one and turned people away—and sent the proceeds to Mrs. MacDowell towards the furnishing of the Pine Studio. My class completely furnished that studio even to a second-hand piano which Mrs. MacDowell resurrected somewhere and she had it marked with a bronze marker. When we undertook the project, it was Mrs. MacDowell who suggested that it be the Pine Studio. It took us several years, but we accomplished it. There are many of my pupils still living who speak of the joy they had doing it.[154]

---

[154] Personal communication to Jenkins.

Mrs. Beach herself became an annual contributor and, when she died, she made the Colony one of her chief benefactors.

It is with the inspiration of the MacDowell Colony that Mrs. Beach returned to composition. In 1921 she produced Suite for Two Pianos, op. 104, based on old Irish melodies. It was dedicated to the Sutro sisters, Rose and Ottilie, who premiered the work in Paris on 25 October 1924, and the John Church Company published it in 1924. She also composed two solo piano works: "The Hermit Thrush at Eve" and "The Hermit Thrush at Dawn." Written at the Colony during the summer of 1921, they represent the composer's development of tunes provided for her by the hermit thrush whose nest was near her studio.

The following year, 1922, the number of pieces greatly increased. "From Blackbird Hills" for piano, based on an Omaha tribal dance, was dedicated to Hazel Gertrude Kinscella, a composer and writer on musical topics, who taught at the School of Music of the University of Washington in Seattle. Many years later, Kinscella recounted her early experiences with the MacDowell Colony and Mrs. Beach:

> First of all, I should mention that my mother, an artist, was at the [MacDowell] Colony very early in its history, probably 1918, and I went along then as "mother's daughter." That year we lived in one of the two houses down across the lower roads; and we ate at the Lower House. I don't recall that Mrs. Beach was in the Colony at the moment. However, I was just beginning to write and was doing many interviews which are published as a sort of series in *Musical America.* So, with Mrs. MacDowell's introduction at hand, I went up to Hillsboro and visited and interviewed Mrs. Beach there. She spoke more of the composer's techniques . . . she spoke of her interest in primitive melodies as possible thematic material; and in view of this I sent her, after our return home to Lincoln [Nebraska], an Indian tune which was and is well-known among our local tribes. She then composed a work for piano upon this "air" which she dedicated to me.[155]

Other compositions from 1922 include the *Te Deum* in F, op. 85; the Christmas carol anthem "Constant Christmas," op. 95; *Benedictus* and *Benedictus es*, op. 103; and the five piano pieces *From Grandmother's Garden*, op. 97. The *Benedictus* and *Benedictus es* were premiered in February 1924 in Emmanuel Episcopal Church in Boston, where she had been baptized and confirmed. During the next few years Mrs. Beach wrote additional anthems and piano music, as well as the cantata *Peter Pan*, op. 101, on a text by Jessie Andrews. *Peter Pan* was first performed by the Cincinnati Women's Club Chorus, to which it was dedicated. The anthem "Let This Mind Be in You," op. 105, was first sung on Palm Sunday 1924 in Emmanuel Episcopal Church, and the piano piece "Old Chapel in the Moonlight," inspired by the painter's studio at the Colony (the Alexander Studio), enjoyed a long period of popularity.

---

[155] Personal communication to Jenkins, 7 August 1959. Mrs. Beach enjoyed a reunion with Miss Kinscella on 10 March 1933 in the Woodstock Hotel next to Town Hall.

While in Hillsboro, Mrs. Beach made the acquaintance of the Rev. Howard Duffield (1854-1941), who served as pastor during the last 50 years of his life at the Old First Presbyterian Church in New York City. Winifred Duffield, his daughter, told her father about Mrs. Beach's interest in birds and bird calls, and Rev. Duffield told his daughter to suggest to the composer that she set Matthew Arnold's translations of texts by St. Francis of Assisi. Sometime later, on Sunday, 3 October 1926, Mrs. Beach attended a service in commemoration of the 700th anniversary of St. Francis' death at Boston's Trinity Episcopal Church, an event which inspired her to take up Rev. Duffield's suggestion. The result is the very popular cantata *Canticle of the Sun*, op. 123, for mixed voices and solo quartet, with either orchestral or piano accompaniment.

Second European Tour (1926-27)

Mrs. Beach's visits to Hillsboro often preceded her days at the MacDowell Colony where, usually, she spent the month of June, or at least part of it, and sometimes also part of the month of September. On 5 September 1926, while at the Colony, Mrs. Beach discovered the symptoms of her first illness of any consequence. After treatment by Peterborough's Dr. Cutler and upon his advice, Mrs. Beach was told to go to Boston. The night before she left, Mrs. Beach asked colonist Helen Sears to pack her studio things, and the evening was spent in front of the fire at the Eaves with the Du Bose Heywards, Mary Column, Willa Cather, Henry T. Gilbert, and "the girls" (as Mrs. Beach called Esther Bates, Mabel Daniels, Edith Orr, and Nancy Byrd Turner). The following day, on September 10, Mrs. MacDowell arranged for Mrs. Beach to be driven to Boston by Emil Tonieri, manager of Colony Hall, in the Colony car. After consultation with Dr. Cobb, Mrs. Beach entered Fenway Hospital and had a hemeroidectomy on September 13—"the worst day of my life, too horrid to remember," as Mrs. Beach later recalled.

Having recovered from the unpleasant episode, Mrs. Beach was discharged from Fenway Hospital on September 30. She went to the Copley Square Hotel for a week, after which she spent a fortnight with her old friend, Amy Brigham, who had accompanied her on her first European trip. Amy Brigham observed that while she was still in the hospital, Mrs. Beach had received in person a poem from Emma Roberts entitled "Birth," which "helped me through a rather bad night," the composer later said with great amusement. Brigham encouraged Mrs. Beach to then set the poem to music.

While at the hotel, Mrs. Beach made arrangements for a second trip to Europe, which would commence from Boston on November 20. She returned to the Parkers in Hillsboro on October 18 to put her affairs in order, and on October 28 signed her final will before Judge Wagner in the Hillsboro County Court House, Manchester, New Hampshire. Then, on November 2, after voting a straight Republican ticket in the local elections, she headed for New York to attend a convention of the American Pen Women. At Stratford House, headquarters of the convention, Mrs. Beach met the singer Ruth Shaffner, soprano soloist of the choir of St. Bartholomew's Episcopal Church, on fashionable Park Avenue. Schaffner informed Mrs. Beach that the composer's *Magnificat* was scheduled for performance Sunday morning and was to be rehearsed before the service the following day. She invited Mrs. Beach to attend the rehearsal, and as Mrs. Beach listened to David McK. Williams work with his choir on her music, she, as composer, experienced for the first time in her career the bringing to life of her music most nearly as she had conceived it. Her introduction to Williams was propitious. For him and his choir, the composer subsequently poured forth sacred choral works, and for Shaffner Mrs. Beach wrote some of her most inspired songs. For the remainder of her life no one performed as often with Mrs. Beach as Ruth Shaffner. Mrs. Beach returned to Boston the following day with a feeling in her heart that she had met two true new friends.

The following week was devoted to final arrangements to sail from Boston for the Mediterranean region abroad the *S.S. Martha Washington*. After a day at the Azores and a stop in Lisbon, the ship passed through the Strait of Gibraltar on November 29 and arrived in Naples on December 2. Before reaching Rome on December 16, Mrs. Beach visited Patros in Greece, then Trieste, Venice, Padua, and Florence. From then until February 24 she and her friends stayed at the Boston Hotel. Christmas 1926 was ushered in by attending midnight Mass at St. Luigi's Church, where they heard music sung by a thrilling boy's choir. Mrs. Beach spent more time in sightseeing in and around Rome than she did professionally, either in composing or in performing. There is no indication that she had a piano in her hotel room on which to practice, but she often mentioned trying this piano or that one in various hotels she visited on her many excursions. On 24 February 1927, however, she did give a joint concert with Mrs. Fitzhugh Prevost, violinist, for the guests of the Hotel Verdi in Rapello. About the piano she had no compliments, but she did manage a Chopin group and one group of her own compositions: "Italian Menuet," "Honeysuckle," "Heartsease," "In Autumn," "Scottish Legend," "Gavotte fantastique," and "Old Chapel by Moonlight." Mrs. Beach, with utmost seriousness, related how the concert was brought to a close by Mr. Prevost, who re-told his tiger-hunting experiences to the audience. Mrs. Beach suggested that, possibly inspired by Nero, Mrs. Prevost fiddled while her husband hunted.

After Rome, Mrs. Beach and her companions spent nearly two weeks in Genoa, and on March 5 they moved to Nice which they made their headquarters until April 7. From Nice they took a week's excursion to Corsica, but the crossing was so rough that Mrs. Beach, who was usually a very good sailor, found it "agonizing." Then the party went to Avignon and Marseilles and spent Easter 1927 in Lourdes. The last half of April was spent in Bordeaux, Tours, and Chartres, and they reached Paris on April 30. This was an especially exciting time to be a tourist in France, for on May 9 Nungesser and Cole made a non-stop airplane flight over the Atlantic and on May 22 Lindbergh landed in France and four days later made his triumphal parade through the French capital.

Despite this brief vacation from America and her career, Mrs. Beach could not escape from involvement in the musical life of her country. The University of New Hampshire wanted to tender her an honorary degree at its June commencement, but she turned it down because of her absence from the country. In Paris she met a Mrs. Hill who, anticipating the days of the WPA Music Project, suggested laboratory programs for composers to stimulate a more wide-spread interest in contemporary music. Mrs. Hill, Mrs. Beach observed, belonged to a school that was against modern music, and her program was her means of counteracting the influences of the new music. Mrs. Beach, in turn, found the Berlioz *Requiem*, which she heard at Notre Dame Cathedral on May 28, "extraordinarily modern but beautiful."

The month of June was spent largely in Belgium and in the cathedral country. On July 8 she visited Mont St. Michel en route to Cherbourg where, on July 12, she sailed for home aboard the *Leviathan*. Among the passengers were the aviators Byrd and Chamberlain. On arrival in New York on the 18th, Mrs. Beach took the Fall River boat for one more night's sailing to Massachusetts. The following day she was once again in her cottage in Centerville, Cape Cod.

Back in America (1927-28)

Besides the unpacking and distribution of numerous gifts purchased on this recent European trip, Mrs. Beach's household followed the Sacco-Vanzetti case in Boston with interest equal to, if different from, that demonstrated over the installation of the first electric water pump bringing water from a deep well into the house. Otherwise, for the next two months, the composer luxuriated in the quietude of the Cape in the presence of cousins from Newton Highlands, Massachusetts, who shared many stays at her Cape home with Mrs. Beach. Reminiscing over her recent European trip to Mrs. Ella Lord Gilbert, Mrs. Beach wrote that "what we digest is what feeds us, not what we swallow."

Mrs. Beach's piano did not remain in the Cape house from year to year; instead, Steinert's of Boston sent down a Steinway grand upon her arrival at the Cape, and, at the end of the season, returned it to their Boston warehouse. This year, their truck arrived on September 10 to pick up the instrument, and five days later Mrs. Beach deposited the Newton cousins in their home before spending the night in Boston at the Copley Square Hotel. The next day she set out for another working session at the MacDowell Colony.

The day after her arrival at the Colony, Mrs. Beach was back in the Watson Studio. She was working on a "jazz" piece, though this has not been further identified. On September 19 she made an additional choral arrangement of "Ah, Love but a Day," and the following three days were consumed with sketching and finishing the men's chorus "Sea Fever," op. 126, no. 2. She also sketched the song "Springtime," op. 124 (later dedicated to Arthur Kraft) and a setting of Psalm 110 for Ernest White. In addition, she borrowed Cecil Forsyth's *Orchestration* (1914) from the library, which she probably used over the next year in completing the orchestration of *Canticle of the Sun*; the short score was completed on December 27. On December 28 she started to write her *Magnificat* and *Nunc dimittis*, which she finished on 4 January 1928.

Although she was to recluse herself and concentrate on her own creations while at the Colony, Mrs. Beach could not refrain from assisting other guests and playing her role as the good citizen. On the afternoon of September 24 she politely listened to the works of another composer-colonist, which she found confused in styles, though they "grew on repeated hearings." On the following day, "a heavenly Sunday," she played hostess to 55 visitors from Hillsboro who came to see the Colony. Most of them were music pupils who belonged to the Junior Beach Club and their parents. She showed them around, brought them to her studio, and played a miniature concert for them.

At the end of September, Mrs. Beach left Peterborough for the 25- to 30-mile drive north to Hillsboro. Later, on October 24, she returned to the Colony to pay a personal call on Mrs. MacDowell, who remained at her residence "Hillcrest" until late in November.

In Hillsboro most of the fall of 1927, the composer first distributed gifts from her recent trip to her many friends. She reported how Clara Belle Miller was so delighted with her present that she pleaded with Mrs. Beach to play for her, which Mrs. Beach did in spite of the Miller's "awful piano." But as another neighbor, Florence Favor, reported, Mrs. Beach was always gracious when called upon to play for friends. And friends extended beyond individual persons, to the Beach Club and to other local groups. On October 15 she played a piece called "Cairo" for the first time at a meeting of the music club named in her honor, and a week later she played six of her piano pieces for the choir of the Methodist church after its night services. Although an Episcopalian, Mrs. Beach was generous to all religious groups and even donated $50 to the Congregational church. [156] Again, she played for the Beach Club on November 19.

Mrs. Beach did not neglect her Boston friends, either. After a recital in Norton, Massachusetts, in early November, she returned to Boston for the Christmas holidays, where she was a guest of honor at a Professional Women's Club luncheon at the Statler Hotel on December 20. She heard her "Constant Christmas" "beautifully given" at the carol service on Christmas Day at Emmanuel Church on Newbury Street, and on 8 January 1928 performances of her *Benedictus es, Benedictus, Kyrie,* and *Gloria tibi* at the same church "went finely." That same afternoon Rose Campana performed the Beethoven C-minor Piano Concerto with the People's Symphony Orchestra and "splendidly played" Mrs. Beach's cadenzas.

Before returning to Hillsboro, Mrs. Beach called upon Madame Helen Hopekirk, a colleague for more than a quarter of a century. Hopekirk's piano pieces were highly praised by Mrs. Beach, and the composer responded by giving Mrs. Beach copies of them. The two women played a two-piano arrangement of a Bruckner symphony before having tea, and had a talk about the Faelton Piano School, in which both women shared great interest.

After another week in New Hampshire, Mrs. Beach went off to New York City. Theodore Steinway sent a "fine Steinway grand" to the Seville Hotel for the composer's use during her stay in New York so that she could practice. She was introduced to the

---

[156] Mrs. Beach even recommended Christian Science to a friend who was ill, but when the friend's health did not improve, Mrs. Beach quipped that perhaps Mrs. Eddy had never forgiven her (Mrs. Beach) for marrying a surgeon.

facilities of St. Bartholomew's Church, including the Community House, library, and choir rooms, which later were to play an important part in her New York life. David McK. Williams and Ruth Shaffner were her hosts at a luncheon in the church's Community House. On February 19, Williams performed her *Benedictus* and *Benedictus es,* and at lunch the next day Mrs. Beach promised to write a *Benedicite* for him. On January 24 she heard a choral arrangement of her "The Year's at the Spring" performed by the St. Cecilia Club. The following night was a "piano dinner" at the Edwin Hughes's with Alton Jones, Arthur Whiting, and Miss Seidlowa joining Mrs. Beach. She described it as "a lovely dinner, we all played all evening, great fun." The next evening Maria Jeritza sang "superbly" Beach's "Ah, Love, but a Day" in a recital at the Plaza Hotel, and on Sunday, January 29, at 4 o'clock, Mrs. Beach heard her *Magnificat* and *Nunc dimittis* for the first time with orchestra at a concert of sacred music at the church of St. Mary the Virgin— "superbly given." Later that same evening she was a guest of honor at a MacDowell Club dinner. In February, at tea, after a four o'clock service at St. Bartholomew's Church, Mrs. Beach accompanied Ruth Shaffner in four of her songs. This was the first of many joint performances the two ladies enjoyed over the next fifteen years.

During these few weeks in New York, Mrs. Beach came into contact with several very important musicians. On February 5 Mrs. Beach spent the evening at Ethel Hier's Studio with Béla Bartók. Bartók and Joseph Szigeti performed his violin sonata, *Hungarian Folk Tunes,* and *Peasant Dances.* She termed the sonata "hideous," while she admired the other pieces. A short time later she went to a piano recital by Percy Grainger at Carnegie Hall and was annoyed by "a couple of drunks" who occupied the box next to the one Mrs. Beach shared as a guest of Marion Bauer. On February 18 she managed to hear Rachmaninoff's recital, which she described as "wonderful playing—best Chopin *Fantasia* I ever heard."

Before leaving New York on a tour of several southern states, Mrs. Beach served on the jury of the Society for the Publication of American Music. On February 25 they chose Bernard Wagenaar's Sonata for Violin and Piano, which Mrs. Beach found to be "good, but not remarkable."

Her southern concert tour began with a recital at Burlington, North Carolina, on March 2. This was followed by one at Greensboro on the third, Winston-Salem on the fifth, and Asheville on the eighth. On March 12 she gave a recital at Converse College in Spartanburg, another on the thirteenth at Columbia, South Carolina, and on the fourteenth a talk at the University of South Carolina. From there she went to Atlanta, where she remained until April 2. She was entertained by many people there, but the most important meeting was with the writer Nan Bagby Stevens, whom she had met at the MacDowell Colony and who eventually would supply Mrs. Beach with the libretto of her opera *Cabildo,* op. 149. From Atlanta she made excursions to neighboring towns for recitals and lectures. For example, on March 21 a Miss Torrence drove Mrs. Beach to Decatur, Georgia, for a recital at Agnes Scott College, followed by a lecture in the college chapel the next day. She also gave a recital at Bessie Tift School in Forsyth, Georgia.

From Atlanta, Mrs. Beach left for Washington, D.C., then continued on to Beaver, Pennsylvania, for a visit with friends, and finally on April 18 played a recital in Pittsburgh at the Pennsylvania College for Women. The following day she returned to the Seville

Hotel in New York City and immediately began rehearsals of her Piano Quintet with the Kneisel Quartet. The performance took place on April 22 in Steinway Hall as part of the program of the annual meeting of the Society of American Women Composers. The business meeting was held the next morning in Mrs. Beach's own hotel room, during which Mrs. Beach resigned as president and was made an honorary president by acclamation. Gena Branscombe succeeded her, and Mary Howe of Washington, D.C., was elected first vice president and Marion Ralston second vice president. Among the other women composers present were Mary Wood Hill, Phyllis Fergus Hoyt, Anne Hull, and Ethel Hier.

On April 25 Mrs. Beach was the guest of the Sutro sisters, who played for her her two-piano suite, op. 104. Immediately afterwards, Mrs. Beach departed for Washington for concerts at the Library of Congress, and was back in New York on the 28th to hear a "wonderful performance" of her *Cantate Domino*, op. 78, no. 3, at St. Bartholomew's. The next day this energetic woman went to Boston where she made plans to return to Europe six months hence. Meanwhile, on May 18 she played the piano part of her Quintet with the Lenox String Quartet in a radio concert broadcast nationally from station WJZ in New York and sponsored by NBC. After another short stay in Hillsboro, where she sketched out the *Benedicite*, op. 121, for David McK. Williams, Mrs. Beach returned to the MacDowell Colony on June 5 and there completed it. From June 11 to 14 she sketched and completed a *Communion Service*, op. 122. Two days later she hurried to Hillsboro because there had been a fire at the Parker's, but she was happy to find that no damage had been done to any of her belongings. The next day the Parkers drove to Durham, the seat of the University of New Hampshire, where, on June 18, she and Mrs. MacDowell each were awarded honorary Master of Arts degrees. That afternoon the two women returned to Peterborough together. On June 27 President Edward M. Lewis of the University of New Hampshire paid a return call upon them by visiting the Colony himself, expressing regrets at "not having given [the] doctor's degree instead of M.A."

Each year, as the 4th of July approached, Mrs. Beach became apprehensive of the noises of celebration associated with the holiday. As Esther Bates recalled (letter to Jenkins, 3 October 1957),

> At Peterborough I noticed how sensitive her ears were. On the Fourth
> she was beside herself with nervous distress over the noises. Almost
> hysterical, and as you know, she was a woman of fine poise. One single
> firecracker drove her wild; a gun shot drove her frantic.

This year, 1928, she was happy to escape to Henniker by accepting Julia Jones's invitation to the Guy Jones farm. Here, on the 4th, she heard the Boston singer Lillian Buxbaum perform "Ecstasy" and "Ah, Love, but a Day" in a radio broadcast. The next day she joined Mrs. Buxbaum in Boston and invited the singer to accompany her to Centerville. Mrs. Buxbaum soon became a regular in Centerville as visitor and singer at Mrs. Beach's home, and eventually the composer willed the place to her.

The excitement of the summer was the installation of a private telephone, at the cost of $865, and attaching electric lighting to the house. With these two new features, Mrs. Beach felt she could remain in Centerville longer, and this year stayed until October 3, when the house was closed for the winter. During this stay in Centerville she completed the orchestration of *Canticle of the Sun* and read publisher's proofs for this work as well as for *Benedicite*, "Rendevous," and the *Communion Service*.

After a week in Boston, where much of the time was spent in going over old letters and destroying many, especially those from her old piano teacher Ernest Perabo, Mrs. Beach returned to Hillsboro for an anniversary meeting of the D.A.R. Julia Jones sang songs by the chapter's distinguished sister. The following week the Junior Beach Club presented a recital at which a young girl performed the composer's "Humming Bird," "remarkably well."

On November 1, Mrs. Beach departed again for Atlanta, Anniston, Asheville, and Chicago. In Atlanta she gave a lecture recital for the Junior Music Club, followed the next day by a recital and talk on the MacDowell Colony at the Women's Club luncheon. On November 9 she gave a recital in Anniston. In Asheville she played a recital on the 16th and spent considerable time with the Crosby Adamses who, with her, were prominent in the Music Teachers National Association. For them she played through the score of *Canticle of the Sun*, which was to receive its premiere at St. Bartholomew's Church on December 9.

In Chicago the Music Teachers National Association was having sessions over the Thanksgiving weekend, and Mrs. Beach performed at their concerts. She also performed at a concert sponsored by the Mu Phi Epsilon Sorority and subsequently, at a luncheon, was made an honorary member.[157] In addition she was heard on a radio broadcast, declined to play her Piano Concerto with the Chicago Women's Symphony Orchestra, and witnessed several of her works performed in the city during her brief stay. She also attended a reception in her honor and gave a talk on the MacDowell Colony. She was in Washington, D.C., on December 6 for a recital at the Washington Club, and the following day attended a supper party at the home of the Washington composer Mary Howe (Mrs. Walter Bruce Howe), where she was called upon to play eleven of her piano pieces for a small and distinguished audience.

Third European Tour (1928-29)

Mrs. Beach arranged to sail to Europe from New York on December 11 on the *S.S. Saturnia*. The two days in New York before sailing were busy with last-minute details and with working out details with G. Schirmer for the publication of "Springtime," op. 124. She also attended a supper at David McK. Williams's home for the English Singers and a party at Olin Downs's for Vladimir Horowitz. Horowitz had played the

---

[157] Mrs. McCormick Ochsner of Chicago was also made an honorary member at this luncheon.

Tchaikovsky piano concerto with the Chicago Symphony Orchestra, and Mrs. Beach had gone to hear the great Russian virtuoso. Horowitz was in a rare out-going mood; he "played snatches of everything wonderfully" to the apparent pleasure of all the guests. Among the guests was another famous pianist, Alexander Silotti, a pupil of Liszt, who was then teaching at the Institute of Musical Art in New York (later known as the Juilliard School). Mrs. Beach also enjoyed performances of her *Benedictus*, the new *Benedicite*, *Benedic anima mea*, and *Canticle of the Sun* at St. Bartholomew's Church the day before she sailed.

With such a send-off, the composer surely was in a happy frame of mind as she left the country. The calm voyage was disturbed only by the news of the death, on December 16, of the poet Elinor Wylie who had been one of Mrs. Beach's closest friends at the MacDowell Colony. At dawn on December 21 the *S.S. Saturnia* docked at Naples, and by mid-afternoon Mrs. Beach and her companion[158] were comfortably settled in their hotel.

The year 1928 closed quietly in Rome with a reception in Mrs. Beach's honor attended by about one hundred persons, despite inclement weather and plague. Unlike her previous visit to Europe when she vacationed and was not professionally active, this visit involved both composition and performance. The first main event in the new year was the completion of her String Quartet, op. 89; except for the final details, the score was finished by January 21. In an inspiring chamber music concert on January 18 she heard the Viennese String Quartet, composed of the "very young" Kolisch, Lehner, Khuner, and Heifetz, playing the Brahms A-minor and the Beethoven C-major quartets "without notes" and with "superb ensemble and much feeling." A string quartet by Mario Labrosa was "dull but less than some."

She herself played for the steady procession of guests, many of them Americans, who came to her room almost daily. In her previous visit to Rome there is no evidence that Mrs. Beach had regular access to a piano; on this occasion, however, a piano must have been a part of her furnishings since she practiced and played daily.[159] On February 23 she visited the American Academy where, before leaving, she played three of her pieces to an audience which included the Steinerts of Boston, the Roger Sessions, Robert Sanders, and other Americans. At a concert at the Academy on March 9, two movements of Sanders's String Quartet were played, and on April 11 the entire work was performed on a concert at which Mrs. Beach's String Quartet received its world premiere.

Although working very hard on her own composition, Mrs. Beach nevertheless attended the weekly Agosteo concerts under Desirée Defauw and other conductors in order to hear what famous European composers were doing. On January 13 she felt that Malipiero's *Impressione del Verdi* was "hideous" and that Prokofiev's *Scythian Suite* was "ultra-modern but strong." Molinari conducted the premiere of Respighi's *Roman Festivals* on March 17, which Mrs. Beach found "superbly brilliant," but she disliked Hindemith's Concerto for Brass and Winds, performed by Klemperer on March 3. At the opera she saw Mascagni conduct his *Amico Fritz*.

---

[158] Jenkins does not indicate who her companion was.

[159] Diary.

Mrs. Beach's principal concert took place at the American Embassy in Rome on 17 March 1929. The rooms were crowded, and the enthusiasm high. Her assisting artist, Edwin Alonzo Bartlett, "sang gloriously." Then on April 30 she returned to Munich, which she had not seen since her departure in 1914. She was met by her old friend Marcella Craft, and after a busy period revisiting old scenes, she departed for Bremerhaven from whence she sailed for the United States on May 15 on the *S.S. America*. On board she met a Mrs. Duke, a black lady from Richmond, Virginia, who entertained informally by singing traditional black songs. One of these, "On a Hill," was copied down on May 19 by Mrs. Beach, who subsequently arranged it and later that year published it without opus number through the Schmidt Company.

Illness and Recovery (1929-30)

A mere two days after her return to America, Mrs. Beach performed a recital at the Longy School of Music in Cambridge. This was at the invitation of Amy Eaton, a long-time friend and fellow pianist. From June 1 to July 4 she was back in Hillsboro, except for many one-day excursions with friends. Once more she spent the 4th of July holiday with Julia and Guy Jones in Henniker, where she rehearsed with Julia many Beach songs including the new Negro song. The following day she returned to her Centerville home by train from Concord, New Hampshire; the Buxbaums and her cousins met her at the West Barnstable station and brought her to the house they had prepared for her.

The summer of 1929 passed quietly. Much time was spent in practicing in anticipation of several winter-season concerts. Many friends and relatives visited her. She subscribed to swimming lessons, for she thoroughly enjoyed the surf and bathing in the invigorating water on the south side of the Cape. Suddenly, on September 9, after the departure of house guests, Mrs. Beach became violently ill with what later was diagnosed to have been a gall-bladder attack. As soon as the Centerville house could be closed, she retruned to Boston (September 15) where, after several recurrences of the attack, Mrs. Beach entered Phillips House of the Massachusetts General Hospital for an operation on October 11. In the meantime concerts had to be cancelled, and the pleasant summer turned into a nightmarish fall. The receipt of many flowers, letters, and visits from devoted friends helped cheer her up, and she received a psychological boost when on November 17 she heard Giovanni Martinelli sing her "Ah, Love, but a Day" on the Atwater Kent national radio concert. In December, however, when an abscess developed in the wound area, Mrs. Beach was forced to return to the hospital for another operation and to spend Christmas there. She was discharged from the hospital once more on 4 January 1930. Three days later she wrote to a friend:

Now I am pronounced cured, but I can do no work, by doctor's orders, this season. I had some fine concerts arranged, but I am so thankful to be well that I can even bear to be idle! My dear friend Mrs. Clifford Brigham has invited me to be her guest thru this month and February and I am very happy to be out here in the lovely Blue Hill region.[160]

Mrs. Beach and Amy Brigham attended many concerts together, including Harold Samuel's recital in Jordan Hall; Glazounov conducting the Boston Symphony Orchestra with Benno Rubinoff playing the Glazounov Violin Concerto; Goosens conducting the Boston Symphony Orchestra (Mrs. Beach found his "string concoction DULL"); a Prokofiev concert by the same orchestra ("terribly modern, exciting, brilliant and *hard*"); Sanroma's "*very* brilliant" piano recital in Milton, Massachusetts; a performance of Strauss's *Rosenkavalier* by the Chicago Opera Company; and productions of Debussy's *Pelleas and Melisande* and Massenet's *Le Jongleur*, both with Mary Garden.

On March 4, Mrs. Beach went to Short Hills, New Jersey, for a private visit; she then spent from April 11 to the end of the month at the Copley Square Hotel in Boston. While in Boston she "worked over" somebody's orchestral parts to "Year's for Toledo," and sent them to Schmidt. On April 25, after having lunch with composers Louise Souther and Mary Howe, Mrs. Beach and her friends attended a Boston Symphony Orchestra concert commemorating Chadwick's 50th anniversary as a composer. The orchestra played his *Sinfonietta*, and afterwards Mrs. Beach enjoyed a reunion in the Green Room with her old friend who had played at her wedding forty-five years earlier in 1885.

At the end of April Mrs. Beach returned to Hillsboro and on May 8 listened to a broadcast of a MacDowell program from New York where Mrs. MacDowell played her husband's *1650* and Ernest Hutcheson played two movements from the D-minor Piano Concerto. She noted in her diary on 12 May 1930 that it was the fifty-second anniversary of her first trip to San Francisco (1878) and this year, 1930, the first performance of *Canticle of the Sun* in Toledo. The work was repeated by Albert Stoessel at Chautauqua, New York, to whose chorus the work was dedicated.

After an absence from the concert stage for half a year, Mrs. Beach played her first public concert for the Junior Beach Club on May 23, and she did so despite severe pains that she had had in her right arm for about a week. On the 27th she was back in Boston at the Phillips House of Massachusetts General Hospital. After extensive examinations, the pain was said to have been caused by a postural weakness causing nerve pressure. Corrective measures were taken, and the pain subsided to the point where she could resume normal activities. She therefore returned to Hillsboro on June 13 and arrived at the MacDowell Colony on the 16th.

For her stay at the Colony in 1930, Mrs. Beach did not reside in the Eaves but rather at the Nebanussit Tea Barn located on the Dublin Road beside the Nebanussit River, a gentle little stream wandering peacefully through the fields before reaching its rock drop nearer the center of Peterborough. Mrs. Beach noted the Sunday night supper

---

[160] Letter from Mrs. Beach dated Readville, Massachusetts, 7 January 1930.

at Hillcrest on June 22; as was common in those days, Mrs. MacDowell had the colonists as guests to supper once a week.

> Sat with Agnes Rourke. Saw Nancy Byrd Turner, Mabel Daniels, the Chard Smiths, Rollo Browns, Mr. Haubiel.[161]

Just before supper "Douglas Moore called. . . . Lovely talk with him."

At this time Mrs. Beach arranged her song "When Soul Is Joined" and her piano piece "The Fair Hills of Eire, O!" for violin.

> The latter is based upon a folk tune given to the composer by Padriac Colum, the great Irish poet, who was working that summer on some translations of some very old Irish songs. The melody was so hauntingly beautiful that Mrs. Beach found it, like the theme of the *Scottish Legend*, taking possession of her until she had given it a setting. This she did without altering the air—so very characteristic with its flat seventh— merely harmonizing and arranging it in a way that brings out its full pathos.[162]

On June 24 she went to Hillcrest to hear Louise Souther play her own music for Mrs. MacDowell. Two days later she finished "Mr. White's Anthem," and the day after that she completed the draft of "Shadows of the Evening Hour," op. 125, no. 1, and began Masefield's "Prayer" for men's voices, completed June 28. On the 30th Nina Maud Richardson drove Mrs. Beach, Mrs. MacDowell, and her sister Anna Nevins to Hillsboro, and that evening Mrs. Beach slipped away to Henniker to the Jones's, who were pleasantly surprised to see her. The next day Flora, one of the Jones's cows, gave birth to a heffer who was given the name "Amy" in honor of their guest. Mrs. Beach returned to the Jones again for July Fourth in order to escape the terrible noise of firecrackers; she wrote:

> Quiet here, but much firing in village night & day. . . . Tried over new songs with Julia. Went well!

The following day, as was becoming the custom, Mrs. Beach left for the Cape where the Buxbaums met her at the West Barnstable station. She found her cousin Mabel at Centerville as "crotchety" as usual and enjoying "uncertain health." Of considerable concern to Mrs. Beach was the news that a new road was to be built that would go near the front of her home and destroy a part of her woods; what was worse was that a filling station was then built there.[163]

---

[161] Diary.

[162] Una Allen, "Composer's Corner," *Musician*, July 1930.

[163] In September Mrs. Beach drafted a letter to the highway commissioner at the Patriot office in protest, and in February she wrote the Barnstable selectmen protesting the filling station. During the summer of 1935 she

After several starts at "Spirit of Mercy," op. 125, no. 2, the music was finally worked out on July 14 and copies were completed by the end of the month. At the same time Mrs. Beach also wrote out "Shadows of the Evening Hour," no. 1 of the same opus. On August 6 she sent copies of the two songs of op. 125 along with "Mr. White's Anthem" to Schmidt. By mid-August the Masefield "Prayer" was finished.

Mrs. Beach arrived at the MacDowell Colony on September 20, and the next day she sketched a four-part version of "June," the third of four songs from op. 51. Besides Mrs. Beach, other pianist-composers in residence in 1930 were Harold Vickers (who was almost blind), Suzanne Armstrong, Celius Dougherty, and Lewis M. Isaacs. She continued to sketch songs, and stayed until the 30th when nearly everyone else had already left.

Once again Mrs. Beach was at the Parker's in Hillsboro, where she plunged into the social life of the town. She was one of the hostesses at a D.A.R. meeting where Julia Jones again sang songs by Beach. Then on October 17 she was back at the Copley Square Hotel in Boston, where she negotiated further publications with Schmidt's representative, Mr. Austin.

New York City as Winter Home
(1930-31)

For some time Mrs. Beach's New York friends had been urging her to make New York City her winter headquarters. She had declined the idea for several reasons, and perhaps most of all she could not bring herself to live far from Boston except when she was on a trip abroad or on an extended concert tour. She found it difficult to realize that the hub of musical activities had moved away from Boston where it had been for so long a time. True, the Boston Symphony Orchestra under Serge Koussevitsky was recognized by nearly everyone, including New Yorkers, as the world's finest orchestra. But otherwise Boston was no longer the leader in musical matters as it had been at the turn of the century.

Even as recently as the first of April she had written: "Gave up idea of staying in N.Y. . . . too risky." What she meant by "risky" is uncertain, but in any case she yielded to the urging of her friends and agreed on August 30 to take a room at the American

---

refused to allow a garage and service station to be built on a corner of her property, but eventually she was forced to accept the fact that the town of Barnstable gave permission for the erection of such a garage and service station on property directly across from hers on Phinney's Lane, facing the new highway. When Mrs. Beach learned, in March 1943, that a liquor store was to be erected opposite the gate to her property, she immediately wrote a complaint to the town selectmen and was able to get a temporary delay.

Women's Association Club House on West 57th Street for three months, beginning November 1.[164] She established herself in room 1128, which she described as "small but very nice." She immediately plunged into the concert activities of the city. One of the first was a Philharmonic concert conducted by Erich Kleiber, whose performance of Tchaikovsky's Fourth Symphony was "much tamer than Boston's," which she had heard the previous week under Koussevitsky. That same day she inaugurated a habit of attending morning services at St. Bartholomew's Church. Except for a brief visit to Helen Fish in Albany from November 4 to 7, she concentrated her activities in New York City and its immediate suburbs until the following April.

By November 12, proofs of "June" were awaiting correction. The next few days were devoted to arranging "Lotus Isles" for three voices and transposing "Spirit of Mercy" to a lower key; all three songs were sent back to Mr. Austin at Schmidt's in Boston. One afternoon during this time Mrs. Beach stopped in the New York office of G. Schirmer on East 43rd Street and met Dr. Carl Engel, editor of *The Musical Quarterly*, Carl Deis, a Schirmer editor, and Florence and Percy Grainger, all of whom she found cordial. Mabel Daniels, the Boston composer, was also there with the lovely singer Clara Edwards. On November 18 Mrs. Beach spoke at the Symposium of the National Federation of Music Clubs in the theater of the Roerich Museum; introduced in the grand manner by Oscar Thompson, she discussed the "Composer's Standpoint." The next Sunday morning she heard her *Benedictus es* sung at St. Bartholomew's, and the following day she noted with sorrow the death of Lynwood Farnham, organist, whose performances of the music of Bach were internationally famous.[165] On November 30 the Sutro sisters played Mrs. Beach's Suite for Two Pianos at the MacDowell Club before a small but enthusiastic audience. Her *Benedictus* in A-flat was sung at St. Bartholomew's on November 30 and December 9. On the 11th she and Ruth Shaffner gave a short recital for the National Opera Club headed by Baroness von Kleuner.

Mrs. Beach, overflowing with Victorian romanticism, seems to have been affected somewhat by the mysteries of the occult. She spent December 12 at Helen Ware's with Gena Branscombe and with her hostess played the ouija board. One message she received from the board was so impressive that she wrote it in her diary:

Be careful. Fight. Mother here high above you each day.

Mrs. Beach was a most devoted daughter, and on several occasions after Mrs. Cheney's death she mentioned the "nearness" of her mother. On one occasion at the MacDowell Colony, I played the ouija board with Mrs. Beach and a group of colonists,[166] and when the table moved and when messages came, Mrs. Beach appeared to take the matter very seriously and ponder the messages as if they had some special meaning for her, which

---

[164] Letter from Mrs. Beach to Ruth Shaffner, dated 30 August 1930.

[165] She attended a concert at St. Bartholomew's on 13 January 1931, in commemoration of the late organist's birthday.

[166] From this point on, Jenkins occasionally inserts his personal reminiscences of Mrs. Beach.

the rest of us failed to understand. She was indignant if we scoffed at the game; we played for fun, it had little meaning for us except as a means of relaxation on a stormy night. The following February Mrs. Beach mentions in her diary that her horoscope was read by a numerologist, and when she returned to Hillsboro in May, she sent to England for her horoscope.

Mrs. Beach's first Christmas season in New York City proved not to be an inactive one. After hearing inspiring services at St. Bartholomew's, whose assistant rector, the Rev. Robert W. Norwood, she had come to love for his fine talks, sermons, and books, she plunged into the writing of an "Alleluia" for David McK. Williams and his choir, which she delivered to him on New Year's Day and to which he responded that he was "crazy about the music." On December 26 her Flute Variations, op. 80, was broadcast nationally from Cleveland, but she found out about it too late to listen. A few days later Mr. Austin informed her that he had sent the score and parts of the *Gaelic Symphony* to Henry Hadley, conductor of the Manhattan Symphony Orchestra, at the request of Mr. Hadley.[167] A performance was scheduled for 25 January 1931. Strangely, Hadley sent Mrs. Beach 500 tickets for her to buy, and a week later she sent him $50. She attended a rehearsal of the symphony on the 24th and lamented the long cuts and the roughness of the playing. However, the concert the next day, "brilliantly played," was a "great success" with "much enthusiasm" on the part of the audience. Friends of the composer who heard a broadcast of the performance said that "it was fine over the radio." Hadley and his players expressed good will toward the composer, and the New York press was generous with its praise of this thirty-four-year-old work.

The day before the performance of the *Gaelic Symphony* the LaSalle String Quartet with Mrs. Beach at the piano performed her Piano Quintet at a concert of the Society of American Women Composers. She also learned at this time that Albert Stoessel had started rehearsals in Worcester, Massachusetts, of her *Canticle of the Sun* for chorus and orchestra for a performance the next October. Meanwhile performances of her music at St. Bartholomew's continued on January 10. She gave two well-received recitals in White Plains, New York—one for the Brahms Club and another for music students and supervisors at the high school.

There were many musicales, lectures, plays, and other entertainments at the Community House of St. Bartholomew's, which Mrs. Beach frequently attended and in which she sometimes participated. For example, on February 4 she and Ruth Shaffner, Elsa Hilgen, and Harry Shub gave a concert there. There were also concerts in the church itself. Four days after her concert with Shaffner, Hilgen, and Shub she heard her *Magnificat* and *Canticle of the Sun* sung at the afternoon church concert, which she termed "phenominal." And during the services themselves Mrs. Beach's music often was performed. For example, on three separate Sundays in March her canticles were sung at services in St. Bartholomew's.

---

[167] Hadley was an ambitious conductor on behalf of American music. His Society of American Composers and Conductors sponsored regular concerts of chamber music by American composers at his studio, a custom continued by his widow after his death.

In mid-February she joined the Kneisel Quartet in the Piano Quintet at the Roerich Museum and three weeks later repeated the piece at a concert of the League of American Pen Women. On March 6 she was in Newark for a radio concert on station WOR; she was assisted again by Ruth Shaffner, as well as a violinist and cellist. On March 12 she attended Elly Ney's recital on which the English pianist played her two "Thrushes." A few days later she attended one of Marion Bauer's lectures on "Modern Music" at Mrs. George Alexander's; she was "not surprised" that Bauer omitted her from the list of modern composers yet enjoyed the lecture, illustrated at the piano by Harrison Potter. At the annual banquet of the American Society of Composers and Publishers (ASCAP) she sat with Victor Harris, who asked the composer to play her *Nautilus* so that he might consider a performance of the cantata in 1932 with the St. Cecilia chorus. Mrs. Beach was again a judge in a contest for a publication award by the Society for the Publication of American Music; the prize in 1931 went to Frances Terry for her violin sonata, and after the March 7 decision she visited one of the losers to console him. Finally, during this season, on April 6, she heard her Flute Variations performed at Mary Wood Hill's studio.

Soon afterwards Mrs. Beach went to Wakefield, Massachusetts, where on April 10 she gave a piano recital. She remained in the Boston area to attend to personal matters and to visit friends and relatives. On the 21st she played for the Boston Professional Women's Club and then went directly to Washington, D.C., for concerts at the Library of Congress. Although none of her compositions was on the programs, the violinist Elena de Sayn gave a separate recital that included the slow movement of her Violin Sonata. The composer was back in Boston in a few days, where she and Lillian Buxbaum gave a radio concert on station WEEI including some of her music. A few days later, on May 1, the two musicians performed at the Bridgewater (Connecticut) State Normal School for an enthusiastic audience.

By mid-May Mrs. Beach was once again in her beloved Hillsboro amidst old friends. She enjoyed the enthusiasm the townsfolk showed her and could hardly turn down an invitation:

> I have promised to play once more for the *Juvenile Beach Club* Thursday
> night. They gave an operetta (so-called) and the tots always want me
> to add to the program. The Juniors did finely last week—a larger-sized
> group, and I also played for them.[168]

But her thoughts were also with David McK. Williams, who was sailing from New York at the end of May. While in Boston, Mrs. Beach had received a poem by Alice Meynell from Williams with a request to set it to music as an anthem. During her month in Hillsboro, Mrs. Beach memorized the poem—"Christ in the Universe"—so that she could set it.

---

[168] Letter to Ruth Shaffner from Mrs. Beach dated 25 May 1931.

Mrs. Beach was at the opening of the MacDowell Colony on 1 June 1931. Among the early arrivals were Nancy Byrd Turner and George Chadwick, while Esther Bates arrived a day later. By June 5 Mrs. Beach had

> finished [the] rough sketch of [the Meynell] anthem except filling in [the] accompaniment. Great Thrill! Used every bit of piano piece, including climax. Took four days here and one in Hillsboro.[169]

Two days later she

> finished [the Meynell anthem] "Christ in the Universe." Six days and ½ in Hibby! Like it so far as proportions is concerned. Rather too emotional.[170]

She sent the manuscript to her copyist on August 19.

Mrs. Beach remained at the Colony the entire month of June 1931, where she was very busy. After sketching the anthem, she wrote four responses for a Methodist publication in Kansas City, then set Dr. Norwood's "Drowsy Dream Town" for soprano and three-part women's chorus, and also wrote a song for Ruth Shaffner on Leonora Speyer's poem "Dark Garden."[171] She also set Katherine Adams's "I Shall Be Brave," and she wrote out a three-part chorus arrangement of "Lotus Isles." She finished the organ sketch of the Meynell Anthem and looked over three piano pieces, op. 128, for publication by Theodore Presser.[172]

Life at the MacDowell Colony was not all compositional work. Mrs. Beach had musicales in her studio, with performances by Mary Howe, Mildred Smith, Charles

---

[169] Diary.

[170] Diary.

[171] She completed both "Drowsy Dream Town" and "Dark Garden" on June 11. Speyer was a fellow colonist.

[172] Mrs. Beach described the compositional activities of June 1931 in a letter to Ruth Shaffner dated June 11:

> What do you suppose I was doing, when your precious letter came this noon? Finishing a song I had begun only this morning for you, using the lovely poem "Dark Gardens" which Mrs. Speyer read to us when we called upon her! I *think* you will like it—I surely hope so! And—also this morning, I had written a little song for you and your girls on "Drowsy Dreamtown"—Dr. Norwood's words! Don't you think two entirely different songs in one day are enough, so I can stop now and write to you? Yesterday I sketched four choral responses for a religious publication in Kansas City, promised last winter. And last week I did the entire poem which David [McK. Williams] had sent! That is what this Colony does to me! I suspect that his Anthem is to the same words he sent me, for he wrote just before sailing that he had sent *his* to the publisher. It is Alice Meynell's "Christ in the Universe." He gave as his excuse (so like him!) that if he wanted to see mine he would never have the courage to publish his! And, curiously enough, *I* feel sure that *his* will be *much* the most appropriate setting of the two! This is the way we quarrel! I, too, have put in a soprano solo, leading the whole work up to it as a close. *Please* do not mention this anthem of mine, as I shall keep it back until I have time to orchestrate it, and that will not be soon! It is a superb poem and I do not wonder that David loved it, as I do.

Haubiel, Celius Dougherty, and herself. There also was a concert in Colony Hall by the MacDowell Chorus and a string quartet which drove up from Boston; this concert was attended by the villagers as well as by the colonists. Mr. and Mrs. Phillip Hale came up from Boston for a short visit, and there were nightly talks with "the girls" at the Eaves. Mabel Daniels, a Boston composer, was among "the girls" and often took small groups of colonists for late afternoon scenic drives to nearby towns. The two composers, although holding high respect for each other's professional accomplishments, often extremely irritated each other; Mrs. Beach was especially upset when Daniels called her "Aunt Amy." Before departing from the Colony for her annual Fourth of July escape to Hillsboro or Henniker, Mrs. Beach offered to have the Colony Hall porches screened as a matter of protection against mosquitos. Her offer was promptly accepted and accomplished, much to the comfort of colonists who liked to congregate there before dinner each night.

After a couple of days at the Parker's in Hillsboro, Mrs. Beach went to Henniker for the holidays, celebrated at the Jones's by picking peas. Then, on July 6, she returned to the Cape via train from Concord, New Hampshire. As usual, Mrs. Buxbaum and the cousins were at the West Barnstable station to meet her. She was delighted, upon reaching her house, that the new porch, which had been built since she was last there the previous fall, was "a howling success."[173] She was distressed, however, at the new state road construction, which was completed on September 4 only after the engineer urged Mrs. Beach to give up more land along her front line for safety on the curve. Just after she reached the Cape she wrote to Ruth Shaffner:

> As soon as I get some real rest, I will copy out the new songs for you. How gloriously you will sing them!

A few days later she added:

> Tomorrow morning I hope to send the package of songs to you, registered, on our way to the swim. I am sending the original MSS to you "for keeps," high key and all, thinking that you might like to have them as a souvenir of our day in Peterborough. However, I am sending also some copyist work for actual use, in the lower keys, excepting in the case of "Drowsy Dream Town" which has not been transposed. . . . My deep love goes with these things to you and my longing to hear you sing them all. I shall send them to Mr. Austin when I succeed in getting all the permissions for use of the copyright. The Norwood poem I have, but the Alfred Knopf people haven't replied, and I am still waiting to hear from Katherine Adams [Walker] in Ireland about hers. She *gave* me her verses, but they had been published by *somebody*.

---

[173] Letter to Ruth Shaffner, July 1931.

That summer, she eventually added one more anthem, "God Is Our Stronghold," on a text by Elizabeth Woodworth. She invited David McK. Williams to visit her in Centerville so she could share with him her new works and was "feeling . . . rather let down" when he wrote that he could not come.

The composer's sixty-fourth birthday on September 5 was celebrated quietly, as were most of these occasions, by a morning swim and a drive with Mrs. McArthur to a tea at West Yarmouth. Here she was greeted by the composer Bainbridge Crist and Mrs. Crist, who summered at Yarmouth. Mr. Crist recalled that he had heard Mrs. Beach perform her Piano Concerto in Berlin on her first trip to Europe before World War I. A few days later, before many of the summer people got away, two women (Miss Crosby and Miss Cornish) representing the Centerville Church called upon Mrs. Beach, lest the composer should overlook her annual contribution of $25 to the church. And, as the ladies expected, Mrs. Beach was soon gone, first to Boston, then to Bath, Maine, to visit her New Jersey cousins, whose summer cottage was on MacMahan Island off the Maine coast.

On September 25 the island cottage was closed and Mrs. Beach and her cousins returned to New York City. Upon her arrival there, Mrs. Beach went to the apartment of Ruth Shaffner, and the two ladies drove to Shaffner's newly acquired country home on the bank of a little stream near Paterson, New Jersey. Brookwillows, as Shaffner called her escape home, is not far from Drew Seminary where she taught, and it was for the girls, Shaffner's choral pupils, that Mrs. Beach wrote "Drowsy Dream Town." During the ensuing years Mrs. Beach would often visit Brookwillows with Ruth Shaffner to escape the city and enjoy the country. The next day they returned to New York to pick up David McK. Williams and brought him back with them to Brookwillows to spend the night. This seemed a very high point emotionally for Mrs. Beach, who played her Meynell Anthem for him.

> He likes it very much. R. sang all new songs and I played.

The following day Williams went golfing (he played 27 holes), and after he returned to New York, Mrs. Beach noted that she was "very tired, but a successful day in spite of depression" at Williams's departure.

On October 1 Shaffner and Beach visited the poet Anna Moody, whose Japanese house and garden were not far from Paterson. There Mrs. Beach played on the "first piano made in Japan." The next day the two musicians drove back into New York City, where Mrs. Beach took up residence once more at the American Women's Association Club House, this time in a corner room, no. 2157. The following day Gray Publishers requested her new anthem on Meynell's poem and also requested David McK. Williams's setting of the same text. That same day Ruth Shaffner went to Williams and told him that Mrs. Beach felt for him as her son. The following day, Sunday, she attended three services at St. Bartholomew's and noted Dr. Norwood's theme that "God is with us when we love, only we must love at its best—consecrate it—lift it up to Heaven." She found Williams's responses "lovely." On October 6, just before taking a late afternoon train to Boston, she had lunch with Williams where they talked about the Holy Land, "he played his anthem" for her, and he was "very churchly and evocative." For her it was "a holy day!"

Canticle of the Sun (1931-32)

After a day in Boston, Mrs. Beach went to Worcester for its annual music festival where her music would be played. She was met at the Bancroft Hotel by Marion Bauer, Mary Howe, Mabel Daniels, and Mrs. Campanoli (Shaffner's pupil) with her mother. Together they attended the opening concert of the Festival that night, 7 October 1931. The second night, after a performance of Gabriel Pierné's *The Children of Bethlehem* for soloists, children's chorus, orchestra, and narrator, Mrs. Beach's *Canticle of the Sun* was premiered in historic Mechanics Hall. As she recalled,

> Wonderful *Canticle* rendering. Volume of choral tone magnificent. Lerch's high notes like stars. Tremendous enthusiasm. Twice to platform & repeated rising from seat. Reception Worcester Club. Much congratulating from [John] Powell whose *Natchez on the Hill* received its premier [*sic*] at this Season's Festival, by Kramer, Stoessel and other musicians.

At 4:30 a.m. the next morning Mrs. Beach wrote to Ruth Shaffner:

> So many thanks for your dear wire, but oh! I was really heart-broken that you & David [McK. Williams] could not have witnessed the thrill of last evening: I can never forget the enthusiasm of that big audience, as well as chorus, orchestra, soloists—everybody! It was one of those *wild* moments that sometimes come to us all, but not often!—I have sent a description to David of the Choral work, as well as the hour could permit! Not being able to sleep, after the first nap of exhaustion, I thought I would write to you both while my impression was vivid. For you are both so intimately associated with this work that it seemed strange indeed to hear it done in another atmosphere than *our* adored church. The chorus is really superb in volume, quality, pitch and accuracy. The climaxes overwhelmed me. They knew every note and evidently loved it. The orchestration proved just what I had hoped it would be. The soloists were fine—*for the concert room*—and everybody was keyed up to the last pitch in their desire to "do me proud." All this was to the good! Now for a few words in strict confidence on account of all this devotion to me and my work. As I wrote David, the point where I longed unspeakably for you both was in some of the tempi—notably in the soprano solo and following quartet section. Dr. Stoessel has a big feeling for the dramatic and could not feel the advantage of a more deliberate tempo for that part of the *Canticle*. It was feverish in its intensity where David gives the stateliness and solemnity of greatness. Miss Lerch's voice is lovely and her high notes carried over chorus and orchestra. She felt the work too, and yet there

was the same lack of *calm*—what I call in your singing of the part the *angelic* quality. In short, where she might have gained from copying you, I noticed not one moment where you might gain by copying her! Doubtless her "rush" in spots was largely induced by the conductor's tempo which she had to follow, and of course, excitement all around accounted for a great deal in every way. I have had the real joy of close association with Mrs. Campanoli and her mother, which has helped immensely in my real loneliness without you. We have seats together and have seen each other often at the hotel. They are both *dears*! I have had a devoted bunch of my "women composer" friends here and all the officials and musicians connected with the performance have tried their best to spoil me!

A critic in a Worcester newspaper the next day could only praise the work.

Of course no woman's name stands out more prominently in the world of American music than that of Mrs. Beach and in the world there is perhaps only one other better known, that of Cecile Chaminade, the very popular French composer. . . . [Mrs. Beach] gives to this magnificent Canticle a setting of no particular period but one of true appropriateness, a setting of dignity and beauty which also displays great technical skill. Nevertheless the outstanding feature of the work, the thing which made itself manifest almost in the opening measure for chorus was the pre-eminently vocal character of the Canticle. For the chorus the work brought out a splendid sonority and richness of tone which surpassed anything previously heard in the festival. The composer was equally kind to the soloists as well and each of the good voices in the quartet, Louise Lerch, soprano, Rose Bampton, contralto, Dan Gridley, tenor, and Frederic Baer, baritone, was heard to fine advantage. Perhaps the most effective part fell to the soprano in the telling obligato solo with the chorus. The tenor too had more of an opportunity to show the full beauty of his voice than the more vigorous and complex Hungarian Psalm afforded him on Wednesday evening.

Mrs. Beach was in the audience and she must have been highly gratified at the spontaneous acclaim accorded to her and her *Canticle of the Sun*.[174]

Another critic, who lavished praise on Mrs. Beach, made a special point that "she has unflinchingly withstood the onslaught of polytonal and atonal modernism, idioms unsympathetic to her musical nature and her personal aim, and gone on her own way."[175]

---

[174] Mrs. Elizabeth C. Regal, in the *Worcester Evening Gazette*, Friday, 9 October 1931.

[175] A. Walter Kramer, in the *Worcester Evening Post*, Friday, 9 October 1931. Another review is by William Place, Jr.

Two days after the performance of the *Canticle*, Mrs. Beach took a train from Worcester to Peterborough, where Jessie Parker met her and drove her to Hillsboro for a two-week stay. Once again there was a Beach Club meeting, followed a few days later by a meeting of the Juvenile Beach Club. As usual, the composer played for both clubs, and this time she told them of her recent experience at the Worcester Festival. Part of one day was spent at the Hillsboro Community House hanging pictures of Auntie Franc and cousin Ethel in the D.A.R. rooms. Mrs. Beach also gave the chapter a blue cloissonné vase in memory of the two women. The Women's Club of Henniker also gave a "Beach Day" program on October 20. The composer was assisted by a trio of women and by Julia Jones, who sang several songs. The next day, before taking a late afternoon train to Concord, Mrs. Beach played for the Hillsboro Benevolent Society, where the "audience was most enthusiastic and their farewell really touching."

Mrs. Beach was in Boston for the premiere performance of the piano concerto by a fellow-colonist, Harold Morris, a piano teacher at the Juilliard School. Mrs. Beach found it "interesting—brilliant orchestration, but solo instrument overpowered." The soloist was the composer, who observed that he felt that Koussevitzky gave a very studied and careful presentation of the score. Before leaving for New York, Mrs. Beach worked with the Boston baritone David Blair McClosky in anticipation of a concert with him the following February. Mrs. Beach considered him a "superb interpreter," and as a result she felt confident in the success of their upcoming performance.

When Mrs. Beach reached the American Women's Association Club House, she was assigned room no. 2403, facing the Hudson River. On her balcony overlooking river activities, she corrected proofs of the Meynell Anthem for Gray and returned them to the publisher on November 2. The second proof arrived on November 13, so that much of this month was consumed by correcting them and proofs of other recent works. The *Canticle of the Sun* was "beautifully performed" at the Brooklyn Church of Our Savior under Mr. Watkins's direction. Mrs. Beach attended the usual services at St. Bartholomew's and many concerts and operas, including a performance of Alban Berg's *Wozzeck* by the Philadelphia Opera Company under Stokowski at the Metropolitan Opera House. She found it "strange beyond words, strong and deeply interesting."

On December 1 Mrs. Beach was in Washington for a recital for the League of American Pen Women. Elena de Sayn performed the composer's Violin Sonata, and the impression it made on Hans Kindler, conductor of the National Symphony Orchestra, who was in the audience, was so great that he immediately made plans to perform the *Gaelic Symphony* the following season.

Back in New York a few days later, Ruth Shaffner gave a recital at the Canadian Club, where she premiered Mrs. Beach's "Dark Garden." This song, along with the two Browning songs, met with "great success." That same day the composer's canticle *Deus misereatur* was sung at St. Bartholomew's on a program that also included Brahms's *Requiem*, and the following Sunday Mrs. Beach's *Benedictus* was sung at the same church. On December 16 the Musician's Club presented an all-Beach concert, which featured the Kneisel Quartet with Mrs. Beach in the Piano Quintet, Ruth Shaffner in several new songs, and the composer playing her own piano works. The year 1931 closed with Mrs. Beach in Detroit for the Music Teachers National Association convention, where she gave a recital

Beach Club of Hillsboro, N.H., with the composer, late 1930s

and a lecture, both of which were received with "tremendous applause." She and Mrs. Crosby Adams returned together to New York on New Year's Day.

At the beginning of 1932 the Meynell Anthem was published, and when Mrs. Beach played the piece for Mrs. Adams and Gena Branscomb at the American Women's Association Club House, they were "deeply thrilled." Mrs. Beach then turned to a revision of the *Jubilate* from the 1906 *Service in A*; she played it for David McK. Williams on January 15, and by spring it was out in a new edition. The day before, the 14th, Mrs. Beach's Flute Variations was performed at the studio of a private music teacher on West 40th Street. The morning of the performance a rehearsal was held at the Club House, but she found the piece not going well—the "viola [was] hopeless." Later she wrote:

> Program went fairly well except mine. Big crowd. Variations dreadful
> but better than rehearsals. People kind but pitying.[176]

Fortunately, ten days later Victor Harris and the St. Cecilia Club performed *The Chambered Nautilus*, which "went superbly," with "great enthusiasm." On January 30 the work was performed again in Boston by George Dunham and the Boston St. Cecilia Club, which repeated it on the night of February 7 at the Boston Public Library. While in Boston Mrs. Beach went back to the Faelton School, playing her Piano Quintet in Huntington Hall. The following day, at the House in the Pines School in Norton, Massachusetts, Mrs. Beach and McCloskey gave a concert for the students, who recalled the composer for five encores. They especially liked "Chipmunk." During the next days she and McCloskey gave a 15-minute broadcast over radio station WAAB, she played at a Mu Phi sorority concert at Mrs. Ollendorf's, she talked about the MacDowell Colony at the monthly meeting of the Boston Piano Teachers' Club, and she played a short recital for the Brookline Society of Allied Arts. Before departing from Boston, she and Mabel Daniels had a long discussion concerning the fate of the Society of American Women Composers and its Washington sessions.

Back in New York City on February 14, Mrs. Beach "was given a superb welcome by the New York Federation of Music Clubs," where she played several piano works. Early in March she played at a musicale at Hiers's studio in Steinway Hall. On the 6th there was another performance of the *Canticle of the Sun* and of *Cantate Domino* at St. Bartholomew's—"the best performance ever." She also performed at a Community House recital of Ruth Shaffner before a very large audience. In the meantime de Sayn had come to New York from Washington on March 6 in order to hear the *Canticle of the Sun* and to rehearse with Mrs. Beach for a radio broadcast, which took place on March 15 on station WABC, and for a recording session of the composer's violin music. The recordings were made at Sterne's. On March 20 Mrs. Beach played her Piano Quintet over radio station WJZ with the Pro Arte Quartet.

Also at the beginning of March, the Boston Symphony Orchestra played Aaron Copland's *Symphonic Ode* in New York. The work was written for the 50th anniversary of the Boston ensemble. Mrs. Beach called the work "hideous," and from this point on

---

[176] Diary.

she had no kind words for America's other great composer. On the 20th of the month she went to a tea in honor of the composer Respighi and there met Giovanni Martinelli, who asked her to dedicate a song to him. On the 29th she deposited songs at his hotel without indicating that she had either written or dedicated any of them to him.

April 1932 proved to be an extraordinarily busy month. At the beginning of the month Mrs. Beach had another radio concert with Ruth Shaffner.[177] On the 7th she gave a recital for the Scarsdale Brahms Club, and the next day she was a guest of honor at the dedicatory dinner of the Doctor's Club on 58th Street. At Gena Bramscombe's choral concert of the National Opera Association, Mrs. Beach's arrangement of her own "The Year's at the Spring" was so well received that it had to be repeated. Her "Christ in the Universe" was premiered at St. Bartholomew's on April 17 as part of the Easter afternoon service;[178] she considered this "My wonderful Sunday" since the performance was "glorious beyond words" and "D. [McK. Williams] was *radiant*."

At the end of the month *Canticle of the Sun* was presented at Mt. Vernon Methodist Episcopal Church in Washington, D.C. Mrs. Beach attended this performance since she was in the capital as a New Hampshire delegate to a convention of the League of American Pen Women. She also heard her *Benedictus es Domine, Benedictus*, and "O Praise the Lord, All Ye Nations" (written in 1891 for the consecration of Phillips Brooks as Bishop of the Diocese of Massachusetts) on April 24 at the Church of the Epiphany in Washington. The next day Mrs. Beach joined the Ferrara Quartet in a "ragged" reading of her Piano Quintet at a chamber music concert at Mrs. Patterson's in Dupont Circle, and on April 26 she performed in a short luncheon program at the White House at which Mrs. Herbert Hoover presided. That night she played three piano pieces and accompanied Ruth Shaffner in three songs in the course of a large dinner at the Arts Club. The following day she was busy at the convention; she nominated Phyllis Fergus Hoyt of Chicago to be the new president of the League, but her candidate lost by a narrow margin to Mrs. Clara Heflebower.

At the conclusion of the convention, Mrs. Beach and Shaffner vacationed briefly in Virginia and then returned to New York by May 3 in order to be present at a concert at Juilliard Hall where Ulric Cole's String Quartet and two string divertimentos were successfully played. Four days later the Rubinstein Club honored Mrs. Beach at a large "white" breakfast at which the guest of honor stood in line to greet thousands of members.

On May 8 the choir of the Riverside Church performed *Canticle of the Sun, Benedictus es*, and the old response "With Prayer" conducted by Harold Vincent Milligan. The music was so well received that Milligan repeated it in the fall.[179] On May 11 Mrs. Beach attended a Philanthropic Educational Organization (P.E.O.) banquet as the guest of Ruth Shaffner, and eventually she joined this fraternity of philanthropically-minded people. The next day the two women drove in Shaffner's car to Bethlehem, Pennsylvania, for three days of the annual Bach Festival, where Shaffner was one of the soloists.

---

[177] On station WOR, Newark.

[178] "Christ in the Universe" was repeated at St. Bartholomew's on May 18 while Mrs. Beach was in Hillsboro. Her *Cantate Domino* was sung at St. Bartholomew's earlier in April.

[179] Letter from Milligan to Mrs. Beach, dated 3 November 1932.

On May 15 Mrs. Beach went to Boston for a few days en route to Hillsboro, where she arrived in time to hear several of her works performed by the Hillsboro Music Club on May 18. The New England Federated Music Clubs met in Hillsboro on the 19th. Mrs. Beach was on hand to welcome guests at the morning session, and, to conclude a varied program in the afternoon, she performed eight of her own pieces. A week later, on the 26th, the annual meeting of the New Hampshire branch of the League of American Pen Women met at Hillsboro, and Mrs. Beach gave a program and reported on her Washington meetings. Two days later the Hillsboro Beach Club sponsored Mrs. Beach and Julia Jones in Municipal Hall.

Cabildo (1932)

Mrs. Beach's eagerness to return to the MacDowell Colony caused her to be the first colonist to arrive there on 31 May 1932.[180] Soon her friends—Mary Howe, Esther Bates, Nancy Turner, Edith Orr, Frances Frost, Mr. Guglielmo, and Carty Ranck—checked in. They were joined shortly thereafter by Edward Arlington Robinson and Thorton Wilder. By the middle of the month the Hiers arrived, and later more friends, including Marion Bauer and Ethel Peyser, then at work on the book *Music through the Ages*. Mrs. Beach composed two Norwood songs, and "Fire and Flame" on a poem by Anna Moody. On June 21 Ruth Shaffner brought Moody to the Colony for one night, both as guests of Mrs. Beach, and the day after they departed Mrs. Beach wrote another song to Moody's verses, this one entitled "To One I Love."

Most of June was devoted to studying an opera libretto by Nan Bagby Stevens entitled *Cabildo*, the musical setting of which would be her main work for the summer. The librettist, also a colonist of other seasons, arrived later in the month, on the 25th, after Mrs. MacDowell gave Mrs. Beach permission to invite her, and stayed until the 29th. Mrs. Beach was anxious to get Stevens's reaction to the libretto and the music that had been written so far. Stevens was delighted with both and was happy at the treatment her opera libretto was getting. Hopes were high for an early completion of the opera, though ultimately Mrs. Beach would never see the work performed.

Mrs. Beach herself left the Colony on June 30 and spent her usual Fourth of July with the Joneses in Henniker. As per usual she left for Centerville the next day after the holiday. She spent most of her working time at Centerville copying the score of *Cabildo* and the songs written that June. Otherwise it was a welcome respite from the

[180] While driving Mrs. Beach to the Colony, Mrs. Jones took Mrs. Beach, who obviously liked farm life very much, to the stock farm of ex-governor Bass in Peterborough in search "for a husband" for one of the Jones's heffers.

hectic activities of the preceding year.[181] It was a warm, clear summer, and Mrs. Beach enjoyed swimming in the splashing surf and "being buoyed up by the salty water."

The house in Centerville had a constant flow of guests, friends of the composer and of her cousins and the Buxbaums, all of whom made up the regular family when she was at the Cape. In order to be able to work, therefore, Mrs. Beach had a studio away from the house, which was uninviting to the guests. It was on the back side of the knoll, some distance down the far slope from the house. It was a small building (approximately 9 feet by 12 feet), with an open porch about the same size as the enclosure. The building faced a little pond of fresh water and projected only slightly from the thick woodland covering much of the countryside thereabouts. After tramps had broken into the studio several times, Mrs. Beach had it moved further back into the woods for greater camouflage. When noise from her neighbors threatened her solitude, she purchased the adjoining six-acre lot "to add to my domain."[182] There were no conveniences at the studio, except for a few comfortable chairs, a couch, and a plain table which served as a writing desk. Mrs. Beach usually spent a part of every day there.

By mid-September Mrs. Beach had closed up her Centerville house, deposited the cousins in Newton Highlands, and, after a night in Boston, repeated her adventure of the preceding year by visiting her New Jersey cousins Margrette and Lillian Wheeler on MacMahon Island, Maine. She returned to New York on the 24th and, after a few days with Ruth Shaffner in Brookwillows and a day in the city arranging for a new room at the American Women's Association Club House and for a piano, the two women set out for New Hampshire where news reached them of the death of their pastor, the Rev. Dr. Norwood. They were both stunned and grief-stricken, for it was he whose inspiring words added great spiritual strength to both women and abetted their musical careers.

The usual activities in New Hampshire filled much of the fall days in Hillsboro, but mainly she enjoyed being in her home state when the fall foliage was at its height. On October 9 Mrs. Beach played for the choir and congregation of the Methodist Church in Hillsboro and for their many out-of-town guests. Beach Day was observed in Hillsboro on October 10 and at Henniker on the 15th. At each of the Beach Club programs the composer heard several of her piano pieces played by aspiring piano pupils of aspiring piano teachers. The New Hampshire Federation of Women's Clubs's annual banquet was held on October 18 in Whitefield, and the following night Mrs. Beach gave a recital and talk on the MacDowell Colony to an audience of six hundred.

A few days later Mrs. Beach was back in Boston en route to New York. She witnessed a performance of her *Benedictus es Domine* at the Church of Our Savior in Brookline on October 30, which she described:

> I attended a service this a.m. in Brookline—a *beautiful* small church, and
> fine sermon and an unusually good choir. By accident they gave my
> *Benedictus es, Domine* (very well) and when I met the young organist
> afterward he nearly fainted!

---

[181] She was still feuding with the Barnstable County Commissioners over the new state highway and wrote to them to remind them of a debt of $50 still unpaid for the corner of her property taken for grading the new road.

[182] She did this in the summer of 1935.

During the few days she was in Boston she visited her cousins and played for Lillian Buxbaum's Club; Mrs. Buxbaum sang six of the composer's songs.

One of the first duties Mrs. Beach performed upon returning to New York was to mail her absentee ballot for Herbert Hoover to the town clerk of Hillsboro. Throughout the years she maintained her official citizenship in Hillsboro and was punctilious about her civic duties. She was also punctilious about voting straight Republican.

Her first musical performance of the fall was with the Kneisel Quartet on November 14 in a concert in Newark. She played four solo encores after the group did her Piano Quintet. On November 23 she and Ruth Shaffner gave a recital over NBC (WEAF) in a series sponsored by the American Women's Association. Her canticle *Deus misereatur* was sung at the four o'clock service at St. Bartholomew's on the 27th, and afterwards that day she attended a reception at the MacDowell Club for Ralph Vaughan Williams, whose lecture at the Juilliard School she had heard a few days earlier. A week later she again attended a performance of one of her pieces (the *Magnificat*) at St. Bartholomew's and then went again to the MacDowell Club where the guest this time was Ernest Schelling, who asked about having some of Mrs. Beach's music, which she delivered at his Park Avenue home the next day. The month of November ended with a memorial service to the Rev. Dr. Robert W. Norwood at the Roerich Museum, at which Mrs. Beach's Norwood songs were sung by tenor Louis Alvarez.

Because she was a celebrity, Mrs. Beach had to take care lest thoughtless strangers take advantage of her, but sometimes they were able to reach her. Two such individuals got to her in early December. For some time a woman of name had asked Mrs. Beach's permission to come and play for the composer, and in a moment of weakness she succumbed to an appointment on the afternoon of December 1, about which she wrote in her diary:

> Seemed anarchistic and half crazy. Played *Fireflies* poorly—very conceited and altogether gone by.

On the 7th,

> A colored man came from DuBose Heyward [author of *Porgy and Bess*].
> Told story of lost money and license. Wanted to go south at once.
> Gave him two dollars.

To her friends, however, Mrs. Beach was always available and with them she frequently went on outings or to special events. For example, one evening in December 1932, Nan Stevens, the Grant Reynards, and Ruth Shaffner dined with her at the Club House, and they all went together to the annual MacDowell banquet of Allied Members, attended by many colonists. She was frequently at her church, not only to hear her music but to be with her friends. On Christmas afternoon Mrs. Beach and Mabel Daniels sat side by side in St. Bartholomew's to hear each other's carol—two childless Bostonian women composers, each adding her offering to celebrate the birth of the Holy Child![183]

---

[183] On the same day Mrs. Beach's carol was also sung at Calvary Episcopal Church in New York under Vernon De Tar.

The Music Teachers National Association convention in 1932 was in Washington, where Mrs. Beach went the day after Christmas in order to read a paper at an afternoon session on the 27th. That night she left the Pan American concert early in order to reach a party before her friends left. She promised that she would play for them, and she had a new piece for the occasion. "Out of the Depths" seems to have made a strong impression, and several musicians present suggested that the piece might advantageously be transcribed for organ. On the 28th, after lunch at Mary Howe's, in the company of a few friends who played their new manuscript pieces for each other, they attended a Library of Congress concert of the Gordon String Quartet with Harold Bauer, pianist. Before leaving the library for the annual banquet of the convention, Mrs. Beach spent considerable time viewing the music manuscript holdings of the library. After several more sessions and a concert by the National Symphony Orchestra under Hans Kindler, Mrs. Beach returned to New York, where she spent a peaceful New Year's Eve reading *Increasing Christhood*.

Mrs. Beach's first social occasion for 1933 was, on January 11, a reception at the Kneisel's for President and Mrs. Moore of Skidmore College, followed by an organ recital by Palmer Christian on the new organ at the Church of St. Mary the Virgin. Otherwise, her days were filled with numerous rehearsals, broken only on the 14th when

> Mrs. Gibson came and read my palms. Told still more remarkable
> things. . . . Lovely predictions.

The next day Mrs. Beach accompanied Shaffner in another recital at the Canadian Club, which included her "The Year's at the Spring." On January 24 the St. Cecilia Society sang *Sea Fairies* in its Town Hall concert, for which Mrs. Beach played the piano part without score in a "superb" performance by Victor Harris. Several days later Harris asked to examine the score of *Peter Pan*, also for women's voices. On the 29th Mrs. Beach and Edwin Hughes performed her Suite for Two Pianos at the Matinee Musicale at the Hotel Astor. That night Nan Stevens was Mrs. Beach's guest at a dinner before a performance of *Canticle of the Sun* at Grace Church on lower Broadway. Ernest Mitchell conducted his boy's choir in a fine performance of the cantata. Two weeks later she and Shaffner gave a recital for the Monday Music Club of East Orange, New Jersey, an organization which had raised money for the MacDowell Colony.

While Mrs. Beach obviously spent a lot of time with music, her interests were wide and she entered into many activities with zeal. Nan Stevens, who was spending much of the winter in New York, took Mrs. Beach to several meetings of the Poetry Society. For some time the composer was also taking bridge lessons and was beginning to enjoy the game; some of her bridge friends persuaded her to join them at a benefit bridge tournament for the crippled children at St. Regis Hotel on January 30, and she won first prize.

Besides the New Jersey concert, Mrs. Beach and her music were heard at numerous events in February. On the 6th the MacDowell Club featured her works and those of Mabel Daniels; Percy Grainger spoke very nicely to Mrs. Beach about her pieces. On the 7th the Mendelssohn Glee Club sang an arrangement by Douglas Moore of "The Year's at the Spring." At the Roerich Museum, Mrs. Beach accompanied Mr. Linscott in several songs and played a group of her piano pieces, and on the 20th she returned there with Ruth Shaffner, who sang seven of Mrs. Beach's songs, including the Speyer songs (Leonora Speyer was also present and read from her own poetry). On February 26 Mr. Gilbert led the choir of the Fifth Avenue Presbyterian Church in her anthems "Thou Knowest, Lord" and "Lord of the Worlds," and a few days later on Ash Wednesday her *Deus misereatur* was sung at St. Bartholomew's.

One of the highlights of the winter for Mrs. Beach occurred on February 18, when she attended a Paderewski recital:

> Too wonderful for words. B flat Mazurka I had remembered for over
> 40 years as he played it! Six encores!

She was less impressed with his compositions. When she heard his symphony performed by the Musicians' Orchestra on April 10 she found it "dull and long." His piano playing on this spring program (Schumann concerto, Schubert Impromptu, and several Chopin pieces), on the other hand, moved her deeply. She was also impressed by a Walter Gieseking recital on February 19 in which he played six or seven encores.[184] On the 25th she enjoyed the debut of Richard Crooks in *Manon* at the Metropolitan Opera; Lucrezia Bori was also in the cast.

Meanwhile Mrs. Beach was concerned with a performance of her new chamber opera *Cabildo*. David McK. Williams and her friend Anna Morgan, who was president of the American Women's Association and a staunch member of St. Bartholomew's, had originally agreed to perform it at the church, but the arrival of a new rector on February 19 changed their plans. Morgan admired both the music and the libretto and was anxious to have the work premiered at a site so important for Mrs. Beach, but Williams was too distraught at the orders for music from the new rector to continue.[185] Mrs. Beach took up the score with Albert Stoessel on 7 May 1934, and she thought his reactions were "very nice."

The month of March continued with concerts and social engagements. On the 8th she attended an all-Beach concert at the home of a Mrs. Bristol in Westfield, New Jersey, and on the following Sunday she heard a large choir under Miss Adam sing the *Jubilate Deo* and the anthem "Lord of the Worlds" at the Church of the Ascension.[186] On the 15th she performed before an enthusiastic audience in Summit, New Jersey, and four days later she witnessed another performance of *Canticle of the Sun* at St. Bartholomew's. On March 22 Ruth Kemper played Beach's Violin Sonata and Ruth Shaffner sang many of her songs at a gathering of musicians at Anna Morgan's home; Olin Downes stayed to the bitter end, a tribute in itself to the composer. A large audience gathered to hear a considerable amount of Beach music accompanying a lecture at the American Women's Association on the 27th. Finally, Mrs. Beach and Ruth Shaffner provided a program for the "big crowd" at another Association meeting on March 30.

---

[184] On 10 March 1934, she heard Gieseking again when she attended a lecture-recital by Olin Downes and Gieseking.

[185] Before leaving for the summer of 1933, Mrs. Beach deposited the score in the safe of the Arthur P. Schmidt Co., 8 West 40th Street.

[186] That evening, Mrs. Beach confessed in her diary, she indulged for the first time in a cigarette, which was not the sort of activity in which a lady of her social standing engaged in at that time.

The composer, meanwhile, frequented many concerts, including, besides the Paderewski concert on April 10, a concert on April 4 at the Beethoven Association in which Ossip Gabrilowitsch played the Chopin E-minor Concerto "beautifully" with the Philharmonic. She traveled to Washington for concerts at the Library of Congress, including the Busch String Quartet and the Busch-Serkin Duo. She heard Schoenberg's string sextet *Verklärte Nacht*, which she termed "lovely." Mrs. Calvin Coolidge was there, recognized Mrs. Beach, recalled their previous meeting at the White House during Coolidge's administration, and was "very cordial." While in the capital she heard the Boston Symphony Orchestra play music by Copland (*Ode for Orchestra*) and Stravinsky, which again, as in the past, she found "horrid." She mentioned music by Hindemith on the same program as "exciting."

Mrs. Beach herself played informal concerts throughout the month, beginning on April 4 for the Yonker's Chaminade Club and the following day for the New York Piano Teachers Association at Steinway Hall. On the 11th she played several pieces for a small, informal audience at a Mu Phi sorority dinner, and on the 20th she and David McK. Williams played her Suite for Two Pianos at St. Bartholomew's Community House. The next day she was off to Boston to hear her *Sea Fairies* performed at the Professional Women's Club and to perform herself seven solos.

While in Boston, Mrs. Beach had lunch at the College Club at 40 Commonwealth Avenue with her old friends Esther Bates and Nancy Byrd Turner, and for a moment she became very homesick, but by three o'clock that afternoon she was on her way back to New York. She was now an important part of the New York music scene and needed to be there to participate in it. Right after her return, for example, Henry Hadley's reorganized "new society for recognition of American composers and conductors" met at the Waldorf Hotel on April 11 and elected Mrs. Beach as Second Vice-President.

The Busy 1930s and the Beach Routine
(1933-36)

The extraordinarily busy life which Mrs. Beach lived during the 1930s would have been impossible for anyone without her unusual verve and energy level. As has been seen up to this point, there was hardly a day in which she was not before the public or her friends as performer or composer, or both, and her generosity inevitably led her to engage in philanthropic and charitable activities way beyond the call of duty. She was ever available not only to her friends and colleagues but also to music students, aspiring composers and performers, struggling women's and music organizations, her church (St. Bartholomew's), and the MacDowell Colony. Still, she found time to compose and to practice, and she was not afraid to indulge herself in some vacations and non-musical enjoyments such as bridge, swimming, and touring the beautiful countryside.

As a performer Mrs. Beach continued throughout the 1930s to give solo recitals for various clubs, societies, schools, and churches in New York, New Hampshire, Washington, D.C., and Boston, but major engagements with major orchestras and in major recital halls still eluded her.[187] Typically, on 20 May 1933 the New Hampshire Federation of Women's Clubs met with Mrs. Beach as speaker and pianist playing seven pieces, and on the next day she performed her music for an informal gathering of musicians. The following January 24 she appeared in a recital in the ballroom of the American Women's Association Club House before an enormous audience including many outside guests; the program "went splendidly." On 9 March 1934, Mrs. Beach played for a group of Oxford piano teachers, who were deeply moved by her skills.

Her friends and associates took advantage of her generosity and willingness to perform for them. One such case occurred on 17 May 1933, when the Hillsboro Music Club entertained Mrs. Ella Lord Gilbert, who spoke on her newly created organization, the New Hampshire Music and Allied Arts Society, which was to serve as a model for many W.P.A. music projects.[188] Mrs. Gilbert brought a Manchester singer and pianist, Alice Broadrick and Harlan Bradford, to entertain during the program, but when she spotted Mrs. Beach in the audience she called on the composer, who could not decline her invitation to perform. On 21 January 1935, when her friend Ruth Shaffner was suddenly indisposed, Mrs. Beach played an entire program at a moment's notice for the P.E.O. at the Bronxville Women's Club.

24 October 1933, the fiftieth anniversary of Mrs. Beach's debut as a pianist, was celebrated quietly by a drive through the first snow storm of the season with the Parkers and a concert at the Junior Beach Club, to which the composer added the coda. A year later, 2 October 1934, was another "Beach" Day in her home town Henniker where, like it or not, she felt compelled to play for her many friends, and the following day she played for the Benevolent Society of her church in Hillsboro. On 17 May 1934, Mrs. Beach participated in a program of the Allied Arts Salon of Boston and played five piano pieces. Upon hearing of the plight of an old acquaintance in the fall of 1934, she volunteered to play a recital, the proceeds of which would be given to her needy friend; and on 3 February 1935, Mrs. Beach went to Glen Ridge, New Jersey, for a program "for poor musicians."

On 10 April 1935, she went to the Oyster Bay high school for a recital. When she entered the auditorium, the entire audience arose, and the composer was presented a bouquet of roses before beginning her recital. The students had been encouraged to write essays about Mrs. Beach in a contest, and so were eager to see and hear her. At the end of the concert Mrs. Theodore Roosevelt held a reception for the composer at her home.

---

[187] It is uncertain what prompted Mrs. Beach to advertise herself; on 4 January 1934 she entertained Marion Bauer and her sister Flora Bernstein at lunch at the Club House and contracted with the former for a $50 professional advertisement to appear for a year in the *Chicago Musical Leader*. It is clear, however, that the ad brought her nothing in return.

[188] Mrs. Gilbert had recently formed the Society to stimulate greater musical activity among the state's musicians and to provide wider scope for the expression of the individual musician's talents. Mrs. Gilbert had long fought for musical causes in New Hampshire.

One of the few fully professional engagements by Mrs. Beach during the 1930s occurred during October 1934, when she was a guest of honor at the Chicago World's Fair. On October 11 she gave a piano recital of her own music and that by MacDowell. She was the house guest of Phyllis Fergus Hoyt, and she found herself in a whirlwind of rehearsals, performances, and social engagements. Following her stay in Chicago, Mrs. Beach gave concerts in Ottawa, Illinois (October 19), and Jamestown, New York (October 26). She was back in Boston on 8 April 1935 to play for the Boston Piano Teachers Association.

Basically, Mrs. Beach continued to play only her own music and that of other Americans, but there were exceptions. When she was at the MacDowell Colony in June 1934, for example, she gave a classical program that paralleled her concerts when she was a concertizing child:

> I gave a program last night at twilight for the Colonists in the lovely
> Savidge Library. Everyone seemed to enjoy it, but it was a pull for me
> to concentrate on Bach, Beethoven, Brahms and Chopin after working
> so hard in the other direction.[189]

At a private recital for a chapter meeting of the P.E.O. on 31 March 1936, Mrs. Beach included Bach and Beethoven on the program.

More frequently than solo recitals, however, Mrs. Beach performed with others, especially Ruth Shaffner and Ruth Kemper. For example, on 3 December 1933, Mrs. Beach and Ruth Kemper performed the Violin Sonata at the MacDowell Club in New York. Two days later, to celebrate the repeal of the Eighteenth Amendment, Mrs. Beach and Ruth Shaffner performed her pieces for a group of friends, interspersed with "wonderful talk." A month later she and Kemper performed the Violin Sonata at the National Musical Benefit Society. Mrs. Beach remarked that Kemper's playing was "superb—best yet." Likewise she was pleased that the audience was so cordial and showed great enthusiasm for the work. A few weeks later, on 28 January 1934, Mrs. Beach with Ruth Shaffner and Ruth Kemper gave the program for the Madrigal Society in New York, and in early February she and Kemper did her Violin Sonata at a musicale at the home of Otis Carroll in Brooklyn. In the evening of 18 February 1934, Mrs. Beach and Ruth Kemper played her Violin Sonata at the Rodin Studio; the composer also talked on the MacDowell Colony. On the following day she went to Hastings-on-Hudson by train for a concert there with Shaffner and John Rasely of the Metropolitan Opera Company and a soloist at St. Bartholomew's. Included in the long list of piano pieces performed was "Out of the Depths," which Mrs. Beach played in memory of King Albert of the Belgians, who was killed the previous day while mountain climbing. On 12 December 1935, she and Shaffner performed for a meeting of the Montclair, New Jersey, chapter of the D.A.R.

The most noteworthy concerts that Mrs. Beach performed with one of her two friends occurred on 23 April 1934 and 17 April 1936. On both occasions Mrs. Beach went to

---

[189] Letter from Mrs. Beach to Ruth Shaffner, September 1934.

Washington and gave a recital with Shaffner at the White House. "Mrs. Roosevelt was wonderfully sweet, and a big crowd attended," according to Mrs. Beach after the 1934 recital.

While Shaffner and Kemper were her favorite associates, Mrs. Beach performed with many others as well. On 27 May 1933, for instance, there was a program of the Beach Club of Hillsboro, in which Julia Jones and Mrs. Beach performed her music. Although she must have wearied of these occasions, she realized that they had a positive impact on the community.[190] On 11 October 1933, at the opening concert of a convention of the League of American Pen Women in College Chapel of Middlebury College, Mrs. Beach and the singer Prudence Fish performed, and they were recalled for five encores. The following evening at a dinner she played ten pieces for enthusiastic Pen women and their friends. The next March 7 she performed an all-Beach program with John Rasely and Katherine Gunn at the Community House of St. Bartholomew's. Mrs. Beach also performed with other singers and violinists when she was in Chicago for the 1934 World's Fair. At an all-Beach concert at St. Bartholomew's Community House on 4 April 1935, she and David McK. Williams did the *Balkan Variations* in its two-piano arrangement, and Ruth Shaffner sang Beach songs. Mrs. Beach also played many piano pieces and assisted in a performance of the Violin Sonata. A "big crowd and much enthusiasm, many encores, flower baskets" greeted her recital with the singer Grace Leslie on 25 April 1935 at Syracuse University. Mrs. Cass sang with Mrs. Beach at a concert in Peterborough, New Hampshire, on 31 May 1935 for a convention of that state's Federation of Music Clubs.

Mrs. Beach also found numerous occasions on which to perform her Piano Quintet with various performing groups. On 9 January 1934, her Piano Quintet was played at the Brooklyn Museum before an audience overflowing the recital hall; she joined a pick-up quartet which had shown great devotion to mastering the work. In mid-March she was at St. John's School where her Flute Variations were played and where she played the piano part in her Piano Quintet. The following year she repeated the Flute Variations and Quintet at her charity concert in Glen Ridge, New Jersey. On 15 April 1936, she performed the Quintet with "four Chicago girls" at another convention of the League of Pen Women in Washington, D.C.

Besides her own performances, Mrs. Beach enjoyed others' interpretations of her compositions. For example, in the spring of 1933 there were several different locales where she heard her music performed by others. On April 29 she attended with Mrs. MacDowell a recital at the studio of Ethel Hier at which her pupils played music by MacDowell and Beach. The two older women responded by playing for the pupils; Mrs. MacDowell played music by both her husband and Mrs. Beach.[191] On May 1, at an organ recital by Dr. William Carl for the American Guild of Organists at the First Presbyterian Church,

---

[190] As Mrs. Beach noted, "it will be decidedly a Beach party even if we are inland! . . . my smile will get a bit tired but it will stay on, as the people and the children *are* so dear. Their *intentions* are wonderful!"

[191] Mrs. Beach enjoyed not only her friendship with Mrs. MacDowell but also her talent. On several occasions she went to performances by Mrs. MacDowell, such as on 18 May 1933; a meeting of the New Hampshire Federated Music Clubs was held in Manchester, and Mrs. Beach along with two Henniker children attended the sessions at which Mrs. MacDowell spoke and played.

Ruth Shaffner sang "The Year's at the Spring" with organ accompaniment before a large audience. Several weeks later Mrs. Beach accompanied the Juvenile Beach Club of Hillsboro to Manchester for a broadcast from radio station WEAF, during which several of her compositions were performed by several children. At the conclusion she herself played several pieces.

In mid-December 1933 the New York Glee Club gave the New York premiere of her *Sea Fever* at a concert at the Club House. On 24 April 1934, the evening after the White House concert, her cantata *Sea Fairies* was "well" performed,[192] and at luncheon with the Pen women the next day more Beach music was played and sung. On the 26th in the afternoon more of her music was played, and that evening radio station WMAL broadcast *Sea Fairies*, which was conducted by a Miss Lincis. Perhaps the most unusual rendition of her music happened on April 24; the composer was at the Marine Band barracks in Washington before ten o'clock in the morning where, on a regular radio broadcast of the band, "The Year's at the Spring" was "well played" under Captain Branson's direction. Yet the largest performance of any of her works occurred on 1 April 1936, when a male chorus of 1800 voices sang the same piece at Madison Square Garden.

In Chicago the next October Mrs. Beach heard numerous songs and other works performed, mostly by Chicago musicians. Her *Gaelic Symphony* was played by the Chicago Women's Symphony Orchestra at the night concert on October 11, after which she was presented with an official Exposition Medal in token of her contributions to musical composition. The Symphony was broadcast the following 13 February 1935, from the Museum of National History in a performance by the New York Civic Orchestra under Eugene Plotnikoff.[193] On 27 January 1935, Ruth Shaffner, accompanied by strings, sang several of Mrs. Beach's songs, and the composer found her singing "superb." The ensuing May 8 the composer was elated when, at Gena Branscomb's Chorale concert, her "Drowsy Dream Town" had to be repeated because of the enthusiasm of the audience, and a few days later she was at Cornell University for performances of her music. On 28 October 1935, the Beatrice Oliver ensemble performed her Variations for Flute and Strings in New York.

Mrs. Beach returned to Boston for a special all-Beach concert on 24 October 1935. The Boston Manuscript Society, of which she had been an active member nearly half a century before, honored Mrs. Beach at the concert performed by students of the New England Conservatory of Music. Following this she was feted at a reception given by the board of the Handel and Haydn Society because of her long and intimate association with it:

> Her mother was a member of the Handel and Haydn chorus, and Mrs.
> Beach attributes her first awakening to music to this influence. She was
> really launched on her public career as a composer in 1892 when the

---

[192] On 13 May 1934, a "big Choral Alliance Festival" was held in Symphony Hall in Boston before a "small but enthusiastic audience." Among the works heard was a cut version of Mrs. Beach's *Sea Fairies*.

[193] The concert was repeated on February 17 at City College auditorium on Lexington Avenue at 23rd Street.

same society gave the first performance to her Mass in E flat, the most ambitious musical creation any woman had produced up to that time, one of which few composers contemporaneous with her were capable.[194]

Although she attended many of the concerts where others performed her music, there were occasions when she specifically turned down invitations to be present. For example, she was invited to meetings of the American Pen Women's League in San Diego in summer 1935, where her music would be performed, and declined since such a trip would not have sufficient meaning for her at this time of her life. The next month she would have attended a performance of her Symphony, led by her friend Albert Stoessel, at Chautauqua had she not feared the heat which she tried to escape by remaining at the Cape. Earlier, in 1933, she had turned down a generous offer to go to Chicago to hear her Symphony because "the entire thing would have taken nearly two weeks, in mid-Western heat, right out of my vacation" (letter from Mrs. Beach to Ruth Shaffner, 6 July 1933). She was apparently not entirely well, for she wrote Ruth Shaffner from the comfort of her Centerville home:

> We go nowhere except for necessities. Dr. Cobb is looking after me, as he did not quite like the way the old engine was pumping. He has already helped with digitalis and "vitamin B" tablets. So I have joined the "Quiz-kids," only I have not yet reached the "Alkaseltzer" stage! I feel so well and hate even to think of leaving this dear place, but I would not wish to stay all winter unless it became necessary for some reason not apparent now.

The composer was still remarkable for her customary energy and good health, and even a sprained ankle acquired one day while walking down the wood path to her studio was only "a nuisance." But before leaving her Cape house for the winter, she wrote one more time to Shaffner that she would have to refuse a theater date in New York "as I *must not* get too tired" and "My head will only hold about so much when I have to work."

The number of Mrs. Beach's works performed at her own church, St. Bartholomew's, surpasses that for anywhere else, thanks largely to her loyal friend David McK. Williams. In some cases she could not attend, but in most instances she was there. On 25 May 1933, for instance, in her absence the St. Bartholomew's choir sang her *Cantate Domino*,[195] and during the afternoon service the following November 12 in her presence they performed her *Magnificat*.[196] Three weeks later her *Deus misereatur* was performed at the afternoon

---

[194] *Boston Globe*, Friday, 25 October 1935. The article goes on to state that "yesterday she presented the Handel and Haydn Society with an autographed score of her Mass."

[195] This was a popular work at St. Bartholomew's. Williams repeated it at the Evensong Service on 18 February 1934, and it was heard again at the church on May 10 at a five-choir festival; Mrs. Beach termed the latter "wonderfully sung." It was sung again on 16 December 1934, 17 February, 31 March, and 25 November 1935, and 8 March 1936.

[196] The *Magnificat* was also performed at St. Bartholomew's on 18 November 1934 and 25 November 1935.

service, but she could not go because she had a concert that evening at the MacDowell Club;[197] three weeks after that, 24 December 1933, they sang her *Benedictus* at the morning service.[198] In March 1934 and 1935, she heard her *Deus misereatur*. Mrs. Beach was always very satisfied with the way Williams interpreted her pieces. She noted that the anthem "Thou Knowest, Lord" was gloriously sung on 18 March 1934, and when it was repeated on 29 March 1936, it was "too wonderful for words." A week later, on Palm Sunday, Williams premiered her new anthem "Let This Mind Be in You," and on April 22 that year he conducted *Canticle of the Sun*.[199] For the centennial celebration of St. Bartholomew's on Sunday, 13 January 1935, Williams performed three of her works: the anthem "Hearken unto Me," *Cantate Domino*, and *Canticle of the Sun*; she found the "chorus and soloists superb, and D[avid McK. Williams] beyond praise."

Mrs. Beach's religious works were greatly prized by other churches as well. For example, on Sunday, 30 April 1933, at a program of the Hymn Society Festival held at St. George's Episcopal Church, Mrs. Beach's anthem "Lord of the Worlds" was sung by a fine choir. On 11 February 1934, Mrs. Beach's anthem "Let This Mind Be in You" was sung at the Sunday morning service at Christ Church on Park Avenue, and Bishop Hughes's sermon on "music" was inspired by a suggestion of Mrs. Beach herself. She missed a performance of her Easter anthem at Christ Church on Easter Sunday night 1934, because of the strenuous activities of the day at her own church, but the following Sunday she heard her *Canticle of the Sun* sung again at the Riverside Church in a performance "a little better than the last."[200] Just prior to her Washington trip, on 15 April 1934, an all-Beach program was presented at the Passaic, New Jersey, Methodist Church. This was the second time that day that Shaffner sang the solo in Mrs. Beach's *Magnificat*, which had also been done at the afternoon service at St. Bartholomew's.[201] Her *Benedictus es Domine* was sung at St. James's in New York on 26 January 1936, in memory of King George of England, whose death occurred six days before.

While at the Chicago World's Fair in 1934, Mrs. Beach attended St. James' Episcopal Church, where Leo Sowerby was organist and choir director. He greeted Mrs. Beach most cordially after the service, for each composer had great respect for the other, different as their approaches to church music may have been. In December 1934 Sowerby performed her *Benedicite* and *Benedictus* at Chicago's St. James' Church, and on 1 March 1936 Sowerby performed her entire *Communion Service* for the first time in Chicago.

---

[197] She was able to attend a performance of *Deus misereatur* sung at St. Bartholomew's a year later, on 2 December 1934, in a program that also included Verdi's *Requiem*. She also heard it there in December 1935, and 15 March 1936.

[198] Williams led the *Benedictus* again on 9 December 1934.

[199] There was a special luncheon that day, attended by nearly a hundred present and past choir members in honor of the retirement of Pearl Jones as one of the choirmothers. Leo Sowerby was there from Chicago and sat with Mrs. Beach at the luncheon, at the concert, and at a supper party by Mrs. Anna (Horatio) Parker for Mrs. Beach and ten of her friends.

[200] The same piece was performed at the same church on 21 February 1936.

[201] In November 1933 the *Canticle of the Sun* was performed at the Old South Church in Boston, but Mrs. Beach did not know about it in advance and did not attend.

There were also a few occasions when she was not satisfied with the interpretation of her work, such as at the 21 November 1933 New York recital by Washington violinist Elena de Sayn, who used Beach's "Berceuse" as an encore. Mrs. Beach expressed considerable concern to de Sayn's accompanist, Miss Lakeman, for the violinist's health, since de Sayn "was tired and played poorly." On 8 May 1935, at Teacher's College in New York, a performance of *Canticle of the Sun* took place with a chorus that "sang well," with soloists that were "bad," and with an "orchestra [that was] dreadful."

A fundamental grievance of hers had to do with transpositions that she had not authorized. At the annual Beach Day in Henniker on 15 October 1935, William R. McAllaster "took the liberty of transposing [her *Stella viatoris*, op. 100] down from A-flat to G-flat" to accommodate the singer, Vera Oxner; after the concert, "Mrs. Beach blasted out" at McAllaster, "What did you do to my song?" Mrs. Beach had absolute pitch, and, as we have shown, since childhood she related certain specific colors to keys; if the song was not quite right for a singer's voice, she herself would transpose it to a proper key (with the proper color)—something McAllaster was unaware of. For anyone other than the composer to alter this was a sacrilege; the music would run the risk of not expressing the same idea that Mrs. Beach intended in the work. Therefore, in recognition of the differences in singers' tessituras, many of Mrs. Beach's songs were published in at least three keys in order that *one* of the keys would fit any voice without destroying the color of the song.

Increasingly Mrs. Beach took advantage of the new technology and performed on the radio. On 11 May 1933, she played over radio station WEEI on the "Silver Lining Hour" of the Boston Industrial Home. At the same time, radio made her aware of the performances of her music by others, sometimes without her knowledge. In July 1934, for example, Dr. Van de Wall "wrote me a nice letter about a broadcast June 10th of my Quintet" (letter from Dr. Van de Wall to Mrs. Beach, 30 June 1934), but she had no idea who performed it. On the other hand, when she could listen to others performing her works on the radio, it gave her pride. Such was the case when Lawrence Tibbett was soloist on the "Firestone Hour" on 7 February 1936, and included "Ah, Love but a Day" among his numbers. Two weeks later Herman Neuman played her Omaha Indian piece "From Blackbird Hills" over radio station WNYC in a piano recital of American music.

While the popularity of her compositions increased during the 1930s,[202] her rate of new works greatly diminished. Mr. Austin of Schmidt's frequently negotiated with her for the publication of her newest songs and piano pieces, which were in demand, and there were requests for new works from various sources. One of the most prestigious came in December 1934; while at Princeton, New Jersey, she met Dr. John Finley Williamson, founder and director of the Westminster Choir School, who expressed the hope that she would write a choral work especially for his group. Apparently most of the new works were conceived during the summer at the MacDowell Colony and in Centerville. In June 1935,

---

[202] If financial reward is any indication, Mrs. Beach's quarterly checks from ASCAP were beginning to become substantial. On 12 April 1935 the composer was elated at the "biggest check ever from ASCAP ($1453.43)." On 23 December 1940 the United States Government forbade ASCAP from interfering with radio broadcasts. Three days later, Mrs. Beach, who that day received her quarterly checks from ASCAP for $2169.13, wrote to the Attorney General in Washington to complain about the ruling.

while at the Colony, for example, she wrote an anthem for Vernon De Tar, "O Lord, God of Israel," op. 141,[203] and some songs. The previous summer she completed her new anthem "Hearken unto Me" at the Colony, which was nearly completed by the time she arrived. She also did a lot of arranging. Upon arrival at the Colony in 1933, for example, she orchestrated the Meynell anthem "Christ in the Universe" and on June 12 began the two-piano arrangement of her "Balkan Variations" and finished it on the 15th. In 1935 she wrote a new postlude to her *Benedictus* which was more appropriate for the vast edifice and huge organ of St. Bartholomew's than the original, which was suitable for most other churches.

Frequently Mrs. Beach was called upon to lecture or participate in discussions. At the end of December 1935, for example, she attended the annual meeting of the Music Teachers National Association in Philadelphia, where she delivered a paper on piano playing. She reflected upon the fact that pianists, for more than a century, had struggled to attain a "singing tone" from their instrument and now many composers were requiring the ten fingers to perform like mechanical hammers to produce the opposite effect: percussiveness. "I believe," she said, "that the piano is an instrument of nobility, dignity, grandeur, and charm when it is made to give of its best, rather than its worst, qualities." Since the Association comprised the most conservative music teachers in America, the audience loudly cheered Mrs. Beach's convictions and enjoyed three of her own works in which she demonstrated them.

Mrs. Beach's fame at this time brought her invitations to speak to various groups. On 15 October 1933 she went to Durham, New Hampshire, where she was a guest of the University of New Hampshire, the poet Agnes Ryan (wife of Henry Bailey Stevens of the University Extension Service), and the local MacDowell Club. On the 16th she spoke before two classes of the music department on the top floor of Nesmith Hall. The following 12 April 1934 Mrs. Beach went to a meeting of the National Opera Club, where she was called upon to speak extemporaneously.

As a composer and performer herself, Mrs. Beach took special interest in new compositions by others and the performances by the most gifted musicians of her time. She did not always approve of the avant garde and was particularly unhappy with the works of Copland, but she sought out the strengths of a new work and, in her terse jottings in her diary, left us with her opinions. On 10 February 1934 she attended the world premiere of Howard Hansons' opera *Merry Mount* at the Metropolitan Opera House with the cast of Lawrence Tibbett, Edward Johnson, Göta Ljundberg, and Gladys Swarthout, with Tullio Serafin conducting. She found the music "very rich and interesting, often beautiful." One month later, on March 10, she witnessed Virgil Thomson's opera *Four Saints in Three Acts*, based on Gertrude Stein's text, and termed the work "queer, with some beauty." A month later, the day after the Sunday after Easter, Mrs. Beach heard an early performance of Ernest Bloch's *Sacred Service* at a Schola Cantorum concert in Carnegie Hall, which she found "expressive and reverent, but too monotonous for concerts." When she attended a Stravinsky program and reception on 7 January 1935, she noted that "the latter [was] very pleasant," but had nothing to say about the music. William Walton's

---

[203] It was sung for the first time at St. Bartholomew's on 16 April 1936.

Belshazzar's Feast impressed Mrs. Beach as a "superb work," as produced by the Schola Cantorum under Hugh Ross on 9 Januray 1935. She found "incomprehensible" a performance of a suite from Alban Berg's opera *Lulu* by the Philadelphia Orchestra under Stokowski on 28 November 1935. On 24 April 1936, she went to a recital of Helen Traubel, who sang a group of "tedious" contemporary songs, of which, according to Mrs. Beach, Marion Bauer's song was the best.

Mrs. Beach took in many concerts of standard repertory works and was often thrilled, but she was not hesitant in criticizing performers or pieces she did not like. For example, on 20 November 1933, she attended a concert by the Manhattan String Quartet with Egon Petri, pianist, at the Beethoven Club and found the performance of the Brahms Piano Quintet—a work which she liked—"dull." But such criticisms were relatively rare. Much more common were her raves, such as for a concert on 12 February 1934 at the Beethoven Club. Mrs. Beach was enraptured by Lotte Lehmann's singing of lieder and by the playing of Myra Hess, Michel Piastro, and Felix Salmon in the Brahms Trio, op. 78. She called Toscanini's performance of Beethoven's *Missa solemnis* on 11 March 1934 "one of the greatest experiences of my life."[204] In mid-December of the same year she heard Bach's B-minor Mass in the Princeton University Chapel conducted by Stokowski; the soloists, "except for Rose Bampton, did not distinguish themselves." She also enjoyed an all-Bach organ recital by Carl Weinrich in the same chapel. A 11 January 1936, recital by Margorie Lawrence she found "superb."[205] Mrs. Beach continued to go to concerts and operas, but from November 1934, when she purchased a new radio, she spent more time in her own room at the American Women's Association Club House listening to broadcasts. Only in 1939 did she also buy a radio for her home in Centerville, though from that distance the radio signal had some interference.

Because of her fame and her openness, much of Mrs. Beach's time was consumed by persons wanting to be heard. Most of these persons tried over songs, but had "worn voices and stupid minds," although they were usually "very appreciative" of the composer's attention. Occasionally a teacher "brought . . . a pupil . . . to sing 'Ah, Love but a Day,' who had a 'superb voice' and was 'very young and *poor*.'" This Mrs. Beach thoroughly enjoyed since, with genuine sincerity, she could encourage a young musician.

Besides public musical affairs, Mrs. Beach remained active in several organizations only tangentially related to her career. Her interest in the Republican Party extended to the Women's Republican Club, where she often dined, attended receptions, and sometimes played concerts. She took an active role in the Pen Women's organization, frequently attending their conventions and performing for them. On 14 October 1933, while attending the Pen Women's convention in Vermont, she stayed at the home of Francis Bailey, Commissioner of Education for the state of Vermont, and she was able to discuss with her host the development of an extensive program of music education for the public schools of his state.

---

[204] She also attended Toscanini's farewell concert with the New York Philharmonic on 26 April 1936, when she remarked "Toscanini was almost blinded by flash-lights at close range" from camera flashes set off by the many photographers in the audience so that he did not come out for a bow at the end.

[205] Miss Lawrence confided to me that she has sung several of Mrs. Beach's songs over a period of years.

One of her principal interests at this time clearly was supporting Mrs. MacDowell's Colony. She lectured about it, went out to raise money for it, played at innumerable MacDowell Club concerts, and became active in its governance. For example, on 16 January 1934, Mrs. Beach substituted for Mrs. MacDowell in speaking on the Colony before the New Jersey Music Teachers Association in Newark; Mrs. MacDowell had become ill. Later that year, while attending the Chicago World's Fair, she spoke to an Illinois composers' group about the Colony, and on 20 November 1934, she gave a talk on the MacDowell Colony to the P.E.O., which would soon extend a membership invitation to her.

It was a typical situation when on 22 November 1934 she played for the Brahms Club of White Plains at a luncheon meeting, followed by a recital for children and high school pupils who demonstrated great enthusiasm for her illustrated talk. The next day her hostess presented Mrs. Beach with a check for her services; in a gesture often practiced, Mrs. Beach turned this check over to one of the several memorial funds for use by the MacDowell Association. On other occasions the money that was raised at a concert was advertised in advance as a donation to the Colony. For example, on 8 May 1934 Mrs. Beach, Shaffner, and Dr. Anderson went to Scarsdale by train for a concert at the Music Club for a benefit of the MacDowell Colony.

The concerts at various local MacDowell Clubs were not directly involved with the Colony, but indirectly they helped keep a line of communication open between the many active participants in those clubs and the special place in Peterborough. Among such concerts there was the one on 15 October 1933, in Durham, New Hampshire, connected with Mrs. Beach's appearance at the University of New Hampshire. That afternoon Mrs. Beach and Louise Souther, a composer and another guest of the Durham MacDowell Club, gave a program for the 150 children of the local public grammar school, and that evening she sat with President and Mrs. Edward Morgan Lewis of the University at the MacDowell Club concert, which was for an overflow audience and consisted of works by Mrs. Beach, Souther, and MacDowell.[206]

Although she was vitally concerned with the Colony for over a decade, it was only at the beginning of January 1934 that Mrs. Beach assumed an official position with it. She was elected, at that time, first vice-president of the MacDowell Association at its annual meeting. Mrs. MacDowell valued her judgement, and so it was only natural that on 29 April 1935 Mrs. MacDowell met with Mrs. Beach in New York City and the former "made me the 'admitting' committee" for the MacDowell Colony's 1935 roster of composers. Later, on June 8 that year, at Mrs. MacDowell's request, Mrs. Beach served as hostess to a group of especially invited guests from among the Colony directors. The weather was bad, but fortunately "Stoessel, Schelling & Erskine have been *very* interesting, & Douglas Moore is always a joy."

The MacDowell Colony afforded Mrs. Beach the chance to socialize with leading creative spirits from many arts, and the after-work hours there meant a great deal to her. In 1933, she remained only three weeks from May 31 to June 21, but she experienced during that time the special camaraderie that was unique to the Colony. One afternoon Mrs. Cleugh, a playwright, visited the Watson studio for Mrs. Beach to play a five-voice

---

[206] Reviewed as a "fine recital" in *Foster's Daily Democrat*, Dover, New Hampshire, 17 October 1933.

fugue for her that she wished to describe in a drama as a "ghostly" fugue. In appreciation, Mrs. Cleugh dedicated the script to the composer, which delighted Mrs. Beach who revelled in mystery and ghost books, plays, and stories. That evening, after dinner at Colony Hall, Edward Stringham, Alfred Kreymborg, Carl Carmer, and Edward Arlington Robinson played pool while the other colonists huddled around the great fireplace, warmed by the fire and thrilled by Esther Bates's tales. Bates was at work on a Christmas play at the time, and she revelled in relating an endless supply of medieval stories to the gathering. Marion Bauer arrived at the Colony the next day and brought with her sketches for a book on twentieth-century music (a novel idea in 1933) and a new version of solitaire for those, including Mrs. Beach, who enjoyed the game. The stay at the Colony in 1935 was highlighted by

> our latest arrival . . . Albert Spalding. He came Tuesday and left this a.m.
> He proved *delightful*. Yesterday a.m. he asked me most politely if I would
> like to play some sonatas with him last evening. Naturally I consented!
> We did two Beethoven's and part of a third, & I did the Andante from
> the Mendelssohn from memory as I have done it for Eugenie [Limberg].

I was among those present in the Savidge Library that night. Some of us musicians followed the scores as Mrs. Beach and Spalding performed, and it was with greatest admiration and respect for Mrs. Beach's musicianship that we listened to a most inspired, yet gramatically correct rendition of the movement from the Mendelssohn work. Spalding himself was utterly inspired by his co-musician that night.

Mrs. Beach had a large circle of close friends seemingly wherever she went. Two of her closest gentleman friends not only caused her great joy during these years but also some anxiety because of their health. In fall 1933, Mrs. Beach became concerned with David McK. Williams's health, and just before Christmas she visited a friend's astrologist who "gave me assurance that D. would live and gain . . . I am not very satisfied."[207] On 22 September 1934, Mrs. Beach gave Williams a copy of her new anthem, and after the composer's *Benedictus es Domine* was sung at St. Bartholomew's the next day, Mrs. Beach noted with distress that Williams seemed so tired and depressed, but she was overjoyed that he had dedicated *his* new anthem to her. She then left New York and went to Brookwillows with her usual concern over Williams. Later she wrote:

> You can see how David, after living in that super-human atmosphere
> long enough to write such music as he *has* written to those words, would
> look rather used-up and find it hard to take up every-day life again!
> We who use our imaginations as the very essence of our material work
> have to guard against carrying such use of our powers over into other
> regions! I have to shut my imagination up into a separate compartment
> and *lock the door*, otherwise I should be worrying about my dearest

---

[207] Mrs. Beach often consulted with astrologists, and other representatives of the occult. Besides the games of ouija mentioned above, she noted in her diary on 30 November 1933 that someone "told my fortune with cards," expressing "very good views, if nothing special."

ones all the time and seeing them in all sorts of dangers and troubles! What a continual *fight* life is anyhow!![208]

Mrs. Beach's relationship to Edward Arlington Robinson was probably just as necessary to her as her relationship to Williams, although she was with him less often. At the Colony she interacted with Robinson a great deal. On 23 June 1934, for instance, after lunch with Robinson in her studio, Mrs. Beach played "3 little *Improvisations*—first time to anyone. He liked them." Robinson's death on 6 April 1935, therefore, was a great blow to Mrs. Beach as well as to the creative arts as a whole. In January 1937, she wrote a paper about him.

Mrs. Beach enjoyed relaxing with a good game of bridge, and her partners were often persons prominent in the arts. On 20 February 1934, despite the heaviest snowfall of the winter, Mrs. Beach went to Mrs. Horatio Parker's house for bridge that evening; the widow of the distinguished composer was, with Mrs. Beach, a devout member of St. Batholomew's Church. But on the 26th the snow was so bad that she was confined to the Club House, where she played bridge with the composer Fannie Dillion and two other neighbors. At the Colony, when the weather was bad Mrs. Beach and the other Colonists entertained themselves not only with artistic matters but also with bridge and pool. Mrs. Beach was ecstatic when she made her debut in pool and won.

Besides games, Mrs. Beach enjoyed observing the world about her, whether countryside or street scenes. Her trips from and to New York, Boston, New Hampshire, Maine, and other areas of the country excited her interest in the beauties of nature which she saw from a car, train, or boat window, and whose impressions she recorded in her diary. On 9 March 1934, after lunching downtown, Mrs. Beach took an uptown, Riverside Drive bus as far as Grant's tomb before returning to her room. At the slightest provocation, she would indulge in such a ride, for she found the trip relaxing and enjoyable.

Throughout these years she continued to spend most of the month of June at the MacDowell Colony, the rest of the summer in Centerville, and the rest of the year in New York. In between would be frequent trips to Boston, Washington, and other familiar haunts. The composer often remarked that the hardest thing in going away was "coming home," where always she was greeted with stacks of mail and many messages, often requiring her to spend a great deal of time in getting "caught up" again. Not having a full-time secretary, the composer, who took great pride in writing personal replies to all her correspondence, dictated letters to a typist only when business matters required more formal replies. At a recent auction in settling the personal estate of Mrs. MacDowell, an acquaintance of mine purchased an old trunk which contained a stack of unopened mail. It turned out to be mail sent to Mrs. MacDowell pending her arrival one summer at the Colony and which somehow had been overlooked by all. My friend opened the letters in search of whatever hidden treasures they might reveal. Except for a single, small check which was returned to the directors of the MacDowell Association, "they were all just chatty letters from old friends of hers, some of them soft-soaping her a good deal." Undoubtedly these letters were similar to the ones which Mrs. Beach received endlessly, for among the letters eventually found in *her* belongings were many of the same soft-soapy nature.

---

[208] Letter from Mrs. Beach to Ruth Shaffner.

Part 4: Mrs. Beach the Philanthropist, 1936-44

England and Illness (1936)

On 8 May 1936, Mrs. Beach and Ruth Shaffner sailed aboard the *S.S. American Farmer* from New York to London for a tour of England. This trip was a present from Mrs. Beach to Shaffner, who was resigning as soloist from St. Bartholomew's Church after many years of service.[209] During her tenure there she had sung in many premiere performances of Beach's church music, as well as in countless recital performances featuring her friend's songs. To show her appreciation, Mrs. Beach decided to show Shaffner the beauties of England. She recorded in her diary the minutest details of their excitement at seeing the coast, the harbors, the sheep in pasture, and the sights of London. She was very impressed with a service at Westminster Abbey.

> May 21: Ascension Day. Service Westminster Abbey. First came part of early service for a boy's [sic] school (St. Peter's College) with a talk by the Dean. Then the full choral Communion Service. Sat close by choir. Long procession of choir and ecclesiastics around Abbey. . . . Choral service by Ireland sung. Most beautiful tone from boys['] voices, perfect pitch, also remarkable male altos and heavy basses. Piano used instead of organ, as latter was being made over for the Coronation.

She was equally impressed with a service at St. Paul's Cathedral on May 24:

> Good seat. Communion. Three long chants to begin, then Te Deum & Benedictus, also Introit (all standing!). Very good but academic. Went to sit in choir for Communion. Choir sang beautifully, especially Sanctus. . . . Temple Church [at] 3. Best boy choir singing I ever heard.

---

[209] Mrs. Beach was overjoyed when she learned in September 1937 that Miss Shaffner had received an appointment as voice teacher and choral director at Drew Seminary near New York City.

It is the otter side
of her profile —
I have, R-S,

Mrs. Beach, a photo owned by Ruth Shaffner, ca. 1935

Beauty of tone and perfect a ca[p]pella rendering of a fine Magnificat and Nunc Dimittis. . . . Met organist afterward. G. T. Thalben-Ball. Very pleasant.

There are many other churches they visited and by which they were impressed. The main secular musical event was a visit to Covent Garden on May 22:

Tristan. . . . Tremendous enthusiasm especially for Flagstad for whom they cheered like a football hero! Reiner conductor and also rec'd much applause. Sandwiches and tonic between acts. People even bro't them into their *boxes* and picnicked!! Royal box occupied by very distinguished looking people.

After an invigorating non-stop tour, the two ladies returned to Boston via the *S.S. American Merchant.* Mrs. Beach remained there while Shaffner continued to New York.

After spending the rest of the summer in Centerville, Mrs. Beach went to the MacDowell Colony on September 15, where she began at once composing and arranging earlier works. On the 19th the Peterborough Women's Club gathered at Colony Hall as Mrs. MacDowell's guest, and Mrs. Beach and Nancy Byrd Turner contributed the program for the large audience. The next day, Sunday, Mrs. Beach discovered "a large bunch in [her] left groin," which was not sore but was "beginning to be felt." Tuesday morning, after a "jolly breakfast" in the Colony Hall dining room, Mrs. Beach "called Dr. Cutler, as bunch had grown." Dr. Crisp, a surgeon in Nashua, New Hampshire, was brought to Peterborough, and early that afternoon he operated on Mrs. Beach at the local hospital. Nine days after surgery a "stitch abcess showed definitely" and it was not until October 13 that she was out of bed for the first time. Only on November 5 was she discharged from the hospital. Mrs. MacDowell loaned her car and chauffeur, Emil Tonieri, to Mrs. Beach, who then was driven to Worcester, Massachusetts, in company with Dr. Cutler and a nurse. There a drawing room car of a train was reserved for her, and together with the nurse she rode to Grand Central Station where, in a wheelchair, she made her way to a taxi and then to the American Women's Association Club House. She found her room laden with bouquets from many well-wishers, and more and more flowers and plants arrived during the next days. Almost daily, friends sent their chauffeured cars to take her for drives in Central Park or along the river.

The composer's bout with surgery did not result in a speedy recovery, perhaps largely owing to the heavy weight she had been cautioned about several months previously.[210] Her temporary poor health also contributed to her withdrawal from frequent attendance at St. Bartholomew's. Without Ruth Shaffner singing at the church, Mrs. Beach found

---

[210] Mrs. Beach had enjoyed excellent health until now, but she had visited physicians on occasion for special problems. Dr. Brackett in Boston ordered footbraces for her in 1933, though a year later she still had not received them. In November 1934, she mentions for the first time her New York physician Dr. Anthony Bassler, who ultimately served her to the end of her life.

less urgency to listen to her music there. On November 8 her *Magnificat* was sung at the afternoon service, but was "not well done"; but on December 6 she was on hand to hear her *Deus misereatur*, which "went beautifully." She felt depressed at the change in St. Bartholomew's. David McK. Williams came to her apartment on the 13th to listen to King Edward's abdication announcement on the radio,[211] and together they played over her arrangement of "Far awa'," which she had rewritten for organ that fall at the Colony and "which he liked." On December 13 Williams directed a performance of Brahms's *Requiem* and Beach's *Cantate Domino* over the radio from St. Bartholomew's, and while she praised the new soprano as having a "sweet and clear" voice, she also noted that it "flatted at the end." Two weeks later she liked Williams's performance of her carol, also broadcast from the church.

The Waning Years (1937-40)

Evidently it became obvious to Mrs. Beach's friends as well as to Mrs. Beach herself, that by the later 1930s there was a waning interest in her music and her playing by most professional musicians and by the public at large. She had been content for so many years to limit her playing before friends and charities that she was virtually unknown to the growing audiences of major concert series and of major symphony orchestras. Likewise, while her music continued to be performed, it was never a major orchestra that did so, and only occasionally did a major soloist include her works—and then often as an encore. "St. Bartholomew's was a boon and a blessing to her, as she was to it," according to her friend Esther Bates, for only there was she sure of a regular performance and full appreciation.

Nevertheless, during the last years of the pre-War years Mrs. Beach was still full of energy and led a very active life. She continued to perform, even if for unpretentious audiences. On 14 March 1937, she played on a radio broadcast for 30 minutes on station WQZR, which elicited phone calls from friends assuring her of the good reception of her program. When the League of Pen Women met in Worcester, Massachusetts, for two days during the middle of October 1937, Mrs. Beach, as was expected, played at programs each day of the sessions. A few days later Mrs. Beach "gave six numbers" at a meeting of the New Hampshire League of American Pen Women in Hillsboro Community House. She and Annie Bryant served as hostesses to the gathering of nearly 30 Pen women. Mrs. Beach received many gifts, including "lovely flowers from the Amy Beach Club of

---

[211] The next day she listened to "the last words of King Edward over the air, with Big Ben tolling. Too sad to believe!" and a few days later she "heard proclamation of King George 6th with trumpets from St. James' palace."

Providence, Rhode Island." Two days earlier, at Henniker, that town's Women's Club held its annual Beach Day, for which she played four pieces. The day before there was a program of the Hillsboro Benevolent Society. There was a

> talk on gardening by an Antrim man, mostly on manure! Heat terrific!
> My playing put after talk when I was exhausted.

Mu Phi Founder's Day was observed on 13 November 1937, and for the occasion Mrs. Beach "gave four pieces and played 'The Year's at the Spring' for a contralto." On November 17, as guest of honor at a luncheon of the New York Branch of the League of American Pen Women, she played for the group of about a hundred women. A year later, 19 October 1938, there was another meeting of the Benevolent Society in Hillsboro, and Mrs. Beach played for them; the next day was Beach Day in Henniker, for which the Manchester Trio played again and Mrs. Beach played seven pieces. She played several pieces on 7 January 1939 for the Osborne Club in Stamford, Connecticut, and four days later she played a long concert for the Harmony Guild meeting in Carnegie Hall Studio 705. A few days after that she played six piano pieces for a Founder's Day gathering of the P.E.O. On 12 March 1939, Mrs. Beach played her new *Five Improvisations* at a concert at the Henry Hadley Studios for the National Association of American Composers and Conductors. On April 16 she gave her last concert in New York of that spring for the Osborne Club, which met in Lillian Carpenter's studio-apartment.

For the next few weeks, while vacationing with Ruth Shaffner at Brookwillows, she gave several concerts in the vicinity, including ones at the Pawling School, Mt. Carmel High School, and for the Brahms Club, which met at Mrs. Austin's home. Additionally she played for school children. Only a case of severe bronchitis kept her from appearing before more local audiences. The following winter, on December 27, back in New York, she appeared as composer-pianist on a program of women composers at the Roerich Museum arranged by Frances McFarlane of the Federal Music Project (WPA). When the Osborne Club met on 28 January 1940, Mrs. Beach played there again before a "delightful" gathering; and when she played before forty persons attending the Mu Phi meeting on February 3 at the home of Barbara Parson in Yonkers, they took Mrs. Beach into the chapter.

Of course, there were many occasions when she performed with her friends. These were frequently at private concerts or parties, such as during July 1937, when Mrs. Beach accompanied Shaffner and Mrs. Buxbaum in many of her duets. Throughout the summer of 1938 scarcely a day passed without visitors calling at the composer's home in the woods of Centerville, and for nearly all her guests Mrs. Beach was easily persuaded to play, often with Mrs. Buxbaum singing her songs and sometimes with the guest as soloist (if the guest was a performer).

Almost as often Mrs. Beach and her friends performed for a public gathering. On 3 November 1937 she gave a concert in Concord assisted by Lillian Buxbaum; the "program went splendidly; half full [hall] and much enthusiasm." On 3 December 1937 she took a morning train to Providence where, at Mrs. Hail's Music Mansion, she "gave a long program" assisted by Mrs. Elsie Lovell Hankins, soprano, and a chorus under the direction of Mrs. Gertrude McGreevy. The next afternoon the Amy Beach Club of Providence presented the composer in a concert and reception.[212] On 22 February 1938, Mrs. Beach and Lillian Buxbaum participated in a concert by the piano teachers' guild of Boston, for which "I gave six numbers."

Although the number of concerts with Ruth Shaffner sharply declined, there were still a few. On 18 January 1939, during Marion Bauer's lectures on music at the Juilliard School, Shaffner, accompanied by the composer, illustrated several Beach songs that were being discussed; on February 15 Mrs. Beach performed her *Thrush Songs* and "Young Birches" for another Marion Bauer lecture. Mrs. Beach and Ruth Shaffner performed on 2 December 1939 for another P.E.O. meeting; on her December 27 concert at the Roerich Museum, Shaffner was soloist in five of Mrs. Beach's songs with Mrs. Beach accompanying; on 7 January 1940, at a private musicale, Mrs. Hudson sang Mrs. Beach's "Fire and Flame" twice, and "Ruth sang and I played two" pieces for the "small but lovely group."

During rehearsals for a concert on April 20 for the WPA Music Project, for which she accompanied Louise Taylor, she found that Taylor had a "hard voice but much power," that she "didn't know [the] songs and learns with difficulty," and that she was an "old time opera singer." Seemingly she grew worse with each practice, but after the concert Mrs. Beach conceded that "L. Taylor did well." Earlier, on 4 April 1939, Mrs. Beach recorded a "song recital" with several singers for broadcast the following day over WABC in a series of recitals of the vocal literature. She had listened to the broadcast recital by Harry T. Burleigh the previous week and wrote him of her enjoyment of it;[213] Burleigh had felt panic at speaking live over the air, had so told Mrs. Beach of his fear, and caused her to pre-record her conversation. The music on the program, however, was presented "live."

There seem to have been far fewer occasions when Mrs. Beach appeared in public with instrumentalists than had been the case before 1937. Her only major appearance with an ensemble occurred when her Piano Trio was first played publicly at a concert of the Brooklyn Neighborhood Club on 19 March 1940. She joined Carl Tollefsen, violin, and W. Durieux, cello, and she found that it all "went well."

On the other hand, others continued to perform her instrumental music. On 12 February 1937 she heard two movements of her Violin Sonata played by Eugenie Limberg at an American Women's Association concert. The Violin Sonata was heard again by the same violinist at the MacDowell Club on St. Valentine's night, and was repeated the following year. Early in March 1939 violinist Eugenie Limberg, accompanied by David McK. Williams, played Mrs. Beach's *La Captive* at St. Bartholomew's Community House, and at the end of the month her "Romance" was on a similar recital there.

On 16 March 1937 Mrs. Beach went to a rehearsal of her String Quartet and remarked that the "rehearsal went very badly." She suspected the performers were sight-reading and decided not to attend the concert. She was perhaps also embarrassed that Roy Harris and his wife were at the rehearsal and would get a false impression. Nonetheless, she was cheered by the "good report of [the] quartet performance." On 6 April 1937 she went

---

[212] In a memorial concert for Mrs. Beach on 24 March 1947 in Providence, Mrs. McGreevy conducted the Amy Beach Singers in many of the same works performed ten years earlier.

[213] Burleigh responded with a thank-you letter to Mrs. Beach dated New York, 2 April 1939.

with the sculptress Bashka Paeff to the Steinway Hall Studio of the Sutro sisters, who played Mrs. Beach's Suite for Two Pianos for a small gathering. The performance "went brilliantly." The night of 31 May 1938 she heard a radio broadcast from WHDH, Boston, of the last two movements of her two-piano suite by pianists Strong and Boardman. Despite poor reception, she commented that a "good biographical sketch" of her was included in the broadcast. The following October, the Manchester Trio (Claire Felch Morrison, violin, Mrs. Whitney, cello, and William McAlaster, piano) played a "fine program" during Beach Day in Henniker, and Vera Oxner had sung "Stella V[iatoris] beautifully on the program." Of Carlton Sprague Smith's playing of the Flute Variations in 1938 she said "beautiful," adding that there was "much enthusiasm" from the audience.

On 12 March 1940, Mrs. Beach was in Boston to hear her *Gaelic Symphony* performed by the Women's Symphony Orchestra under Alexander Thiede. After a large, progressive dinner party at Esther Bates's home for about 15 Colonists, they all went to Jordan Hall to hear the music.

> Mr. Thiede's Women's Orchestra gave my *symphony* (but cut). Great enthusiasm. Met many friends.

According to Mrs. Bates, however, "the critics were chilly and patronizing, and I do not think [Mrs. Beach] went back to N.Y. very happily."

As popular as these instrumental works were, it was her songs that were most often performed by others, though not always perfectly. Her "Ah, Love, but a Day" was dreadfully sung at the National Opera Club on 11 February 1937. On the other hand, on March 6 she heard Giovanni Martinelli sing the same song wonderfully on the "Ford Sunday Evening Hour" radio broadcast, and it elicited this letter from Percy Goetschius, the retired music theorist and long-time admirer of Mrs. Beach:

> We had the great pleasure last night of hearing Mr. Martinelli sing your "Ah, Love, but a Day" at the Ford Sunday Evening Hour, and I want you to know that I was deeply impressed with the beauty of your song. I do not know *all* of your many significant compositions (woe's the pity!), but I believe this song ranks with the best you have done; it is impassioned, and yet noble, and is so finely wrought. Mr. Martinelli interpreted it well, as far as I could judge. He is a fine singer, unquestionably.
>
> It was a rare pleasure to be brought thus again into contact with your musical spirit; it occurs far too rarely.
>
> We are both well, and as contented as advancing years, with the infirmities they inevitably bring, make it possible for us to be.
>
> I hope, most fervently, that you too are enjoying the best of health, and fostering your enthusiasm for all that is *really good* in music (and I *don't* mean Stravinsky and his ilk)![214]

---

[214] Letter from Percy Goetschius to Mrs. Beach, dated Manchester, New Hampshire, 7 March 1938. Mrs. Beach continued to keep in contact with Goetschius. When, in late August 1943, he celebrated his 90th birthday, she sent a letter for the "birthday broadcast celebration." He died three months later.

Another broadcast of "Ah, Love, but a Day" and "The Year's at the Spring" over radio station WABC by Margaret Downs and Mary Howe occurred at the beginning of 1939. They "gave a most appreciative sketch of my work." In mid-April she attended a recital by pupils of Ruth Shaffner in which four of her own songs were sung and "people [were] enthusiastic." From the husband of one of the singers the composer received a "lovely bouquet" as a touching tribute from a thoughtful admirer. On 22 May 1939 she heard "Ah, Love, but a Day" sung in broadcast by Margaret Speaks, and about the same time she heard Mrs. Buxbaum sing her "Hymn of Trust" with violin obbligato by "a young American violinist." The song "went well except [for] lack of expression due to short rehearsal."

Canticle of the Sun was performed at the Juilliard School of Music on 25 March 1938, and although Mrs. Beach had grave reservations during the rehearsal, she and David McK. Williams felt that at the concert it was a "good performance of the Cantata." In October 1939 there were two broadcasts of Beach music from New York over radio station WNYC. One was a WPA Music Project concert lasting 30 minutes; the other was an hour concert. A third broadcast on December 16 included piano music, songs, and the Trio; Mrs. Beach considered that all "went finely."

As usual, Mrs. Beach's music was frequently performed at St. Bartholomew's Church. Her Cantate Domino was sung there on 21 February 1937, along with Williams's Piper and the Reed. A week later Cantate Domino[215] and Canticle of the Sun were heard there again, and "both were superbly given." Mrs. Beach found Shaffner's replacement, Dorothy Baker, "appealing in solo and duet by her childlike, innocent rendering." Canticle of the Sun was performed once more on 6 March 1938, and on the following May 26 Canticle was heard there on a program also including "superb" performances of Vaughan Williams's Te Deum and Horatio Parker's St. Christopher. Canticle of the Sun continued to be a popular work at St. Bartholomew's. At the next performance of it on 26 February 1939, Mrs. Beach remarked that "the duet went badly, but otherwise [the performance was] good; David [was] much upset."

The anthem "Hearken unto Me" was sung at St. Bartholomew's on 18 April 1937, and the next day Williams called to say how happy he was with the performance. The anthem "Let This Mind Be in You" was sung there on Sunday, 20 June 1937.[216] On November 14 the choir sang Mrs. Beach's Magnificat. After hearing her Deus misereatur again on November 28, Mrs. Beach arranged with Williams to play her new anthem "Lord of All Being" for him; on 29 January 1939, Williams premiered the new anthem at St. Bartholomew's. St. Bartholomew's choir gave Mrs. Beach's Benedictus a "heavenly" performance on 16 January 1938.[217]

David McK. Williams considered many of the composer's church compositions too lengthy for practical service use, despite their effectiveness, and recognized their more

---

[215] Cantate Domino was repeated there in 1937 on April 25 and December 5, Palm Sunday 1938, Palm Sunday and 16 December 1939, 17 March 1940, late March 1942, and 12 December 1943.

[216] It was repeated on 26 February 1938 and 18 June 1939.

[217] It was repeated on 20 February 1938 and again on January 14 and the end of April 1940.

obvious value as concert works. In this latter category he frequently programmed Mrs. Beach's sacred choral music. Between concerts and services Williams, more often than anyone else, was the chief interpretor of Mrs. Beach's religious music—music which he prized. The comparatively brief anthem "I Will Give Thanks," op. 147, written in 1939, prompted Williams's enthusiastic description: "a darned good anthem." When Williams performed her *Communion Service* on 4 February 1940, Mrs. Beach thought that it was "wonderfully given; David [was] so lovely."

Other churches followed St. Bartholomew's lead, though not so regularly. On 9 February 1937, Dr. Milligan played the organ at a performance of *Canticle of the Sun* at the Riverside Church following an American Guild of Organists dinner, and this performance was an "improvement" over previous performances by the Riverside forces. Beach's *Agnus Dei* was performed on Easter Sunday 1937 at New York's fashionable St. Thomas' Church on Fifth Avenue. She regretted that she was not in New York City on 23 May 1937 to hear her *Canticle of the Sun* performed at Grace Church under Mr. Mitchell. Vernon De Tar gave her *Benedicite* at Calvary Church on Palm Sunday 1938, and on 29 January 1939 he performed *Canticle of the Sun* there. Mrs. Beach found "Mr. de Tar just like David [McK. Williams] in tempo," which was a very high compliment. On Sunday, 21 January 1940, Hugh Porter gave the composer's "Lord of the Worlds" at the Marble Collegiate Church on Fifth Avenue. The soprano soloist was the daughter of Mrs. Carl Alves, a prominent singer of an earlier generation, who sang in the premiere of Mrs. Beach's Mass and had introduced several of Mrs. Beach's vocal works to metropolitan audiences in the 1890s.

On 11 July 1937 Mrs. Buxbaum sang "Evening Hymn" at the Union Chapel service in Centerville, and the following October 10 Mrs. Beach heard her song "I Sought the Lord," written especially for Ruth Shaffner, sung for the first time by Lillian Buxbaum at her church in Boston. On November 7 Mrs. Buxbaum repeated Mrs. Beach's "Evening Hymn" at the same church with the composer in the congregation.

Although the number of new works continued to diminish during the later 1930s, there were several major new compositions. When she sailed from New York to Boston on 7 May 1937, she met with Henry R. Austin from Schmidt's,[218] who was enthusiastic over her compositions, and she graciously accepted many practical suggestions for future publications. She frequently met with Austin over the years, and he encouraged her to revise as well as compose new works.[219] She spent June 1937 at the MacDowell Colony fulfilling many of Austin's requests. She made an organ arrangement of *Far Awa'*, cuts in the *Barcarolle*, revisions of the *Thrush* pieces, proofs of the *Benedictus* postlude, a new variation for the *Balkan Variations* based on an old orchestral one never previously used,

[218] Mrs. Beach had complete faith in Schmidt's. On 30 April 1937, Mrs. Beach left the score and parts of her String Quartet, Violin Sonata, and Piano Quintet at the New York office of Schmidt's for safekeeping in the company's safe. In turn, Schmidt's had complete faith in Mrs. Beach. Miss Una Allen of the publishing house once remarked that Mrs. Beach was one of the few composers she had known who could read what was printed and not limit her vision only to what she wanted to see.

[219] For example, in early November 1941 Austin suggested to Mrs. Beach and she followed up the suggestion with "arrangements for new editions, albums, etc."

a choral arrangement of the song "After," and other changes in other pieces as well. .Mrs. Beach usually spent only one month in Peterborough, but in 1937 she returned to the Colony in September in order to finish works left undone the previous June. It is then that she began the anthem "Lord of All Being" to a text by Oliver Wendell Holmes; she finished a draft on September 18 and then turned to some of the piano *Improvisations*. The anthem was finally finished on December 9 and sent to her publisher on 10 January 1938. Her Colony stay in June 1938 resulted primarily in the writing of the Trio, op. 150, for piano, violin, and cello, and the completion of the five piano *Improvisations*, op. 148. The Trio was premiered on 15 January 1939 at the MacDowell Club in New York. With violinist Eugenie Limberg and cellist Phyllis Kraeuter, the Trio "went finely," and there was "much enthusiasm and [were] many fine comments" concerning the new work.

When Louise Taylor gave a recital of Mrs. Beach's songs for the WPA Federal Music Project in the Chamber Hall of Carnegie Hall, the *New York Times* interviewed the composer and printed the following:

> A woman who takes pride in the fact that she has many friends between 70 and 90 who are doing creative work and having a good time is Mrs. H. H. A. Beach. At 70 she has the distinction of being one of this country's leading women composers. . . . "Working successfully in a field that you love helps to keep one young and well" Mrs. Beach said after explaining that she expects to spend the summer on compositions that now are buzzing in her mind and which she hopes will come to life at the MacDowell Colony in New Hampshire.
>
> "I can't work in New York," she said. "I have too many friends here and there are far too many concerts. And there's the distraction of watching these ships." [The reference is to the view of the river from her apartment.]
>
> She spoke of a performance that the WPA orchestra recently gave of her Gaelic symphony and said she was glad that good concerts now are open to the people who have little money to spend for tickets.
>
> "Music has been a blessing to our country in recent years and I'm glad I had a hand in composing it," she said.

As in her previous years in New York, Mrs. Beach went to many concerts and operas and formed important impressions of other composers' music. She attended the first performance of Albert Stoessel's opera *Garrick* at the Juilliard School on 27 February 1937; she called it "an interesting work well given." Stoessel, who had conducted Mrs. Beach's works and espoused her cause, was very appreciative that she had attended and approved of the piece. Increasingly she also listened to music on the radio. On 25 May 1939, she purchased her first radio for her home in Centerville, and listened that evening to a broadcast of Harold Morris's Piano Concerto, which she found "deadly dull." She had expressed herself similarly before over this work, and another hearing had not endeared the piece more to her.

Clearly she was not fond of most new music, and her loyalties to her old friends from forty years before remained with her. On 4 March 1937, Mrs. Beach wired congratulations

Left to right: **Mable Pierce, Harriet Oldfield (standing), Mrs. Beach (sitting),
Lillian Buxbaum, photographed by Mr. Bachrach in Centerville, 1938**

to fellow-composer Arthur Foote on his 84th birthday; although their paths had not crossed
for many years, she never forgot his loyalty to her. Five weeks later, on April 10, he
died in Boston, but before he passed away he wrote the following to Mrs. Beach:

> Your letter came just after mine had gone, delayed until I had your
> address. I am glad that my rememberings brought back good days to
> your mind—for they were that, as you say. It is probably natural that
> there should be every now and then an understanding group, but such
> a falling off of quality and ideals as we see just now is not encouraging;
> and there is so much "ballyhoo"—and societies to do this and that—As
> to the new ideas, polytonality, atonality, "linear" counterpoint, etc.,
> what of value there may be will contribute to our musical vocabulary,
> and be lasting, what is silly will disappear—there may be something
> worthwhile left—it seems to me the only sane attitude to take. And
> your story about Otto Dresel is to the point. He was such a wise, truly
> musical [man] in the highest sense—that his feelings about Brahms
> always puzzled me: especially as he was such a fervent Schumannite,
> one would have said that Brahms would have been sympathetic to
> him—it is odd. I must say you started well with that B minor piece,
> op. 78—at that time—(I have the best time of all piano music with op. 76,
> 117, 118, 119). Why is it that one never tires of them—and always finds

fresh pleasure! (as with Bach)—Dresel was very kind and helpful to me with advice and criticism—a strong influence which was missed after his death—and he did know so much. At that time John S. Dwight stated that [William] Sterndale Bennett would have written a better symphony than the first of Brahms.

I am pleased to have the St. Bartholomew program, with your very fine *Cantate Domino* and know how you must have listened to it done as it would be done there. One is human, after all, and that others appreciate and value our work does mean a lot, I think. . . . Nowadays I don't ask myself "Is it correct?" "Is it good?" "Is it original?" but "Does it bore me," (as the ugly extreme things do)—or, simply "Do I like it?"

The *Canticle of the Sun*—that must be a real inspiration—I wish I had been there.

She also formed opinions on the new performers of her later years. She had long been a patron of the Harlem Philharmonic Society and often attended its concerts. At the beginning of November 1938 she attended a Harlem Philharmonic program featuring Marjorie Lawrence, whose performance was "good." On 20 January 1939 she was the Society's guest of honor at its breakfast-concert, at which John Charles Thomas was the recitalist. On the Thursday after Easter, she attended a Harlem Philharmonic concert featuring the very young Eugene List, whom she found "*wonderful*," though of the nine-year-old pianist she also wrote "talented but utterly spoiled in the forcing process." No doubt Mrs. Beach recalled her own precocious youth as a prodigy pianist.

On 27 January 1938, Mrs. Beach accepted the invitation of Alec Templeton and his parents to tea and a musicale at their suite in the Buckingham Hotel. The occasion was "all very quiet and delightful." She found Mrs. Templeton "lovely" and Alec a "marvelous boy" whose "wonderful playing and personality" captivated her. In due course she was called upon to play for the assemblage and chose the *Thrush* pieces, which so intrigued Alec that he requested them for his own repertory.

On 27 December 1938, after lunching at the Beethoven Association, Mrs. Beach accompanied me to Jacques Abram's debut in the MacDowell Piano Concerto with the Philadelphia Orchestra. She described the playing as beautiful, and it was a pleasant surprise to discover, years later, that Mrs. Beach also recorded in her diary that I had been a "delightful host" that afternoon. On 26 February 1939 she attended Paderewski's recital in the NBC Concert Hall, for which 19,000 tickets had been refused. Mrs. Beach's comment on the recital was that the pianist was "*very old and feeble, even in playing; so pathetic; great enthusism.*" On 13 February 1937, following a pupil's recital at Adelaide Gescheidt's, where Mary Williamson "sang well," Mrs. Beach was a guest at a dinner at the Albert Smith home. The English pianist Winifred Cecil dined there also and "was nice about my music but a go-getter," according to Mrs. Beach.

On Good Friday 1939 Mrs. Beach attended a performance of *Parsifal* at the Metropolitan Opera House, where the "superb" performance with Flagstad, Melchior, Schorr, and Lenz made a "tremendous impression" on her. In February 1940 she saw Flagstad and Marjorie Lawrence in *Lohengrin*. She was obviously a Flagstad admirer, and after hearing the great soprano in a Norwegian song recital on 13 March 1940, she wrote that Flagstad was "marvellous." On 28 February 1940 Mrs. Beach heard Dorothy Maynor's recital at Town Hall, when the contralto included "Ah, Love, but a Day" as an encore. The composer wrote "The whole program was beautiful beyond words."

On 21 January 1940 Mrs. Beach attended a member's concert at the Beethoven Association, featuring Joaquin Nin-Cummel. Of him she spoke in glowing terms, both as a composer and pianist, but of his vocal assistant Mrs. Beach could not restrain her criticism that "she was awful." Usually Mrs. Beach was cautious in her remarks about singers. She had come to depend upon Shaffner and Buxbaum to perform her own music according to her personal and musical satisfaction, and she strove not to make vocal comparisons with other singers lest she stir up a hornet's nest. Usually she went out of her way to compliment the singer, such as on 16 February 1940 when, at a MacDowell Club recital by Nora Hellen, she noted that the recitalist "sang very well . . . fine voice and good artistry." Therefore, when Mrs. Beach did speak out in criticism of a singer, the provocation must have been well deserved.

There were many other concerts whose performers she admired both from afar and from close up. On 21 February 1938, Mrs. Beach went to Boston as an honored guest along with Nadia Boulanger at a luncheon at the Hotel Vendome. Of her colleague Mrs. Beach wrote that "Mlle. was charming." She felt that Nathan Milstein and the National Orchestral Association under Leon Bargin were "superb" in a concert in February 1940. She attended a matinee of an all-Brahms program by the New York Philharmonic on 1 March 1940, and after dinner, with a group of friends, set out to a concert at Town Hall by the Durieux ensemble with Evelyn Limberg, violist, in the Mozart *Sinfonia concertante*. She also attended regularly the concerts at the Community House of St. Bartholomew's, where, for example, she heard Eugenie Limberg and David McK. Williams on 6 March 1940 in a recital.

Throughout these years Mrs. Beach retained her lively interest in the MacDowell Colony. At a Colony musicale in March 1937, at Mrs. Prince's, Mrs. Beach heard Douglas Moore give a "delightful" talk on the Colony. During the month she was there in 1937, she heard Mary Howe and her three children give a concert of madrigals and recorder music at Colony Hall for the benefit of the Colony, and Thornton Wilder joined "the girls" in their social activities. On 26 June 1937, about a hundred invited guests were entertained by Mrs. MacDowell. Mrs. Beach was one of the hostesses. The program was given by Wilder, who read from the works of Edward Arlington Robinson and Elinor Wylie; by Douglas Moore, who gave an address; and by Mrs. MacDowell, who gave a progress report of the Colony's activities and needs.

Mrs. Beach had access to some wealthy philanthropists who were unknown to Mrs. MacDowell. Such a philanthropist was Mrs. William Schofield of Peterborough; she and Mrs. Beach were both widows of Harvard professors, and Mrs. Beach often sought her generosity on behalf of the Colony.[220]

Mrs. Beach attended a memorial program at Columbia University on 27 April 1938, commemorating the thirtieth anniversary of the death of Edward MacDowell, its first music department head, whose virtues the university had failed to acknowledge during his lifetime. Mrs. Beach wrote in her diary:

---

[220] Mrs. Schofield's large New Hampshire estate on the hill opposite the MacDowell Colony became the home of Kendall Hall for girls, and then the Harvard University School of International Studies.

> Mrs. MacDowell played beautifully. Met many Colonists. My manu-
> script displayed well.

The manuscript was that of *Canticle of the Sun*, included in the exhibit of works representing MacDowell colonists. Two days later she and Mrs. MacDowell appeared together on the program of the Teachers' College Chapter of Sigma Alpha Iota. Songs by Mrs. Beach were sung by Mrs. Gaskill and, substituting for Carl Carmer who was ill, Mrs. Beach appealed for funds for the Colony.

When she arrived at the Colony on 1 June 1938, Mrs. Beach greeted fellow colonists Nancy Byrd Turner, Frances Patterson, Marion Bauer, John Gould Fletcher and his wife Chalie May Simon, Mr. Haubiel, Mr. Stringham, Mr. Jenkins [this author], "and a new face." On 21 September 1938 a terrible hurricane hit New England; although her Centerville property suffered no damage, Mrs. Beach was informed that the Colony had severe damage. When she reached the Colony in mid-October to assess the damage, she found that "the destruction [was] *far* worse than I had imagined." Many colonists helped restore the place, and Mrs. Beach was no exception. On December 27 Mrs. MacDowell wrote to her:

> I don't know how to tell you how grateful I am! but you know you ought not to have sent that second wonderful check. I am so grateful.
>
> I imagine you are listening to the MacDowell Concerto at this very moment. It did seem cruel that I could not be with you, but I am really not well enough. This cold has lingered so long. I really have not much of a one, but I could easily get more, and the doctors shut down absolutely on my going.

At the annual meeting of the MacDowell Association, on 14 January 1939, presided over by Thorton Wilder, Mrs. Beach noted that her friend Mrs. MacDowell seemed to be "*dear*, but so sad and feeble." In April she gave an hour "talk and playing on the Colony" at Steinway Hall for the New York Piano Teachers' Convention. In October 1939 Mrs. Beach sent a box of choice books to the library of the MacDowell Colony from her Centerville collection.

It was during these years that Bashka Paeff persuaded Mrs. Beach to sit for a bust sculpture. Thus, on 6 to 26 April 1937, Mrs. Beach sat nearly every day. Paeff sent the model to the MacDowell Colony, where she finished it the following summer; Mrs. Beach sat almost daily during her month there. Before Mrs. Beach departed from the Colony on June 30, Paeff and her subject invited Mrs. MacDowell and Thornton Wilder to see the model of the bust; both were "delighted" with the unfinished model and commented on its likeness. In mid-December Mrs. Beach attended a musicale at the studio of the sculptor, which served as a reunion of colonists during the past summer; one of the musicians, Raphael Silverman Hillyer, who later was the violist of the Juilliard String Quartet, was Paeff's nephew. Mrs. Beach occasionally had to do further sittings for the completion of the bust, the last one on 24 February 1939. The unveiling took place on March 16 that year in Paeff's Carnegie Hall Studio. The studio was

full of nice people. Ruth [Shaffner] sang four songs. I played four
[pieces], and Bashka's brother[221] played "Captive."

In addition to the bust, there were two other formal portraits made of Mrs. Beach. On 28
April 1937, Chidnoff took formal photographs of Mrs. Beach for use by ASCAP. On 2
September 1941, for $200, Mrs. Beach bought an oil portrait of herself, made from a Bachrach
photo, from a Mr. Calcutt. She donated it to the Henniker Beach Club on Beach Day that
fall, though this year she found it too hard to go there in person.

Mrs. Beach remained a close friend of the sculptress. Although Mrs. Beach, who was
then in Centerville, could not attend Bashka Paeff and Professor Samuel Waxman's marriage
in New York on 1 June 1940, the event occupied her mind that day, since her affection for
the sculptress had become very sincere. Paeff, too, spent the summers on Cape Cod, and
in her many rides around the Cape, none was more pleasant for Mrs. Beach than that which
took her to the studio of the sculptor. In 1941 she wrote to Ruth Shaffner,

> Saturday we drove to Bashka Paeff-Waxman's studio in Greenbush, near
> Scituate, for a "tea" and to see her summer home and studio. The
> Professor is a perfect dear, and they seem so happy. The house is a
> made-over barn that would delight your very soul, and the studio is
> a little apart in the garden, really built on to his garage. We loved seeing
> her and him and the beautiful work.

Mrs. Beach continued her association with many non-musical organizations, such
as the D.A.R. On 23 May 1937, she marched with the D.A.R. women who attended a
memorial service at Union Church in Hillsboro, and on 8 October 1938 she attended a
D.A.R. meeting at the President Pierce Mansion.

Thornton Wilder had taken the place that Robinson had held. In February 1938, Mrs.
Beach attended a performance of his new play, *Our Town*. A few days later, Mrs. Beach
wrote to her fellow colonist, who responded:

> Stevenson said that an author's works are letters that he sends to his
> friends for which the public pays the postage. And in this case I'm
> not only eager to call you friend, but to remember that you are such
> a friend of that part of New Hampshire.
>
> The producer ran in a number of curiosities—that you must have
> been surprised to hear that nocturnal Bob-White, and that line about
> the Biggest fools in the world coming from Boston. You must know
> what it is to hear your work deformed, and can imagine how I shudder.
>
> But on the whole I think the production is very faithful.
>
> I hope next summer I shall be able to thank you all over again.

---

[221] In actuality, it was her nephew, Raphael Silverman Hillyer, who at that time was a member of the New
York Philharmonic.

MRS. EDWARD MacDOWELL — BY BASHKA PAEFF   3591

Sculpture of Mrs. MacDowell by Bashka Paeff

**Backside of postcard of Paeff's sculpture of
Mrs. MacDowell, addressed to Jenkins
and signed by Paeff**

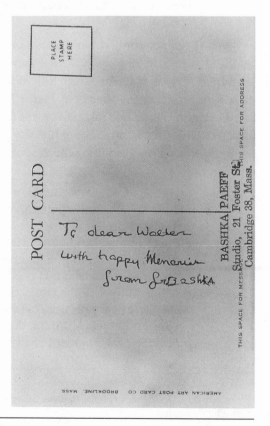

She enjoyed another performance of *Our Town* at the Cape Playhouse in the summer of 1939, with both Wilder and Martha Scott heading the cast. On 29 December 1938 a benefit performance of Wilder's *Merchant of Yonkers* took place with Jane Cowl. Mrs. Beach, together with Mrs. MacDowell, Bashka Paeff, Ethel Hier, and other friends, found the play "very funny and good; everyone happy." Proceeds were given the Colony as an aid in recovery from the September hurricane.

Mrs. Beach had been scheduled to sail for Europe from New York on Ash Wednesday, 2 March 1938, but a fire aboard her ship, the *Berengaria*, indefinitely postponed the sailing. It cut out what would have been her last trip abroad.

Mrs. Beach was an avid reader, and this was especially heightened when the author was someone she knew personally. She read Marquand's *The Late George Appley* in early June 1938, just after her arrival at the MacDowell Colony, and found the book "dull"; she very likely was influenced negatively toward Marquand because of his portrayal of a Dr. Beech in the book who resembles Dr. Beach.[222] She then turned to John Gould Fletcher's autobiography *Life Is My Soul*, which she described as "amazing" and "extraordinary." With the author then in residence at the Colony, his beautifully written book enjoyed a round of popularity.

In 1938 Mrs. Beach requested that Schmidt's send complimentary copies of her music to Bernard Tuthill, who was preparing an article on her for the *Musical Quarterly*. This article appeared in the July 1940 issue, and her reaction was that it was "good (mostly)."

Mrs. Beach was now watching close personal friends and relatives age and die. Her cousin Fannie Pierce, who with her sister Mabel had spent many summers with the composer at the Centerville home, died on 9 May 1939, and Mrs. Beach promptly left for Boston to attend the funeral and visit with her old friends.

On 6 June 1939 she noted in her diary that her first trip to New York had occurred exactly 55 years before. She also began to indicate her concern with events in Europe. On September 3, Franklin Roosevelt announced this country's neutrality, which was clear could not last long.

The Last Years (1940-44)

Besides concerts and operas, Mrs. Beach attended plays and lectures. She rarely went anywhere unescorted, except to church, but she had a large coterie of friends who would accompany her to the theater. She subscribed to the McMullin lecture series on world affairs; on 29 February 1940, for example, she learned that "Finland is desperate but not hopeless." But the continual rounds of concerts and other social activities and

---

[222] Cf. p. 14, n. 20.

entertainments finally overtaxed Mrs. Beach and resulted, in early March 1940, in several days of confinement to her room. Even during these days she received an array of callers that would have exhausted a less endurable person. Just as soon as she had recovered, however, she was back at concerts. A few weeks later she suffered again with a bronchial cold, and on May 6 Dr. Bassler "came and gave [a] thorough examination." He warned her that her heart was not well—the first indication that the composer was suffering from a condition which might have far-reaching affects. On May 8, while still recuperating from bronchitis, her physician

> let me go to my Town Hall banquet for program 200. Wonderful reception and speeches. Kittens gave "Romance" and Trio (with Phyllis K.). Saida Knox "Ah, Love." D[avid McK. Williams] played. He so dear! Dr. Sargent gave fine speech, also Mrs. MacDowell, Douglas Moore, Olga Samaroff, and chairman Mr. Watkins. I spoke. People liked it. . . . Held out well.

The next day she received a copy of *Notes on the Tribute Dinner to Mrs. H. H. A. Beach at the Town Hall Club on May 8, 1940.*

Mrs. Beach was now, like most Americans, very concerned with the war in Europe, and her diary has many entries reflecting this. On 10 June 1940, she notes that Norway had capitulated and Italy declared war on France; three days later she laments the French surrender ("dreadful news"), and on July 5 she records that the French fleet had been captured by the British. When she recalled on December 11 that it was Phillips Brooks's birthday, she also observed that both Germany and Italy declared war on the United States that day. Later, in the summer of 1942, much of her evening life circled around playing checkers or bridge and listening to the latest war news on the radio. A dramatic incident occurred on May 2 when, during church,

> air signals started during the sermon before Communion. David [McK. Williams] used the note as an organ-point and calmly improvised. We sang "He Leadeth Me" and went on with the sermon and service.

By summer 1943, Mrs. Beach was weary of the tension and excitement that the war had brought to the Cape. Camp Edwards was nearby, which brought too much noise and confusion to Centerville. Of course, she was anxious for the war to end lest there should be greater destruction in the world abroad, but, as we have seen, she was also someone who could not tolerate noise.[223] Even escape to Hillsboro, Peterborough, or Henniker, however, would have been futile, since the whir of planes in transport or the thuds of

---

[223] Her diary is full of references to noisy neighbors, and she tried to avoid parties or other situations where noise would be present. For example, on her last New Year's Eve, she complained that there was a noisy party next door that went well past midnight so that she was able to fall asleep only sometime between 2 and 3. At the end of March 1944, her neighbors gave her a "dreadful night" by throwing a cocktail party that lasted all night, and she had to make numerous complaints to the night clerk.

practice bombings in nearby New Boston would have been worse. But though she continually was upset from the "many planes" she heard flying over Paterson, New Jersey, she was concerned continually with what was going on in Europe, and was cheered on 4 June 1944 by the "wonderful news [that] Rome [was] in allied hands!" Despite poor health, she attended a special luncheon at the Town Hall Club on 10 October 1944, "in honor of liberated Luxembourg, Belgium and Holland," where she listened to "heartbreaking" speeches by representatives of those countries.

Mrs. Beach was always thoughtful about others. During June 1941, for example, Mrs. MacDowell was distraught over the injuries of her companion Nina Maud Richardson, who was confined to a hospital in Northampton, Massachusetts, and, according to Esther Bates (letter to Jenkins, 3 October 1957):

> she asked a group of us Colonists to drive to Northampton at least once a week with gifts and devotion. It was a long, hot, boring drive. Mrs. Beach knew that four of us had to go, and to make our journey less burdensome she put $12 into the hands of one of us and bade us go to the Northampton Inn and have ourselves a grand dinner with cocktails.

Of Mrs. Beach's thoughtfulness Bates also recalled:

> All her gifts and pleasures that she contrived for her friends were special recognitions of their tastes and dreams. She gave me a scarf, handwoven from the Churchill Weavers. I have it still and wear it with pleasure.

On 1 November 1940, after learning that one of her devoted Centerville friends, Mildred McArthur, wanted to build a house nearby, Mrs. Beach contacted her and gave her a corner of her own property for McArthur's home. In Boston, on November 19, she added a codicil to her will that made it official. The following year the "very inexpensive but good" house was completed, and when she returned to Centerville in July 1941, she noted that "Mildred [was] ecstatic over [the] house." And, to her good and faithful friend Lillian Buxbaum, Mrs. Beach eventually gave all the remaining property about and under the Centerville house.

Summers continued to be spent in Centerville and winters in New York. In Centerville, Mrs. Beach was surrounded by numerous old and devoted friends, many of whom lived in the vicinity or would come to visit her from Boston or New York. Her last few weeks on the Cape in September 1944, however, were anything but peaceful. Another hurricane came on the 14th and caused extensive damage, which she observed and noted in her diary:

> Terrific hurricane during the evening and night. Great damage. Sleep impossible. . . . Mr. Johnson came to start the pump and clear the driveway. No electricity. Reported beach cottages ruined and small ones washed from beach to hill. No mail train or paper . . . many trees

Mrs. Beach, Cape Cod, ca. 1938

down, including big white pine by pond. . . . Craigville and Long
Beach indescribable, also Main Street . . . at least half the trees are down,
especially near pond. The lovely white pine gone.

On September 21 she bade good-bye to her Cape Cod home forever and left Hyannis
at 9:45 on the New York-bound train.

For several years she retained her residency at the same American Women's Association
Club House where she had been ever since she moved to New York. Upon her return to
New York in October 1942, however, Mrs. Beach chose not to return there, but instead to
rent an apartment at the Barclay Hotel. Here she was honored and well tended to, though
she sometimes had to complain about noisy neighbors. Indicative of her respect among
the hotel staff is that shown by the musicians who entertained in the hotel dining room.

Mrs. Beach's violin piece "Berceuse" had caught the fancy of these musicians, and on 2 and 10 February 1944, as the composer entered the dining room for dinner, the piece was played by the ensemble. "The men were very nice about it" and "played it beautifully." When in September she returned for the last time from Centerville to the Barclay, the dining hall musicians welcomed her back with yet another performance of her "Berceuse" as she came to dine.

Mrs. Beach's life began to slow down considerably once she reached the 1940s, but as much as she could she continued with her favorite activities. She continued attending the meetings of her favorite organizations. The P.E.O. met on 6 January 1941 for a ritual rehearsal, which Mrs. Beach termed "tiresome" and long-lasting in rooms that were "hot, and many had colds." She herself developed a cold and had to be confined; the P.E.O. sent her a floral dish from its January 18 luncheon, perhaps to atone. A few weeks later the P.E.O. celebrated the seventh birthday of Chapter R, and Mrs. Beach took an active part. She was also active in the Osborne Club, which she entertained at her home on 16 February 1941; on 31 January 1942, she joined Shaffner, Lillian Carpenter, and Caroline Parker at David McK. Williams's home for a meeting of the Osborne Club at which Shaffner sang songs by Mrs. Beach. On 10 May 1941, Mrs. Beach went to the luncheon of the New York Federation of Women's Clubs at Scarboro, New York. Near the end of her life, on 29 December 1943, Mrs. Beach attended a luncheon of the Town Hall Alumni Association, where "they gave me a corsage and made me an Honorary Member of the Association."

In the summer of 1940 Mrs. Beach followed the Republican Convention in Philadelphia with great interest in the nomination of Wendell Willkie, for whom she prepared an absentee ballot that was mailed to Hillsboro on November 1. Four years later she listened on the radio with great interest to the acceptance speeches of Dewey and Bricker at that year's Republican Convention, and when Wendell Willkie died on 8 October 1944 she was "too grieved to go out" and listened instead to "beautiful Willkie tributes" over the air.

Her particularly ardent support of the MacDowell Colony continued. During the summer of 1940 Mrs. Beach did not go to the Colony, owing to her health and the damage the hurricane had done to the Colony, but on 7 June 1941 she returned. Immediately, her creative senses revived, and within two days after her arrival she had already written a song based upon a psalm paraphrase "Though I Take the Wings of Morning" by Bishop Spencer, with which she was "very happy." This was to become the composer's last published opus (152).[224] The following day she added some details to the song and revised the Norwood song "My Lover Came through the Fields." She then wrote a "little piece for wind instruments, a part of the woodwind *Pastorale*," a Quintet, op. 151.

On 13 March 1941, Mrs. Beach renewed her contract with the *Musical Courier*,[225] she solicited aid for the MacDowell Colony.

---

[224] Composer's Press, not Schmidt's, published it at the end of October 1941.

[225] She continued to renew her advertisements in the *Musical Courier* for the remaining years of her life.

To the Editor of the Musical Courier: May I make, through your kindness, an appeal to bird-lovers in memory of Hermit Thrush. He once lived near a studio at the MacDowell Colony, in Peterborough, N.H., where I was trying to compose music, only to be constantly interrupted by his beautiful cascades of song.

Finally, I decided to use his incomparable notes in as close an approximation as I could find on a piano. The result was two pieces which people have apparently found suggestive of the bird, recognizing his lonely but appealing voice.

Two years ago the hurricane was cruel indeed to the Colony. In spite of Mrs. MacDowell's heroic efforts toward reparation of buildings, the chimney of the studio is still a danger to the ones who may be fortunate enough to work there.

If everyone who remembers with any degree of pleasure my efforts as private secretary to that bird companion would send me even a very small sum of money, that lovely work-shop will again be able to welcome composers and birds alike.

The appeal, which was widely circulated, met with positive results. Many checks arrived, and on April 24 Mrs. MacDowell wrote to Mrs. Beach from Peterborough:

How darling an appeal you have made for our "Hermit Thrush." Perfectly lovely. And I am sure many will hear his song.

The composer's interest in birds and their songs had not diminished over the years, and one of her great pleasures at Centerville was sitting on her porch in view of the bird baths and feeding stations, observing their play and their vocal exhibitions.

Mrs. MacDowell could continue to rely on Mrs. Beach's avid support of the Colony. On 12 May 1941 Mrs. Beach went to Drew Seminary, where she "gave [a] one hour talk to the School about the Colony." The Junior College gave her a $2.45 brick for the Watson Studio. Problems of the MacDowell Colony involved several meetings with Mrs. MacDowell and other directors at the beginning of 1942, and Mrs. Beach was appointed chairwoman of the "committee to raise money for studio maintenance." On 4 May 1942, an all-Beach program was held by the Mu Phi fraternity, at which Harriet Henders "sang beautifully"; donations were accepted and $21.58 raised toward Mrs. Beach's solicitations for the MacDowell Colony. She collected the money and sent it to Eliza Willetts and advised Mrs. MacDowell of the amount.

Mrs. Beach continued to be involved in the running of the Colony until the end of her life. On 8 January 1944 she attended the annual MacDowell Allied Members supper and meeting at the Town Hall Club, although she found the "people lovely but tiring." On October 17, Mrs. Beach went to a MacDowell luncheon, which was

crowded. Marion Bauer took me. Speeches and a fine lunch. Esther [Bates] home with me. Lovely call. Great occasion.

Two days later, when she phoned Mrs. MacDowell to talk about the luncheon, Nina Richardson (Mrs. MacDowell's companion) related how very tired Mrs. MacDowell was, "but coming along." She then had to postpone a call upon Mrs. MacDowell on October 23 because Mrs. MacDowell "was so tired."

When Mrs. Beach decided in 1943 to publish her organ piece *Pax vobiscum* with Gray, she prepared for them a very condensed biography that should accompany announcements of the new work. In longhand she wrote:

> Mrs. H. H. Beach (Amy Marcy Cheney), born Henniker, N.H. September 5, 1867. Studied in Boston. Debut with orchestra as pianist 1883. Continued in active concert work most of life. Played own concerto and chamber music with foremost organizations in Europe and America. Composer of more than a hundred songs, many piano pieces, besides cantatas, part-songs, sonata for violin and piano, piano quintet, variations for flute and strings and the Gaelic Symphony. Medals from the Chicago Expositions of 1893 and 1933. Honorary member Boston Browning Society. Master of Arts degree University of New Hampshire 1928. Sent to Gray June 14/43.

Although its brevity modestly hides the extraordinary quality of her musicianship and of her contributions to American music, what it shows clearly is that at this point Mrs. Beach already acknowledged that her career was at least ten years past. She rarely played the piano before any audience, and when she did play it was briefly for friends. She wrote to Ruth Shaffner on 10 October 1941:

> My illness was severe, indeed, but I feel well now if I am very careful not to overuse my strength. The doctor is still unwilling for me to play in public and I am saving all my energy for another New York winter, which is strenuous without public performances.

She and Ruth Shaffner performed a group of her songs for the P.E.O. chapter in Scarboro, New York, on 10 May 1941. Following this, Mrs. Beach did not perform in public for more than a year and a half, owing to her poor health. On 5 January 1943, however, she took up just where she had left off; she accompanied Shaffner at another meeting of the P.E.O. in a group of her own songs. Then, for the next year and a half, she did not play for anyone, but on 6 July 1944 she accompanied Lillian Buxbaum in *Pax vobiscum* in Centerville.[226]

Since she could no longer perform her own music publicly, except on the rarest occasions, Mrs. Beach now had to depend entirely on others if her music was to be heard at all. Fortunately, she had devoted followers who kept her music in the concert repertory, and there were also other, mostly younger, musicians, who were continually discovering her music.

---

[226] "First playing in two years," she wrote in her diary.

It was not always possible for her to be at the performances of her music. She missed a performance of her *Gaelic Symphony* by the Boston Women's Symphony Orchestra in Newport, Rhode Island, in July 1940; possibly her earlier experience at the performance in Boston by the same group led her to avoid the summer one. Her *Gaelic Symphony* was performed by the Pennsylvania Symphony Orchestra in Harrisburg under conductor George King Raudenbush in November 1942; but although she wanted to go, she did not want to risk the disappointment of an unexpected illness at the last minute, so she declined Raudenbush's invitation to be there. After the performance Mrs. Beach was cheered by a "nice letter and notices of symphony performance in Harrisburg from Raudenbush." The composer was aware that the work was beginning to slip from the repertory of orchestral concerts and was being displaced by newer works by younger composers speaking with a louder musical vocabulary. Thus, a now rare opportunity to hear the piece was missed.

She also missed a concert including her Variations for Flute and String Quartet, op. 80, performed in Grand Rapids, Michigan, in early January 1941.

> St. Cecilia Program Recalls Composer's Earlier Visit. Mrs. H. H. A. Beach, whose quintet . . . will be the feature attraction on the Chamber Music guild concert at the St. Cecilia Auditorium Friday evening, appeared here several years ago on a St. Cecilia program on which occasion she presented a piano program devoted entirely to her own compositions. . . .
>
> Mrs. Beach is a thoroughly American product. . . . "A very sweet and unassuming person, whose work in theory and composition was done principally by herself," is the description of Mrs. Beach offered by Mrs. Helen Baker Rowe of this city, who has for many years maintained a close friendship with the composer-pianist.
>
> The composition to be heard Friday evening is distinctly in the modern idiom. Mrs. Beach has developed her theme through a series of six variations.
>
> William Rose, flutist, who will assist the Guild String Quartet in presenting Mrs. Beach's compositions, has had most of his training and experience in Grand Rapids. . . . He has occupied first chair in the flute section of the Grand Rapids Symphony Orchestra since its organization.[227]

During Mrs. Beach's last years, the Flute Variations was a popularly performed work. A performance of it had gone well at a concert at the Haubiel studio in New York on 25 May 1942, but since she was in Centerville, she could not attend. In April 1944, Marianne Kneisel Kahn, head of the Marianne Kneisel Quartet and daughter of Franz Kneisel, whose quartet had often performed with Mrs. Beach years before, called upon

---

[227] *Grand Rapids Press*, 8 January 1941.

Mrs. Beach to discuss with her the Flute Variations which John Wommer, first flutist of the Philadelphia Orchestra, was to perform on May 9. Mrs. Beach went to the concert and was thrilled by his "marvellous" tone. Two days later she "heard Flute Variations most beautifully given over WQXR by Mr. Wittgenstein and [a] string quartet on [the] American Music Week program."

Mrs. Beach was at the concert on 8 December 1940, when Ruth Kemper with Gilmer King, pianist, played her Violin Sonata at Mr. Haubiel's studio. On 4 November 1941, Mrs. Beach heard a radio broadcast of the last movement of her Piano Quintet, op. 67, by students at the Eastman School of Music in Rochester, New York. A Town Hall performance of her Piano Trio by the Hudson Trio in early December "went finely," and the work was played twice more at supper concerts in the American Women's Association Dining Hall on December 8 and 21. The Trio was heard over radio station WNYC on 3 January 1942, in what Mrs. Beach termed a "good" performance, and at a request from a listener it was repeated on the station on April 6 that year. WNYC broadcast the Trio again, along with the violin "Romance," on 13 February 1943, in what the composer termed a "perfect" performance, and she heard another performance on NBC on 12 April 1944. When E. Power Biggs played her Prelude on Sunday, 10 September 1944, in his weekly radio broadcast recital from the Busch-Reisinger Germanic Museum at Harvard University, Mrs. Beach commented that it was "interesting on [an] old-style organ and well played."

On 17 December 1941, Shaffner sang Mrs. Beach's new song "Though I Take the Wings of Morning" at Charles Haubiel's Composer's Press Studio. Mrs. Beach wrote to Bishop Spencer about the music and had sent to him an autographed copy; he responded appreciatively:

> I . . . assure you how grateful I am for your having given those words their wings. I do not know music, but our organist played for me, and I hope soon to hear it sung. Dr. Mabelle Glenn told me she thought your setting very lovely as she "would expect from Mrs. Beach." Soon I hope to hear the song on our radio here, and I think it may cause a demand for the music in this city, where my long residence makes me known. And for you, you are a resident of all the far reaches where music goes to bless and inspire.
>
> I am sending you under separate cover a meditation of mine for Altar Guilds; but, again, you build an Altar of sweet harmony, and the meditation is for you also.

As usual she heard her "Ah, Love, but a Day" sung on the last day of the year 1941 by tenor Nadeau, and the following October she heard Margaret Speaks sing it on the Wallenstein Radio Hour in what she termed a "good performance."

In mid-January 1942, at a pupil's recital at Shaffner's studio, songs by Mrs. Beach were sung "beautifully." All the singers joined in the song "Prayer for Peace." An all-Beach concert at the American Women's Association Club House on 8 March 1942, as part of the regular series of concerts, "went finely" and "brought much enthusiasm."

Shaffner's pupils continued frequently to sing Mrs. Beach's songs.[228] On May Day 1943, at a Town Hall concert by the Golden Hill Chorus, "Ah, Love, but a Day" was "well sung."

Eugenie Limberg performed Mrs. Beach's "Romance" for violin on 27 March 1942, at a birthday party for the Rev. Dr. Norton at St. Bartholomew's Community House. Mrs. Beach heard her music at a Canadian Club concert at the Savoy-Plaza on April 10, and at the St. Cecilia concert, following a dinner at the Victor Harris's, Mrs. Beach's *Nautilus* was "well given" by the chorus and "many friends came to the box." On the 19th, at a musicale at the Haubiel studio, Mary Burnett sang five of Mrs. Beach's songs and "made [a] general[ly] good impression." Two days later, at another Haubiel musicale, with a "good audience and much enthusiasm," her Piano Trio "went finely," as did four of the composer's songs, including "Ah, Love, but a Day," with violin obbligato. The Trio was repeated at the MacDowell Club on April 25.

During the winter of 1943 to 1944, her last, Mrs. Beach's music was performed in New York on several occasions. At the American Women's Association, on October 24 on a regular concert at the Club House, Nora Hellen sang "Though I Take the Wings of Morning" "beautifully."

Mrs. Beach's new *Pax vobiscum* was sung at the baccalaureate service at Drew Seminary, where Ruth Shaffner was musical director, on 4 June 1944:

> All liked it and Dr. Watter spoke especially of it. I stayed home.
> Headache.

At the commencement exercises the following day,

> *Pax* began the program. Also *Hymn for Peace*. Both well received. Girls loved the *Pax*.

However exhilarating it must have been to know that so much of her music was being played, it was the special concerts for her 75th birthday anniversary that was the highlight of these last years. In Washington, D.C., in 1942, the Phillips Memorial Gallery recognized the composer's 75th birthday anniversary with two concerts of her music on November 27 and 28. Again Mrs. Beach was forced to decline an invitation to be present for this auspicious occasion, but a scrapbook of programs and clippings was presented to her afterwards. The first program opened with the Violin Sonata, played by Elena de Sayn, now musical director of the gallery, accompanied by Mme. Julia Elbogen, piano. William Leach, baritone, then sang the three songs "Across the World," "My Star," and "The Wandering Knight." Kenton F. Terry, accompanied by the Sayn String Quartet, played the Variations for Flute and String Quartet, op. 80, in the Washington premiere of the work. Another Washington premiere was the *Balkan Variations* for piano, op. 60. Bernice Rickman Gordon closed this program with three more songs, *Stella viatoris*, "Mirage," and "Rendezvous." Ray C. B. Brown wrote that:

---

[228] For example, in March 1943, at Charles Haubiel's Studio.

America's most distinguished woman composer, Mrs. H. H. A. Beach, who completed her seventy-fifth year on September 5, was pleasantly congratulated last evening. . . . Miss de Sayn deserves much credit for the tireless zeal with which she prepared this tribute to a woman whose long career has passed through the phases of a child prodigy at the keyboard, an acclaimed pianist in this country and abroad, and a composer honored both by the performance and praise of her numerous works.

It has been the lot of Mrs. Beach to be better known to the general public by one of her songs, *The Year's at the Spring*, than by her important compositions such as her *Gaelic Symphony* and her two [sic] piano concertos. The two concerts arranged by Miss de Sayn help to remedy this by acquainting local music lovers with some of the chamber music works and selections of songs. Last evening's program began with the sonata for violin and piano, op. 34, a melodious and grateful work charged with poesy and exalted emotional feelings.[229]

First local performances were given of the theme and variations for flute and strings and the piano variations on Balkan themes. The former was written for the Chamber Music Society of San Francisco, and I vividly recall the premiere in that city with Elias Hecht as flautist. It is a work of imagination in content and of ingenuity in structure, a rather elegiac theme being treated in moods of nostalgic meditation, gayety, romantic sentiment and humor. The alternation of moods has a charming effect, as the theme is varied to the purposes of an extended reverie. The set of piano variations, on the other hand, is a more deliberate display piece, technically exacting, brilliant, and highly stylized.[230]

The second concert of the Beach anniversary celebration was held on Saturday night, 28 November 1942, and consisted of the Piano Trio, the "Romance," the one-movement String Quartet, and the Piano Quintet. According to Brown, "It was a premiere performance of the quartet from manuscript and the trio was played for the first time here."[231] Continuing, he noted that

It has been an enjoyable experience to hear a number of Mrs. Beach's compositions successively and thereby to become better acquainted with her wholesome and optimistic nature. Her music is very personal

---

[229] Glenn Gunn thought that:

The most important of the concerted numbers was the violin-piano sonata, which is a fine example of Nineteenth Century romanticism, filled with alluring melodies, the problems of form and of joint utterance of the two instruments all worked out with scholarly resource.

[230] *Washington Post*, 28 November 1942. Alice Eversman wrote another review in the *Washington Evening Star*, and Glenn Dillard Gunn's review appeared in the *Times-Herald* of 28 November 1942.

[231] Ray C. B. Brown, *Washington Post*, 27-28 November 1942.

and underivative because she is self taught in composition. . . . This independence in education was matched by her detachment from musical fashions of the day. She has always been a romantic in the best sense of the word—a devotee of beauty and a follower of the gleam. She has not been tempted into impressionism or atonality, nor has she strayed into the jungle of dischords. Her music has a timelessness that should make it enduring. . . .

Glenn Dillard Gunn added (*Washington Times Harold*):

The art which this remarkable woman has created in a career that has filled 70 of her 75 years is many-sided. Yet for all its variety it defines a musical personality which the cultured world cannot afford to ignore, despite an Anglo Saxon origin. It is an art of active and highly original imaginative gift. It is also an art of wide and expert technical resource. We have much fine American music but not so much that we can disregard any worthy part of it.

Besides these two anniversary concerts, Mrs. Beach was honored by the Friday Morning Music Club at a concert of her music on December 4 at Baker Hall of the Washington YMCA. Once again, Miss de Sayn and Julia Elbogen performed the Violin Sonata and the latter played the *Balkan Variations*. Norma Simonson, soprano, sang her songs and a vocal sextet performed the part-songs for women's voices. In addition to these official concerts, the Covenant First Presbyterian Church performed her anthem "Let This Mind Be in You" on November 29 under the direction of Theodore Schaefer. To help commemorate the occasion, the Phillips Memorial Gallery in Washington displayed Bashka Paeff's bust of Mrs. Beach where Paeff's portraits of Supreme Court Justices Brandeis and Holmes had also been exhibited.

Visits from young musicians who were familiar with her music, and especially those who performed it, became increasingly important to Mrs. Beach at this time. The composer was very aware that her style of creativity was rapidly being replaced by a less dated style. If time was passing her by in her later years, she was well aware of this, and the flattery that she received from young musicians did much to bolster her musical self-esteem. A glance at the flow of bank checks from ASCAP at this time would indicate that, in terms of monetary receipts from her compositions, she still fared well. Many a less-dated composer would have been happy at Mrs. Beach's receipts from royalties and performances.

The most frustrating experience Mrs. Beach endured during her last years concerned the premiere of her opera *Cabildo*. On 24 August 1940, Professor Hugh Hodgson, head of the music department of the University of Georgia, paid Mrs. Beach a visit in Centerville in order to meet her and discuss with her the possibility of performing her opera *Cabildo* at the University of Georgia, and also at Agnes Scott College the following March. A few weeks before, Nan Bagby Stevens, the librettist of the opera and a colonist from Atlanta, had written Mrs. Beach (letter dated 4 June 1940):

About two weeks ago, I heard the annual concert of the University of Georgia Glee Club, which included . . . the one act operetta, TRIAL BY JURY, with a good cast. The Glee Club was outstanding and all in all it was the best performance I have ever heard. The credit is due to Hugh Hodgson, the director, who is a sensitive and fine pianist. He reminds me of David [McK. Williams] and that is higher praise.

The more I heard, that night, the more convinced I was that Mr. Hodgson could give our opera a beautiful premiere. . . .

I wrote to Mr. Hodgson that you had written an exquisite score for my one act libretto and I thought you would be willing to let him have the premiere at the University. I enclose his reply. As you see, he wishes to see the score. I believe he will be deeply interested in your having the piano as leading instrument and from my memory of the other instruments you have used, I think he has them in his chamber ensemble. The students are sophomores and juniors so they will be with him next year. . . .

Do let me know what you think about the opera, dear Amy. I am all excited over it.

After several years of delay, Professor Hodgson wrote to Mrs. Beach that the opera was "to be given this fall" (1944), but the performance, for one reason after another, was postponed until 1945, too late for the composer ever to know of its successful premiere under Hodgson's direction.

Whatever frustrations she had to suffer over the opera, Mrs. Beach was fortunate that her sacred music was continually performed, especially at her own church, St. Bartholomew's. On 19 May 1940, Mrs. Beach heard the first performance of her new and last anthem, "I Will Give Thanks," based on Psalm 3, at St. Bartholomew's. Her *Communion Service* was sung there on December 1 in the morning,[232] and her *Deus misereatur* at the Evensong Service. The following February 2 the anthem "Let This Mind Be in You" was sung there, but David McK. Williams told Mrs. Beach not to come, since at the last minute, owing to an auto accident, the soloist Glen Darwin was unable to sing and his baritone solo was taken over by Saida Knox.[233] *Canticle of the Sun* was performed in the church on 16 March 1941; Mrs. Beach proudly "wore [an] orchid sent by Mr. Lucius Menz," one of the St. Bartholomew soloists.[234] On May 18 her *Benedictus Domine es* was

---

[232] It was repeated there on Palm Sunday, 6 April 1941, with the Agnus Dei omitted, and it was "wonderfully" presented on Pearl Harbor Day, 7 December 1941. There were additional performances on 3 May and 6 December 1942.

[233] She heard this anthem when it was performed at St. Bartholomew's at the end of March 1942, and again on 7 March 1943 and 2 April 1944.

[234] It was repeated on 15 March 1942 and on 21 March 1943, in a "wonderful performance." The performance on 5 March 1944 was not so good; David McK. Williams was "rather depressed over the performance," and she noted that one of the soloists was "weak but sweet."

"beautifully given," and on November 13 it was repeated.[235]   The *Magnificat* was sung there on October 5.   The anthem "Hearken unto Me" "went gloriously except for [the] soprano" at St. Bartholomew's on 11 January 1942.   On Sunday, May 10, her *Benedictus* was "beautifully" sung at her church.   At her last Christmas service at St. Bartholomew's in 1943, her "Constant Christmas" was sung.   When the *Canticle of the Sun* was performed for the Four Choir Festival on 18 May 1944, she met many old friends and some of her colleagues, including Carl Ruggles, Gallup, and Salter.

Other churches continued to program her music as well.   On Christmas Eve 1940, Mrs. Beach heard her Christmas carol sung at Calvary Episcopal Church after she had attended a "wonderful candlelight service" at St. James' Church.   She returned to Calvary Church on 26 January 1941 to hear her *Canticle of the Sun*, preceded by her *Benedictus* and *Deus misereatur*.   The composer was especially appreciative of the cordiality of the choir and its director, Arthur Friedel, at a reception following the performance.   At Riverside Church on April 27 her *Benedictus Domine es* was sung on an American Guild of Organists program of music by New York composers, and on November 13 *Canticle of the Sun* was heard for the eighth time at that church.   On 1 February 1942 Mrs. Beach heard at the Church of the Ascension not only her *Communion Service* and the anthem "Let This Mind Be in You" sung at the morning service but also, in the afternoon, *Canticle of the Sun*, *Benedictus*, *Magnificat*, *Deus misereatur*, and the anthem "Lord of All Being." It "went beautifully."   She missed a performance of *Canticle of the Sun* on 1 March 1942 at this church, but she did get to performances of her *Benedictus*, *Deus misereatur*, and her new organ piece the following November 29.   *Canticle of the Sun*, which surely was one of Mrs. Beach's most popular works, was repeated at Calvary Church on 7 March 1943, and it was also performed at the Central Presbyterian Church a few days earlier, on 29 February 1943, with a "small but very good chorus; a really lovely performance."   On November 7 that year, her anthem "Thou Knowest, Lord" was "beautifully given at Christ Church with Gladys Meyers."

Because of her illness, Mrs. Beach had composed nothing in 1940, but the next year she wrote:

> It was grand to be again at work and with my old zest for it.   A new song is now to appear published by the Composer's Press, New York, and a Pastorale for wind instruments is also in the same publisher's hands.

We mentioned above how within the first days of her return to the Colony in 1941 she was busy with new compositions.   When she went to Centerville in July 1941, Mrs. Beach wrote a "chorale" which she sent to David McK. Williams for his consideration. He replied that he liked it and "would present it to [the] committee on Hymnal revision next month."   In October she wrote out a draft of the hymn "Pax vobiscum," to words

---

[235] It was sung again on 25 January 1942 and 24 January 1943.

by Dr. Earl Marlett of Boston University's Theological School, and the following summer of 1942 at Centerville she finished it.[236] Although she did not spend much time this summer in her studio on the Cape, she was able to work in her home and, in addition to the hymn, she revised her *Eskimo Pieces* for piano, op. 64, and wrote an organ piece on the "Eire" melody for Billy Strickland, who told her "the organ piece is a gem." In October 1943, Mrs. Beach revised her *Hymn of Freedom* and, when requested by the publisher and university to do so, she "sent the new version of *Hymn of Freedom* to Schmidt and the MS. to Washington University at Pullman."

Even during the last few months of her life, Mrs. Beach continued to compose. Ruth Shaffner visited the composer in Centerville for several days toward the end of August 1944. Before she left, she suggested a poem for Mrs. Beach to use as the text for a P.E.O. song. The next day the composer "wrote [the] sketch of [a] song while [the] girls were in Hyannis all p.m." She finished the song on September 2.

At the end of August 1944, the American Guild of Organists invited the composer to prepare guild tests for their annual examinations. Accordingly, she "wrote out three tests for the organ guild" and several others which were mostly completed by September 2. One was a five-voice fugue, which she decided afterwards not to send to the Guild. The remaining tests were sent to Arthur Friedel of the Guild on September 28.

During her last four years, Mrs. Beach remained avidly interested in the musical performances around her, even if she could not easily attend them any more. On 29 March 1941, Mrs. Beach heard a concert of the National Orchestral Association and made no comment, but when she attended another concert of theirs on 28 February 1942, she was not inspired by the prize-winning works by American composers premiered. She admitted Sowerby's work was "interesting," but Nicolai Berezowski's she termed "dreadful." On another occasion, in 1941, she thought the singing of an unnamed Requiem by the Dessoff choirs to be "clear and brilliant but soul-less" and the soloist Rose Dirman "good but too light a voice." On Valentine's Day 1942, she attended an organ recital at the Juilliard School by her friend and fellow Osbornite, Lillian Carpenter. Her fascination with Wagner continued when she attended Eric Leinsdorf's farewell as a Metropolitan Opera conductor on Good Friday 1943; *Parsifal* was "wonderful" and the "music impressive," especially as sung by Lauritz Melchior, Kerstin Thorberg, Julius Heuhn, and Igor Kipnis.

Mrs. Beach continued to take a strong maternal interest in all of David McK. Williams's activities, and, of course, she was greatly indebted to him for the truly wonderful and many performances he gave of her music. When he wrote his opera *Florence Nightingale*, he consulted with her. The 4 May 1943, premiere of the opera, she noted,

> went finely. . . . Music has distinction and beauty. . . . Good orchestra and fine chorus. . . .

[236] When Marlett visited Mrs. Beach in New York on 13 January 1943, she played her setting of his poem for him in her room and he was "delighted." In March that year she arranged a three-voice version of the hymn for Miss Shaffner, who had asked for this particular arrangement for her chorus at Drew Seminary.

On 22 October 1944, the last section of Mendelssohn's *Elijah* was given at St. Bartholomew's. Mrs. Beach had not heard the first section of the work the previous week, and she was determined not to miss this part of the famous oratorio. She was happy with the performance, but expressed concern over the health of Williams, who "coughs and looks badly."

Mrs. Beach learned of the death of Cécile Chaminade on 18 April 1944. She was the only other woman composer to have enjoyed as widespread a reputation as herself. Chaminade, although less prolific or versatile in her writing than Mrs. Beach, became well known to thousands of American piano students, whose teachers assigned "Scarf Dance," equalled in popularity only by Percy Grainger's "Country Gardens." Born six years earlier than Mrs. Beach, Chaminade also began to compose music at an early age. Although the two women were acquainted with one another, this acquaintanceship could be termed only casual.

On 23 December 1942, Shaffner took Mrs. Beach to a performance of Thornton Wilder's *The Skin of Our Teeth*, about which Mrs. Beach commented:

> Remarkable play even for him. Beautifully given. Theater packed. He is now a Captain.

Immediately, upon returning home, she wrote to the author, who replied on 27 December 1943:

> Your letter made me very happy.
> So many persons have found themselves "put off" by the play—including many for whom I have great regard—that I have become resigned to incomprehensions and am all ready to believe that I might have stated these matters in other ways. And then a letter like yours restores me to my first resolves!
> But then, in addition, it was a pleasure to hear from you, to remember our talks, and to start looking forward to the day when we can resume them.

Mrs. Beach's admiration for Wilder was not uncritical, though she herself presumably evolved in her literary-dramatic taste. Her close friend Esther Bates commented that Mrs. Beach

> had no appreciation for a book like Thornton Wilder's *Heaven's My Destination*. I gave it to her. She wouldn't read it through. . . .

Bates prefaced these remarks with:

> She had fine, cultivated literary tastes—unusually discerning—unusually wide. I have often wondered how she came by them, unless during her Boston days she moved with a group of what might, in another time and place, have been termed Academicians. But her taste stopped short of freedom of speech. . . .

Mrs. Beach regularly celebrated her birthdays in Centerville with her closest friends and neighbors. Her 74th birthday, on 5 September 1941, for example, was spent with her cousin Mabel Pierce, her maid Mrs. Cheney (no relative),[237] and "many friends . . . each with a gift." Her last birthday in 1944 was a quiet affair, interrupted only by the terrible noise of war planes.

Mrs. Beach was saddened by the death of Du Bose Heyward, playwright and colonist, on 17 June 1940, and a few days later Mrs. MacDowell wrote that his widow "Dorothy had come to the Colony as the only place she could bear to be just now." Many of her old friends were now dying. Miss Palmer died suddenly at the end of December 1941. Clara Belle Miller died in Hillsboro in March 1943, and in May that year Albert Stoessel, who had frequently conducted her music, died while conducting a concert at the Juilliard School, where he taught. These deaths and many others made her aware of the passage of time.

Mrs. Beach's own health was now of major concern. She had enjoyed great vigor and stamina for more than seventy years, but by 1940 her heart was threatened by her excessive weight. Dr. Bassler, Mrs. Beach's New York physician,[238] had asked Mrs. Beach to check with Dr. Cobb of Centerville soon after her arrival there at the end of spring 1940, in order for the composer's chart to be kept current during the summer. Dr. Cobb had been her neighbor and friend as well as local physician for many years. Accordingly, Dr. Cobb called on Mrs. Beach on June 2 and seemed to Mrs. Beach to be discouraged. He recorded her weight at 200 pounds, the greatest of her lifetime and much above that desired by both physicians. He therefore put her immediately on a diet, which reduced her weight by thirty pounds by the time she returned to New York in the fall, and by another ten by the following February. When she returned to Centerville the following summer, she was down to 157½ pounds and gradually lost more. But her weight had already caused damage. On 17 July 1940, she "had heart flutterings but got through [the] day comfortably." Dr. Cobb kept close watch over her condition, and at this time there was no reason for undue concern by the occasional "poor turns" in her health. When Mrs. Beach was back in New York in late November, Dr. Bassler examined her and then confided to Ruth Shaffner that he was pleased with her condition.

During the winter of 1941-42 Mrs. Beach suffered greatly from lameness due to rhumatism. At a check-up with Dr. Bassler on 1 May 1942, he "advised against New Hampshire and wanted me to get away [to Centerville] as soon as possible." She even had to forgo her usual spring visit to Boston. It was not until May 16 that she was able to leave the city, and then circuitously to the Cape via Brookwillows and the Hier's in Lakeside, Connecticut, arriving finally in Centerville on the 18th. At the end of September she wanted to go to Hillsboro, but Dr. Cobb forbade her from doing so since his examination of her heart ended in "not a favorable verdict." He advised her to remain at the Cape as long as possible because of the agreement of its climate over that of the city, but on October 22 "Dr. C. prescribes N.Y. as soon as possible." She first went to Boston and

---

[237] She was succeeded in 1943 by Miss Leksin.

[238] Her close friendship to Dr. Bassler was confirmed when he had her for Christmas dinner in 1940, 1941, and 1943.

then to New York, where Miss Parker met her with a wheelchair. A few days later Dr. Bassler visited her and was "rather encouraging." Apparently Mrs. Beach was getting strong, so Dr. Bassler approved her helping Mrs. MacDowell celebrate her 85th birthday on November 22 and "doing more." Her recent illnesses during the past year had somewhat frightened Mrs. Beach into being overly cautious about her health, and her physician's advice seemed to release within her a great deal of energy to meet forthcoming events. She started attending concerts, though the bitter cold weather of this winter forced her to stay at home more than she would have liked.

During 1943 Mrs. Beach was able to get about New York at times and visit not only St. Bartholomew's but other places as well. She and some of her friends would occasionally make excursions to the seaside or country to relax and renew strength. This continued into 1944. On February 5, for example, she and Miss Shaffner went to the Half Moon Hotel for a few days of relaxation at the Long Island resort, enjoying its "lovely view." Her energy was quickly sapped in the city, and she had come to find this spot, a short way from New York City, a haven of rest, which always produced in her a great feeling of re-vitalization.

Her health seemed to have stabilized, and her only complaint early in 1944 was that on February 22 she visited her dentist, bruised her face, and was "feeling weak." Within a few days, however, she had recovered sufficiently to attend a World Prayer meeting and to hear Dr. Coleman's noonday talk at her church. A few days later, on February 27, she enjoyed a performance of her "Old Cabin" at one of Ethel Hier's musicales. Nonetheless, she was clearly aging, and frequently she had to give up attending concerts and dinners at the last minute.

It may have been only coincidental, but Mrs. Beach, after expressing concern over the death of her colleague Cécile Chaminade on 18 April 1944, underwent extensive physical and eptometric examinations. Recently she had had some misgivings concerning her eyesight. She was relieved when Dr. Seward reported "no signs of cataracts or other diseases," and when Dr. Bassler prescribed full activity, she was jubilant. A month later Dr. Bassler was "encouraging as to heart but nervous condition poor; gave good advice," and told her to give up several of her social engagements.

When she returned to Centerville on June 21, Dr. Kinney, who had replaced Dr. Cobb upon his death on 30 May 1944, called on her and advised her to walk more, which she did with Miss Leksin. By September 5, her birthday, she was down to 145 pounds, the lowest it had been in many years, but Dr. Kinney was "not quite so enthusiastic about [my] heart, but nothing serious . . . overtired."

A regular physical check-up with Dr. Bassler took place on October 27. He was "satisfied with my condition" and found that her "blood pressure [was] that of a young girl." At 4:30 the next morning she had an "attack . . . of bad breathing after [a] glass of milk," from which she recovered later that morning, and she resumed her more or less normal activities. The following day she attended a performance of Mozart's *Requiem* at St. Bartholomew's, and the next afternoon Miss Shaffner's brother Tom, who was visiting from California, drove the two women to Coney Island, Jones Beach, Floyd Bennett and LaGuardia Fields, and elsewhere. But again, on November 2, at 3:30 a.m., Mrs. Beach suffered "another spell of hard breathing," which lasted several hours. When she called Dr. Bassler, he sent stronger pills to her, and she felt well again by the next day. That was election day, and she sent her absentee ballot again to Hillsboro; of course, she voted straight Republican. That evening she suffered "bad aches in hip and leg," and the next day she felt better and received visitors.

On Sunday, November 5, she was unable to attend morning service at St. Bartholomew's, which included her music, but she went to the afternoon service at which music by Frances McCollin and Horatio Parker (*23rd Psalm*) were "both lovely." In the evening she had dinner at Miss Shaffner's new apartment, and she found

> brother Tom delightful. I played three songs for Ruth to sing. Home by 9:30. Tom brought me.

Later, in describing this evening, Miss Shaffner spoke of Mrs. Beach as being more her old self than she had been for a very long time:

> She insisted on playing, although she had scarcely touched a piano for a couple of years. That night she was truly inspired by her own songs. I shall never forget the experience, for I felt that I was in the presence of a great moment.

Surely this was the case, for on the next day Mrs. Beach recorded her last diary entry: "Not feeling well; hip aches." She remained in bed that day, and over the next few weeks her condition continued to worsen. Nursing care was provided around the clock. Eventually, in early December, she was moved to a larger room at the Barclay, where she could be made as comfortable as possible during the remaining weeks of her life, which ended on December 27. Of these final days, perhaps the most sensitive description came from Esther Bates (letter to Jenkins, 3 October 1957):

> The most beautiful memories I have of her were of her last days. She was within a week of the end when I went down to New York largely to see her, and not knowing how ill she was, I wouldn't have intruded, but she was glad to see me (very briefly) and my memory is that she wished me to take the sacrament with her (but I do not think I did). Her face was lovely, her presence indescribably frail, as of another world than this. My stay was brief in moments but very enduring in my mind.
>
> She was sitting up in bed (for breath probably), said little, but conveyed a great deal. Presently Mrs. MacDowell arrived and I withdrew by the nurse's wise orders. But Mrs. Beach asked me to return. The nurse shook her head gently. So I stayed out in the entry-way, silent and motionless, and looked through the door at Mrs. MacDowell seated beside her. There was some music over the air: it was actually a concert in memory of Lewis M. Isaacs, and the two, bound by so many ties and so dear to each other, listened in silence, hand in hand.
>
> Mrs. Beach said, "Is Esther out there? Tell her to come in." But the nurse again shook her head, and I stayed away.

I never saw Mrs. Beach again. But she was a great lady and a great musician. . . .

David McK. Williams described the final days in more general terms.

Here is the story of our beloved Amy—

Early in November she was sent to her bed because of her heart condition. The heart was getting very unequal to her needs. It had enlarged to its limits and she had several attacks during which breathing was very difficult.

About three weeks ago she changed to a two-room apartment in the Barclay and had a day and a night nurse who served her faithfully. She was kept comfortable with injections when needed. It was only a case of waiting until the end came. She was in a beautiful state of mind, and was free of pain. For about 40 hours she was in a coma.

We had a beautiful service yesterday and then her body was taken for cremation. Later on Dr. Sargent and I will take her ashes to Boston for burial—without any more services.

I think that is the whole story, except to add that Amy was angelic until she lost consciousness. She had a truly Christian life and death.[239]

Mrs. Beach's ashes were placed beside those of her late husband, Henry H. A. Beach, in Boston, on 3 October 1945.[240]

If, as has been remarked, "Time was passing her by in her later years," history must acknowledge that Mrs. H. H. A. Beach stands as a milestone among native-born, native-trained American musicians at the turn of the century. Even if, in terms of Edith Wharton's tale, Mrs. Beach's creations were more *A Backward Glance* than prophetic, they nevertheless did much to establish the place of women in the sphere of musical composition. Her nobility and genius paved the way for women composers who have benefitted directly from her efforts in the years since her death.

The esteem with which Mrs. Beach was held at the time of her death is shown in the widespread national publication of her obituaries. Perhaps the most appropriate memorial took place six weeks after her death. It was an anniversary performance of her Mass in E minor, sung by the Handel and Haydn Society of Boston in honor of the first performance of the work 52 years earlier to the day. For, we may recall, it was after the initial performance of the Mass in 1892 that Julia Ward Howe wrote so prophetically in the *Women's Journal* that Mrs. Beach was the "first of her sex who has given to the world a musical composition of first order as to scope and conception."

---

[239] Letter from David McK. Williams dated 30 December 1944.

[240] Records of Forest Hills Cemetery, Boston, Massachusetts. Previous to this, they had been retained in the vault of St. Bartholomew's Church in New York City.

Some Recollections
of Mrs. H. H. A. Beach[241]

My recollections of Mrs. Beach go back to the early 30s, when as a music student I became aware of her as an American composer, native to my own state of New Hampshire. The idea that one day I might seriously be concerned in evaluating her place in the history of American music did not enter my mind then. Several years later, when we both were composers at the MacDowell Colony, I began to discover what a remarkable person and composer she was.

Amy Beach was then highly regarded as a creative craftsman by her fellow composers, even by those younger composers who considered her music hopelessly old-fashioned. This did not disturb her since she WAS old-fashioned by the standards of younger composers of that time. She was born into the last third of the 19th century, when Romanticism was still a common vocabulary of musical expression.

In manner, Mrs. Beach was gentle, kind, sincere, and generous, with a considerable maternal instinct (although she never had any children of her own), yet regal in bearing. She was not tall in stature, but toward the end of her life she suffered from being overly heavy. Her manner of speech was always quiet, but when she became agitated her voice modulated to a precision of emphasis, which left little doubt about her feelings. In her dress she was moderate. She wore only the jewelry of her wedding ring and one small other ring on her right hand given her by her husband, Henry Harris Aubrey Beach, M.D.

She never failed in her devotion to her husband, whose tragic death in 1910 sent her into deep mourning for many months. She related that her life with Dr. Beach had been "arduous" but most rewarding since he provided an almost ideal surrounding for her activities as a composer. Mrs. Beach is primarily remembered as a composer of songs of exquisite beauty and tremendous emotional impact. She told me of several solo songs written to texts by Dr. Beach; others were dedicated to him.

Probably one of the most puzzling aspects of the composer's style was the reading problems created by her considerable use of chromaticisms and enharmonics, which seemed quite confusing in terms of the key signature of most of her scores. It would be, of course, equally confusing had she changed the key signatures every time the chromaticisms seemed to set up a new key. I never did mention this habit to her, and now, in retrospect, I think she would have been surprised that it would concern a musician familiar with the chromaticisms of Brahms, Franck, Wagner, Liszt, and others, into whose camp Mrs. Beach crept when she was launching her creative career. But once one turns away from the printed page, the aural response to her music moves along in an orderly fashion and the chromaticisms are heard normally and naturally.

---

[241] The following chapter was not originally intended to be in Jenkins's biography but can serve as a fitting conclusion to it. It was written by Jenkins on 1 August 1981, in Rye Beach, New Hampshire.

Mrs. Beach considered her instrumental works simply an extension of her melodic and harmonic sense as found in her vocal writings, characteristically in the style of the instrument for which they were intended. Much of her music for piano was of virtuoso nature since she, herself, was a concert pianist, even a prodigy pianist during the earlier years of her life.

Today it is not strange that this music was written by a woman, but at the time of her death in late 1944, she was among a handful of women composers who could be taken seriously for their creative efforts. Of them, Amy Beach was at the top of the list. At the same time, she never spared any efforts to encourage countless other women composers in setting forth a distinctive coterie, legitimizing women, today, as musical composers. She was not specifically a Women's Rights advocate; instead "the value of one's accomplishments should determine one's acceptance, not one's sex."

If one were to think that life for Amy Beach was all work and no play, such would hardly be a true vision of her. If she was most conscientious in her composing, so also was she in her recreation. At the Colony late in the afternoon she would rustle up a game of croquet, usually winning with the most determined players. Her tour de force came, however, after dinner in the Colony's Great Hall before a roaring fire in the huge fireplace when she initiated the most intellectual game of anagrams with such literary personages as Thornton Wilder, Elinor Wylie, Jean Starr Untermeyer, and Edwin Arlington Robinson. The winner, yes, usually Amy Beach! Later she might then challenge some less literary colonist to a game of pool. Here again she showed enviable skill.

A splendid bust likeness of the composer, now on display in the Special Collections Room at the University of New Hampshire, was done by sculptress Bashka Paeff. When Mrs. Beach sat for the bust in Paeff's Carnegie Hall studio, the sculptress welcomed me at the same time to sit for a bust of Edward MacDowell (at the request of Mrs. MacDowell). As we both sat in the studio, Mrs. Beach's sense of humor made time pass quickly for all of us. She aimed her humor particularly at non-musicians who looked upon her as an oddity because she both wrote and played music. To those who had never encountered a female composer, she was unfathomable. To those today who know her music, Mrs. Beach's remarkable accomplishments are a significant reminder that worthwhile music is more dependent upon musical ideas and craftsmanship than upon the sex of the composer.

Appendix

Analysis of the *Gaelic Symphony*
by the Composer

Mrs. Beach wrote out in longhand the following analysis of her symphony. She intended to include 28 musical examples, to which she referred by successive numbers but which she and Jenkins did not supply. The editor has added the probable measure numbers of those examples according to the orchestral score published by Arthur P. Schmidt of Boston in 1897 and reproduced by G. K. Hall in 1992 in *American Orchestral Music: Late Nineteenth-Century Boston*, edited by Sam Dennison, Three Centuries of American Music, 10.

I. Allegro con fuoco (6/8). Orchestra: 2 flutes, 2 oboes, 2 clarinets in A, 2 bassoons, four horns and two trumpets in F, three trombones & bass-tuba, kettledrum in B, D, & E, and strings.

The movement begins *pp* with a murmuring chromatic figure which is extensively used throughout as an accompaniment to the principal theme [meas. 1-21]. It is first given very softly by the strings, gradually increasing in force and fullness of instrumentation as it ascends higher and higher until the full orchestra ushers in a portion of the first theme, used as horn and trumpet calls [meas. 13-25]. A subsidiary legato phrase in the woodwind against a pizzicato accompaniment in the strings [meas. 26-35] leads to the murmuring figure now associated with the first theme in its entirety. The latter is divided among the horns, woodwind instruments, and trumpets and is always accompanied by the soft rustling of the strings. The last half of the theme is at once repeated by the violins in octaves, with a richly-harmonized accompaniment for wind and brass instruments. A full close on the tonic is preceded by a measure of ritardando in 2/2 time, which will be found considerably extended in the Coda [meas. 69-71]. A loud horn call leads through the key of the dominant to a second subsidiary [theme; meas. 71-75], soft and delicate at first, [it] afterwards works up to a climax for full orchestra [meas. 73-100]. After a fragment of the first theme played by the horns, the murmuring strings introduce and accompany the second theme in G major, "poco piu tranquillo," given out by the solo clarinet [meas. 107-29]. It is immediately followed by a modified version played by the violins in octaves, leading to a conclusion theme in G major of Gaelic folk-song character [meas. 131-64].

This is announced by the oboe, answered canonically by the flute, and finally dies away in the strings, bringing the first part of the movement to a close. There is no repeat, and the free fantasia begins with resumption of the chromatic murmuring by the strings, tempo primo. Both of the main themes, as well as the chromatic counter-subject and the subsidiaries are worked out at great length and with minute detail of augmentation, diminution, and double counterpoint. From a gentle beginning the full orchestra is finally employed in all the strength until there comes a rapid downward arpeggio in the strings followed by a few bars of continually decreasing force, and then a measure of silence. A short recitative for the clarinet, accompanied at intervals by the rustling strings, leads to the recapitulation, which bears a close resemblance in its development to the first part of the movement, save in the modulations. Here the second theme occurs in A-flat major, and the conclusion theme in E major. This theme is now extended by the violins after its appearances in the flute and oboe (the order is reversed from that in the first part) [meas. 439-63]. A few bars, *molto piano*, lead to the Coda, which is long and contrapuntally brought to the maximum of fullness of tone. Near its close there are eight bars in 2/2 time (suggested by that one previously found in the first part), which will again appear with further modifications in the last movement of the symphony [meas. 539-46]. Nine bars of 6/8 time, *ff*, in which the murmuring figure and the horn-call are prominent, bring the first movement to an end.

II. Alla Siciliana (12/8); Allegro vivace (2/4). Orchestra: 2 flutes, 1 piccolo, 2 oboes, 1 English horn, 2 clarinets in B-flat, 2 bassoons, 4 horns in F, triangle, kettledrums in F, G, & C, and strings.

With four introductory bars, in which the horn and strings prefigure the appearance of the principal theme, the second movement in F major begins. The melody is played by the oboe, accompanied by clarinets and bassoons, the flute and horns being added in one phrase where a crescendo is demanded [meas. 5-18]. At its close, the tempo and time change to "Allegro vivace, 2/4," and after a short free prelude of trills in the first violins and chromatic pizzicato chords in the other strings, the rapid movement continues in F major with a variation of the Siciliana theme played by the violins [meas. 36-55]. This new subject is very fully developed and modulates into many keys, major and minor. Fragments of the original theme appear in the minor, played by the French horn, clarinet, oboe, and English horn in turn, to a rapid accompaniment in the strings [meas. 56-74].

After a gradual crescendo "poco a poco piu animato," a sudden upward chromatic rush of the wood instruments, followed by an abrupt chord, *ff*, and a bar of rest, bring a return of the Siciliana in its original tempo. The key, however, is changed to D-flat major, and the melody is played by the English horn against a high tremulous background of divided violins, rhythmically punctuated by pizzicato chords in the low strings. The phrase does not end in that key, but soon modulates to F major, where the oboe takes the theme as at the beginning, with a counter-theme played by the English horn and the pizzicato chords continued in the strings. A crescendo leads to a fully scored climax, then a dialogue between the two clarinets, followed by one between the oboe and English horn, which gradually fades in intensity until a few measures of the rapid Allegro, very softly played, complete the movement.

III. Lento con molto espressione (6/4). Orchestra: 2 flutes, 2 oboes, 2 clarinets in A, one bass clarinet in A, 2 bassoons, 4 horns and 2 trumpets in F, 3 trombones & bass tuba, kettledrum in B and E, and strings.

A short introduction, founded upon a fragment of the first theme, forms the beginning of the 3rd movement. It is worked out by the horns and wind instruments, among which are prominent a sombre trio of clarinets, frequently heard throughout the movement. A long descending scale of soft pizzicato notes in the celli and contrabassi introduces a cadenza for the solo violin, perfectly free in tempo until it is finally joined by the other strings, which are muted. Here the first theme enters, played by the solo cello, to which is added later an accompaning phrase for the solo violin, with the harmonic background supplied by the muted strings. The first half of the melody closes on the tonic, and the answering phrase being taken up by the oboe in G major, with an accompaniment of wind instruments and strings, finally reaching a fully scored climax. Four bars of decrescendo, in which the two solo instruments are supported only by the muted strings, bring a *pp* close in E minor [meas. 35-39]. A brisk reminiscence of the introduction now appears in C major (*f, più mosso*) leading at once to B minor and its dominant, F-sharp major, thence to B major. In this key a short and vigorous new theme is given out by the trumpets and violins, in canonic imitation, with the addition of the full orchestra including trombones and tuba [meas. 44-50]. Then follows an extended development in single and double counterpoint of the first and 2nd themes [meas. 51-82]. A portion of the introduction, including a new cadenza for the solo violin, ushers in the second theme in E major, which is here extended far beyond its former length. Its character is wholly changed by its manner of rendition; instead of trumpets and trombones with all their brilliancy, we now hear only the strings playing as softly as possible (the mutes have been removed), and the folk-song character of the melody is at last clearly apparent. It lasts though but five bars, when it ends on the tonic and is at once repeated, with certain changes, in the woodwind and horns, to which are subsequently added the strings [meas. 93-105].

After another gentle close on the tonic, a long working-out is begun, at a slightly increased tempo, during which the second theme is still further extended and enriched by the clarinet [meas. 112ff]. The celli and bass clarinet play the theme, which is answered canonically by the first clarinet with a soft accompaniment of high tremulous strings and low subdued horns. One phrase which I have indicated by the [symbol for] "marcato" (in [the example just given]) is repeated many times by the violins and wind instruments, reinforced by the full brass choir; the intensity of expression and volume of tone constantly augmented, until a strong climax is reached, followed by a gradual diminuendo. The violins descend step by step in triplet notes from the highest point of the discord until they serve as a low, soft, syncopated accompaniment to the horn which plays the "marcato" phrase in the minor [meas. 125-27].

The first theme is once more heard in the bass clarinet against the low shuddering tremolo of the strings, whose harmonies have become strange and gloomy. The last return of the second theme (now in the minor), softly played by the strings, followed by a series of obbligato phrases for the solo violin, solo cello and bass clarinet, lead to the close of the movement "molto Adagio e pp" [meas. 129-46].

IV.   Allegro di molto (2/2).   Orchestra: flutes, oboes, clarinets in A, bassoons, horns & trumpets in F, trombones, tuba, kettledrums in F-sharp, B, & D, and strings.

The Finale is in sonata-form and opens at once with the first theme* given out by the full orchestra, ending in C major [meas. 1-9].   A sudden change from *ff* to *pp* ushers in a rapid, broken accompaniment figure in the strings, which continues through twelve bars, and then serves as a background to a more extended version of the first theme played by the wind and brass instruments, in various combinations [meas. 9-25].   The subject is fully developed, leading through several keys and with many rhythmical changes in the melody.   There is no subsidiary theme or phrase that is not the direct outcome of the principal subject in some of its modified forms.   One of these is played by the clarinet, canonically answered by the horn, to a simple harmonic accompaniment in the strings [meas. 75-83].

The second theme occurs in B major (poco più lento) and is more melodic in character than the first.   It is given by a composite voice, made up of the cello, viola, and bassoon tones in unison, to which are added horns where an increase of power is demanded. The accompaniment is supplied by the strings, in syncopated rhythms [meas. 107-27]. This theme is also fully worked out, and used, in connection with the first, to close the first part of the movement, there being neither conclusion-theme nor repeat.   The free fantasia is comparatively short, owing to the extensive development of the themes when first presented.   The second theme undergoes many harmonic changes, in its various combinations and alternations with the first [meas. 152-274].   At the climax of tonal fullness the two themes are simultaneously employed [meas. 251-61].

A resumption of the rapid, broken accompaniment phrase in the strings brings the Recapitulation, which is regular in form though shorter than the first part of the movement. The second theme occurs here in G major, played by the violins in octaves, supported by a syncopated accompaniment in the wind instruments, horns, and low strings.   At its close, it is repeated insofar as its form is concerned, by the celli and horns, with additions by wind and strings, but with its harmonic coloring completely changed [meas. 361-81].

It modulates through many keys, finally reaching the tonic through G major, by means of a very quiet phrase for the strings and the clarinet in its low register.

The Coda begins very softly, with fragments of both themes played by horns and low strings, against a tremolo of the violins.   A crescendo soon follows, and after *f* is reached the full orchestra is almost continually employed, to the end.   The second theme returns in E major for a third rendering, in an augmented form, given by all the strings (except the contrabassi) in unison.   Above this is played the first theme by the flutes, oboes, and trumpets as a countersubject, the harmony being supplied by the wind and brass choirs [meas. 480-531].   From this point until the end the key of E major is maintained, and with fanfares of trumpets and trombones, surrounded by rapid *ff* figures in the strings, and full chords in the wind instruments, the symphony is brought to an energetic close.

---

* This theme will be recognized as a repetition of the phrase in 2/2 time previously heard near the close of the first movement.

Bibliography

Other Writings on Mrs. H. H. A. Beach

The most important writings about Mrs. Beach published before 1980 are listed in Adrienne Fried Block's entry on the composer in *The New Grove Dictionary of American Music* (1986). From the bibliography in these works one can find additional studies, reviews, and commentaries on Mrs. Beach. Particularly noteworthy in this list is E. Lindsay Merrill's "Mrs. H. H. A. Beach: Her Life and Music" (University of Rochester dissertation, 1963). An extremely valuable source is *Mrs. H. H. A. Beach*, published by the Arthur P. Schmidt Co. of Boston in 1906, as part of their promotion of her compositions which they published; besides being a collection of music reviews of her works, it contains a 12-page essay on her importance by Percy Goetschius. For early writings concerning Mrs. Beach, consult also Thomas E. Warner, *Periodical Literature on American Music, 1620-1920* (this publisher, 1988). Block also gives a valuable list of Beach's music and a succinct biography that agrees with Jenkins's for the most part. At the present time Block is preparing a major psychoanalytical study of Mrs. Beach which also takes into account her role in the feminist movement and the musical education of women in 19th-century America.

The following bibliography presents the major writings on Mrs. Beach and editions of her music since 1975.

Recent Publications
on Mrs. H. H. A. Beach

Block, Adrienne Fried. "Amy Beach's Music on Native American Themes." *American Music* 8 (1990): 141-66.

—————. "Arthur P. Schmidt, Music Publisher and Champion of American Women Composers." *Musical Woman* 2 (1984-85): 145-76.

—————. "Dvořák, Beach, and American Music." In *A Celebration of American Music: Words and Music in Honor of H. Wiley Hitchcock*, ed. Richard Crawford, R. Allen Lott, and Carol J. Oja, 256-80. Ann Arbor: University of Michigan Press, 1990.

—————. "Why Amy Beach Succeeded as a Composer: The Early Years." *Current Musicology* 36 (1983): 41-59.

Bomberger, E. Douglas. "Motivic Developments in Amy Beach's *Variations on Balkan Themes, op. 60.*" *American Music* 10 (1992): 326-47.

Bracken, Patricia J. "A Guide for the Study of Selected Solo Vocal Works of Mrs. H. H. A. Beach (1867-1944)." D.M.A. diss., Southern Baptist Theological Seminary, 1992.

Eden, Myrna G. *Energy and Individuality in the Art of Anna Huntington, Sculptor, and Amy Beach, Composer.* Metuchen, N.J.: Scarecrow, 1987.

Feldman, Ann E. "Being Heard: Women Composers and Patrons at the 1893 World's Columbian Exposition." *Notes* 47 (1990): 7-20.

Flatt, Rose Marie. "Analytical Approaches to Chromaticism in Amy Beach's Piano Quintet in F Minor." *Indiana Theory Review* 4 (1981): 41-58.

Hubler, Lyn Helen. "Women Organ Composers from the Middle Ages to the Present." D.M.A. diss., Stanford University, 1983.

Kelton, Mary K. "The Songs of Mrs. H. H. A. Beach." D.M.A. diss., University of Texas, Austin, 1992.

Mann, Brian. "The Carreño Collection at Vassar College." *Notes* 47 (1991): 1074-75.

Miles, Marmaduke Sidney. "The Solo Piano Works of Mrs. H. H. A. Beach." D.M.A. diss., Peabody Institute of Johns Hopkins University, 1985.

Pettys, Leslie. "*Cabildo* by Amy Marcy Beach." *Opera Journal* 22 (1989): 10-20.

Tawa, Nicholas E. *The Coming of Age of American Art Music: New England's Classical Romanticists.* New York: Greenwood, 1991.

Thomas, Jennifer Swinger. "Two American Composers of the Early Twentieth Century: Amy Cheney Beach and Ruth Crawford Seeger." *Journal of American Culture* 5 (1982): 27-33.

Recent Editions

American Orchestral Music: Late Nineteenth-Century Boston. Ed. Sam Dennison. Three Centuries of American Music, 10. Boston: G. K. Hall, 1992. Includes *Gaelic Symphony*.

American Sacred Music. Ed. Philip Vandermeer. Three Centuries of American Music, 7. Boston: G. K. Hall, 1991. Includes the Kyrie and Gloria from the Mass in E-flat.

Children's Album, op. 36. Ed. Sylvia Glickman. Bryn Mawr, Pa.: Hildegard Publishing Co., 1990.

Children's Carnival, op. 25. Ed. Sylvia Glickman. Bryn Mawr, Pa.: Hildegard Publishing Co., 1990.

Five Improvisations, op. 148. Northbrook, Ill.: Composers Press, 1982.

The Life and Music of Amy Beach. Ed. Gail Smith. Pacific, Mo.: Mel Bay Creative Keyboard Publications, 1992.

Peace on Earth, for Christmas. Washington, D.C.: C. T. Wagner, 1980.

Piano Music. Ed. Sylvia Glickman. Women Composers Series, 10. New York: Da Capo, 1982.

Quintet in F-sharp Minor, for Piano and Strings, op. 67. Ed. Adrienne Fried Block. New York: Da Capo, 1979.

Romantic American Art Songs. Ed. Richard Walters. New York: G. Schirmer, 1990.

Sea-Fairies. Vocal score. Reprint, Huntsville, Tex.: Recital Publications, 1992.

Sonata in A Minor for Violin and Piano, op. 34. Ed. Rose-Marie Johnson. Women Composers Series, 19. New York: Da Capo, 1986.

Sonata for Violin and Piano, op. 34. New York: C. F. Peters, 1984.

28 Songs. Huntsville, Tex.: Recital Publications, 1985.

Twenty-three Songs. Ed. Mary Louise Boehm. Women Composers Series, 25. New York: Da Capo, 1992.

Two Short Anthems. Ed. Philip Brunelle. New York?: Headon Music/Boosey and Hawkes, 1992. Includes Choral Responses and "With Prayer and Supplication."

Discography

All Woman Composers. Selma Epstein, piano. "Dreaming" and "Out of the Depths." Chromatica, 198?.

An American Music Sampler. Ronald Alan Turner, tenor; Sandra Chucalo Turner, piano. "Though I Take the Wings of Morning." Southern Baptist Theological Seminary, 1993.

The American Romantic. Alan Feinberg, piano. Argo, 1990.

The American Virtuoso. Alan Feinberg, piano. "Scottish Legend," "Tyrolean Valse-Fantasie," and "Fireflies." Argo 436 121-2, 1992.

Art Songs by American Composers. Yolanda Marcoulescou-Stern, soprano; Katja Phillabaum, piano. "Empress of Night," "The Blackbird," and "The Year's at the Spring." Gasparo GSCD-287, 1991.

Bauer, Beach, Boulanger, Chamide, Tailleferre. Arnold Steinhardt, violin; Virginia Eskin, piano. "Invocation," op. 55. Northeastern, 1985.

Blue Voyage, in American Piano, vol. 2. Ramon Salvatore, piano. "Five Improvisations," op. 148. Premier Recordings, 1992.

Carolyn Heafner Sings American Songs. Carolyn Heafner, soprano; Dixie Ross Neill, piano. *Three Browning Songs.* Composers Recordings CRI SD 462, 1981.

Chamber Music for Flute and Strings. Doriot Anthony Dwyer, flute; Manhattan String Quartet. Theme and Variations, op. 80. Koch International Classics 370, 012, 1990.

Chamber Works by Women Composers. Trio for Piano, Violin, and Cello, op. 150. Macalester Trio. Vox Box CDX 5029, 1991.

Concerto for Piano and Orchestra, op. 45; Piano Quintet in F-sharp Minor, op. 67. Mary Louise Boehm, piano; Westphalian Symphony Orchestra, Siegfried Landau, conductor (concerto); Kees Kooper, Alvin Rogers, violin, Richard Maximoff, viola, Fred Sherry, cello (quintet). Vox Turnabout PVT 7196, 1991.

Four American Women. Virginia Eskin, piano. "By the Still Waters," "A Humming-Bird," and "From Grandmother's Garden." Northeastern Records NR 102, 1981.

Grand Mass in E-flat major. Michael May Festival Chorus, Michael May, conductor; Elaine Bunse, soprano; Barbara Schramm, mezzo-soprano; Paul Rogers, tenor; Leonard Jay Gould, baritone; Daniel Beckwith, organist. Newport Classic NCD60008, 1989.

Historical Anthology of Music by Women. "Elle et moi." Laurel Goetzinger, soprano; Anna Briscoe, piano. "A Hermit Thrush at Morn." Virginia Eskin, piano. Indiana University Press cassette, 1991.

Music for Flute and Strings by Three Americans. Theme and Variations, op. 80. Diane Gold, flute; Alard Quartet. Leonarda Productions, 1980.

Music for Piano by Amy Beach and Arthur Foote. Virginia Eskin, piano. Northeastern NR 223-CD, 1987.

The Piano Music of Mrs. H. H. A. Beach. Virginia Eskin, piano. Genesis GS1054, 1975.

Piano Quintet in F-sharp Minor, op. 67, in *Americana,* vol. 3. Mary Louise Boehm, piano; Kees Kooper, Alvin Rogers, violins; Richard Maximoff, viola; Fred Sherry, cello. Turnabout TV-S 34556, 1974.

Quintet for Piano, op. 67. Pihtipudas Kvintetti. Edition Abseits, 1993.

School for Scandal, by Samuel Barber. *Gaelic Symphony,* op. 32. Detroit Symphony Orchestra, Neeme Jarvi, conductor. Chandos CHAN 8958 CD, 1991.

Sonata in A Minor for Piano and Violin, op. 34, in *Recorded Anthology of American Music.* Joseph Silverstein, violin; Gilbert Kalish, piano. New World Records NW 268, 1977.

Sonata in A Minor, op. 34. Duo Pontremoli. Centaur, 1992.

Songs and Violin Pieces. D'Anna Fortunato, mezzo-soprano; Joseph Silverstein, violin; Virginia Eskin, piano. Northeastern Records NR 202, 1982 = *Dark Garden*, NR 9004-CD.

Symphony in E Minor (Gaelic), in *Music in America.* Royal Philharmonic Orchestra, Karl Krueger, conductor. Musical Heritage MIA 139, 1968; reissued 1991 by Audio-Forum.

Symphony in E Minor (Gaelic). Detroit Symphony Orchestra, Neeme Järvi, conductor. Chandos 8958 (CD), ABTD 1550 (cassette).

The Toledo Trio Paints Three New England Portraits. Toledo Trio. Piano Trio in A minor, op. 150. Musical Heritage Society 312283H, 1988.

When I Have Sung My Songs, in *Recorded Anthology of American Music.* "The Year's at the Spring." Emma Eames, soprano. New World Records NW 247, 1976.

Indices

Works by Mrs. Beach
Cited in This Biography

This is not a complete list of works by Mrs. Beach, since Jenkins does not cite every one of her compositions. In general the titles of works and the opus numbers correspond to those found in Adrienne Fried Block, "Beach," in *The New Grove Dictionary of American Music* (1986). There are some additional works which were known to Jenkins but not to Block in 1986, and in a few cases there are some minor discrepancies which Mrs. Beach herself or her publishers created (for example, Mrs. Beach in her letters and diaries often uses cryptic language to refer to a particular work; op. 75 is different, there were two separate op. 78 publications; and "Song of Welcome" is the title on the first page of music but "A Song of Welcome" is in the advertisements and on the cover).

"Across the World," villanelle, op. 20: 34, 36, 158
"After," op. 68: 63, 142
"Ah, Love, but a Day," op. 44, no. 2: 47, 75, 91, 93-94, 97, 125, 127, 139-40, 145, 150, 157-58
Alleluia, op. 27: 43
Alleluia (1930): 102
"America" = "A Prayer," op. 52
"Ariette," op. 1, no. 4: 25, 33, 36

"Baby," op. 69, no. 1: 63
Bal masque, op. 22: 33-34, 37
Balkan Variations, piano version, op. 60: 55-56, 62, 79, 121, 141, 158-60
Balkana, orchestral version of *Balkan Variations*: 62
Ballad, op. 6: 23, 43, 53
"Barcarolle," op. 28, no. 1: 141
Benedic, anima mea, op. 78a, no. 4: 96
Benedicite omnia opera Domini, op. 121: 93-96, 124, 141
Benedictus: 55
Benedictus, op. 103, no. 2: 88, 92-93, 96, 101, 109, 124, 126, 140-41, 161-62

Benedictus es, Domine, op. 103, no. 1:   88, 92-93, 101, 112, 114, 124, 129
"Berceuse," op. 40, no. 2:   44, 111, 125, 153
"Bethlehem," Christmas Hymn, op. 24:   33, 43
"Birth":   89
"A Bit of Cairo":   92
"The Blackbird," op. 11, no. 3:   25, 29, 33
Browning Songs (3), op. 44:   54
Burns Songs (5), op. 43:   47

Cabildo, opera, op. 149:   93, 113, 117, 160-61
cadenza, Beethoven Piano Concerto No. 3, movement 1, op. 3:   22, 92
"Cairo" = "A Bit of Cairo"
"A Canadian Boat Song," op. 10, no. 1:   33
"Candy Lion," op. 75, no. 1:   80
Cantate Domino, op. 78a, no. 3:   94, 111-12, 123-24, 136, 140, 144
Canticle of the Sun, cantata, op. 123:   89, 91, 95-96, 98, 102, 107-09, 111-12, 116-17, 124-25, 140-41,
        144, 146, 161-62
"Canzonetta," op. 48, no. 4:   52-53
The Chambered Nautilus, cantata, op. 66:   63-66, 80, 103, 111, 158
"Chanson d'amour," op. 21, no. 1:   34, 36, 54
"Chipmunk":   111
"Christ in the Universe," op. 132:   103-04, 106, 111-12, 126
"Christmas Hymn" = "Christmas Carol" = "Constant Christmas," op. 95
"Come, ah, Come," op. 48, no. 1:   52
Communion Service, op. 122:   94-95, 124, 141, 161-62
"Constant Christmas," op. 95:   88, 92, 115, 162

"Danse des fleurs," op. 28, no. 3:   35, 53
"Dark Garden," op. 131:   104, 109
"Dark Is the Night," op. 11, no. 1:   25
"Dearie," op. 43, no. 1:   47
Deus misereatur, op. 78a, no. 2:   109, 115, 117, 123-24, 136, 140, 161-62
"Dolladine," op. 75, no. 3:   80
"Dreaming," op. 15, no. 3:   29, 31, 53
"Drowsy Dream Town," op. 129:   104-06, 122

"Ecstasy," op. 19, no. 2:   29, 31-33, 43, 49, 74, 94
"Ein Tag nur Verschied" = "Ah, Love"
"Eire" = Prelude on an Old Folk Tune, op. 91
"Elle et moi," op. 21, no. 3:   32-34, 36, 54, 65, 74
Eskimos, piano, op. 64:   63, 163
"Evening Hymn" from *Six Piano Duets* (1901):   51
"Evening Hymn," op. 125, no. 1:   99, 100, 141
"Extase," op. 21, no. 2:   32-33

The Fair Hills of Eire, O! = Prelude on an Old Folk Tune, op. 91
"Far Awa'," op. 43, no. 4: 47, 136, 141
"Festival Jubilate," op. 17: 30-31
"Fire and Flame," op. 136: 113, 138
"Fireflies," op. 15, no. 4: 29, 31, 36, 53, 56, 75, 115
Five Improvisations = Piano Improvisations
Five Songs = Burns Songs
Flute Variations = Variations for Flute and Strings
"For Me the Jasmine Buds Unfold," op. 19, no. 1: 32, 34
"The Four Brothers," op. 1, no. 2: 23
Four Children's Songs, op. 75: 82
"From Blackbird Hills," op. 83: 88, 125
From Grandmother's Garden, op. 97: 88

Gaelic Symphony, op. 32: 13, 37-43, 58-60, 76, 78-80, 82-83, 102, 109, 122-23, 139, 142, 155-56, 159
"Gavotte fantastique," op. 54, no. 2: 62, 90
"Give Me Not Love," op. 61: 55
"God Is Our Stronghold," op. 134: 106
"Good Morning," op. 48, no. 2: 51-52
"Good Night," op. 48, no. 3: 51-52
"Good Night" from *Six Piano Duets* (1901): 51

"Harlequin": 36
"Hearken unto Me," op. 139: 124, 126, 140, 162
"Heartsease," op. 97, no. 3: 90
"The Hermit Thrush at Dawn," op. 92, no. 2: 88, 103, 138, 141, 144, 154
"The Hermit Thrush at Eve," op. 92, no. 1: 88, 103, 138, 141, 144, 154
Hibernia: 62
"Honeysuckle," op. 97, no. 5: 90
"Humming Bird," op. 128, no. 3: 90, 95
"Hush, Baby Dear," op. 69, no. 2: 63
"Hymn of Freedom," op. 52: 163
"Hymn of Peace" = "Prayer for Peace"
"Hymn of Trust," op. 13: 51, 140

"I," op. 77, no. 1: 80
"I Dreamt I Loved a Star": 74
"I Send My Heart up to Thee," op. 44, no. 3: 47, 83
"I Shall Be Brave," op. 143: 104
"I Sought the Lord," op. 142: 141
"I Will Give Thanks," Psalm 111, op. 147: 141, 161
"Ich sagte nicht," op. 51, no. 1: 53
"In Autumn," op. 15, no. 1: 29, 31, 34, 90
"In Blossom Time," op. 78, no. 3: 80
"Italian Menuet" = "Menuet italien"

"Jasmine Buds" = "For Me the Jasmine Buds Unfold"
"Jeune fille, jeune fleur," op. 1, no. 3:   15, 75
Jubilate: 36
Jubilate Deo, from *Service in A*, op. 63:   111, 117
"June" = "Juni"
"Juni," op. 51, no. 3:   53, 74-75, 100-01
"Junitage" = "Juni"
"Just for This," op. 26, no. 2:   34, 36

"Katydid" from *Six Piano Duets* (1901):   51

"La Captive," op. 40, no. 1:   44, 111, 138
La Fille de Jephte, op. 53:   51
"The Last Prayer," op. 126, no. 2:   99, 100
"Le Secret," op. 14, no. 2:   29, 51
Les Rêves de Columbine, op. 65:   62, 75
"Let This Mind Be in You," op. 105:   88, 124, 140, 160-62
"Little Brown Bee," op. 9:   31, 34
"Lord of All Being," op. 146:   140, 142, 162
"Lord of the Worlds Above," op. 109:   117, 124, 141
"Lotus Isles," op. 76, no. 2:   101, 104

Magnificat, from *Service in A*, op. 63:   90-91, 93, 102, 115, 123-24, 136, 140, 162
"Mamma Dear":   63
"March" from *Six Piano Duets* (1901):   51
Mary Stuart, op. 18:   30, 33, 51
Mass in E-flat, op. 5:   23, 25-29, 33, 51, 92, 123, 141
Mazurka, op. 40, no. 3:   51
"Meadowlarks," op. 78, no. 1:   80
"Menuet italien," op. 28, no. 2:   34-36, 47, 90
"A Mirage," op. 100, no. 1:   158
"Mr. White's Anthem" (1930):   99-100
"My Lassie," op. 43, no. 5:   47
"My Lover Came through the Fields" (1941):   153
"My Star," op. 26, no. 1:   34, 83, 158
"My Sweetheart and I" =? "Elle et moi"

"The Night Sea," op. 10, no. 2:   33
"Night Song at Amalfi," op. 78, no. 2:   80
Nunc dimittis, from *Service in A*, op. 63:   91, 93

"O Lord, God of Israel," op. 141:   126
"O Praise the Lord, All Ye Nations," Psalm 117, op. 7:   25, 112
"O Were My Love Yon Lilac Fair," op. 43:   47

"Old Chapel by Moonlight," op. 106:   88, 90
"On a Hill," Negro melody (1929):   97
"Out of the Depths," op. 130:   91, 116, 120

Pastorale, quintet for winds, op. 151:   153
Pax vobiscum, organ, op. 145:   155, 158, 162-63
"Peace I Leave with You," op. 8, no. 3:   29
Peter Pan, cantata, op. 101:   88, 116
"Phantoms," op. 15, no. 2:   31, 36
Piano Concerto in C-sharp minor, op. 45:   47-49, 62, 65, 75-76, 79-82, 95, 159
Piano Improvisations, op. 148:   137, 142
Piano Quintet, op. 67:   34, 63-64, 75, 78-80, 94, 102-03, 109, 111-12, 115, 121, 125, 141, 155,
      157, 159
Piano Trio, op. 150:   138, 142, 150, 157-59
"A Prayer," arrangement of "America" = "Hymn of Freedom," op. 52
"Prayer of Peace":   157
"A Prelude," arrangement of "America," op. 71, no. 1:   66
Prelude on an Old Folk Tune ("The Fair Hills of Eire, O!"), organ, op. 91:   99

Quintet for Winds = Pastorale

"Rendezvous," op. 120:   95, 158
Responses (Methodist), op. 133:   104
"Robin Waltz" from Six Piano Duets (1901):   51
"Romance," op. 23:   31-32, 34-35, 43, 57, 138, 150, 157-59
Rose of Avontown, op. 30:   36, 43-44, 46-47, 49-50

"Scottish Cradle Song," op. 43, no. 2:   47
"Scottish Legend," op. 54, no. 1:   75, 83, 90, 99
Sea Fairies, cantata, op. 59:   55, 116, 118, 122
"Sea Fever," op. 126, no. 1:   90
"Sea Song," op. 10, no. 3:   34
"The Secret" = "Le Secret"
Serenade, piano transcription of the Strauss work (1902):   52-53
Service in A, op. 63:   62
"Shadows of the Evening Hour," op. 125, no. 1:   99, 100, 141
Six Piano Duets (1901):   51, 141
"Sleep, Little Darling," op. 29, no. 3:   36
Sonata for Piano and Violin in A minor, op. 34:   43-46, 49-50, 54-55, 72-74, 103, 109, 111, 117,
      120-21, 138, 141, 155, 157-60
"Song of Liberty," op. 49:   82-83
"A Song of Love" = "Chanson d'amour"
"Song of Welcome," op. 42:   44, 53
"Spirit of Mercy," op. 125, no. 2:   100-01

"Spring Song," op. 26, no. 3: 34, 49, 61
"Springtime," op. 124: 91, 95
Stella viatoris, op. 100, no. 2: 125, 139, 158
String Quartet, op. 89: 96, 138, 141, 158-59
Suite for Two Pianos, op. 104: 66, 88, 94, 101, 116, 118, 139
Suite française: 62-63, 74
"Sweetheart, Sigh No More," op. 14, no. 3: 31, 51
Sylvania, cantata, op. 46: 51, 55-58

"Tarantelle" from *Six Piano Duets* (1901): 51
Te Deum, op. 84: 55, 88
"Though I Take the Wings of Morning," op. 152: 153, 157-58
"Thou Knowest, Lord," op. 76, no. 1: 66, 117, 124, 162
Three Flower Songs, op. 31: 43
Three Little Improvisations: 130
Three Piano Pieces, op. 128: 104
Three Shakespeare Songs, op. 39: 43
Three Vocal Duets, op. 10: 23
"The Thrush," op. 14, no. 4: 25, 44, 52
Thrush Songs for Piano = "The Hermit Thrush at Dawn" and "The Hermit Thrush at Eve": 138
"To One I Love," op. 135: 113

Valse-Caprice, op. 4: 22-23
Variations for Flute and Strings, op. 80: 80, 102, 111, 121-22, 139, 155-59
"Villanelle" = "Across the World"
Violin Sonata = Sonata for Piano and Violin

Waltz Fantasie on Bavarian Folk Songs for Piano (1912): 73
Wandering Clouds = *Mary Stuart*
"The Wandering Knight," op. 29, no. 2: 158
"When Soul Is Joined to Soul," op. 62: 55, 59
"Wilt Thou Be My Dearie?" op. 12, no. 1: 25
"Wind o' the Westland," op. 77, no. 2: 80
"Wir Drei," op. 51, no. 2: 53
"With Prayer and Supplication," op. 8, no. 2: 112
"With Violets," op. 1, no. 1: 23
"Within Thy Heart," op. 29, no. 1: 36
"Wouldn't That Be Queer," op. 26, no. 4: 36

"The Years at the Spring," op. 44, no. 1: 47, 55, 61-62, 66, 74-75, 79, 83, 93, 98, 112, 116, 122, 137, 140, 159
"Young Birches," op. 128, no. 2: 138

Titles by Opus Number

---

op. 1: songs
    no. 1: "With Violets" 23
    no. 2: "The Four Brothers" 23
    no. 3: "Jeune fille, jeune fleur" 15, 75
    no. 4: "Ariette" 25, 33, 36
op. 2: songs 22, 33-34
op. 3: cadenza to Beethoven's Third Piano Concerto 22, 92
op. 4: Valse caprice 22-23
op. 5: Mass 23, 25-29, 33, 51, 92, 123, 141
op. 6: Ballade 23, 43, 53
op. 7: "O Praise the Lord" (Psalm 117) 25, 112
op. 8: *Choral Responses*
    no. 2: "With Prayer and Supplication" 112
    no. 3: "Peace I Leave with You" 29
op. 9: "Little Brown Bee" 31, 34
op. 10: *Three Vocal Duets* 23
    no. 1: "A Canadian Boat Song" 33
    no. 2: "The Night Sea" 33
    no. 3: "Sea Song" 34
op. 11: *Three Songs*
    no. 1: "Dark Is the Night" 25
    no. 3: "The Blackbird" 25, 29, 33
op. 12: *Three Songs*
    no. 1: "Wilt Thou Be My Dearie?" 25
op. 13: "Hymn of Trust" 51, 140
op. 14: *Four Songs*
    no. 2: "Le Secret" 29, 51
    no. 3: "Sweetheart, Sigh No More" 31, 51
    no. 4: "The Thrush" 25, 44, 52
op. 15: *Four Sketches*
    no. 1: "In Autumn" 29, 31, 34, 90
    no. 2: "Phantoms" 31, 36
    no. 3: "Dreaming" 29, 31, 53
    no. 4: "Fireflies" 29, 31, 36, 53, 56, 75, 115
op. 17: *Festival Jubilate* (Psalm 100) 30-31
op. 18: *Mary Stuart* = *Wandering Clouds* 30, 33, 51
op. 19: *Three Songs*
    no. 1: "For Me the Jasmine Buds Unfold" 32, 34
    no. 2: "Ecstasy" 29, 31-33, 43, 49, 74, 94
op. 20: "Across the World" 34, 36, 158
op. 21: *Three Songs* 32-33
    no. 1: "Chanson d'amour" 34, 36, 54

op. 21: *Three Songs—continued*
    no. 2: "Extase" 32-33
    no. 3: "Elle et moi" 32-34, 36, 54, 65, 74
op. 22: *Bal masque* 33-34, 37
op. 23: "Romance" 31-32, 34-35, 43, 57, 138, 150, 157, 158-59
op. 24: "Bethlehem," Christmas hymn 33, 43
op. 26: *Four Songs*
    no. 1: "My Star" 34, 83, 158
    no. 2: "Just for This" 34, 36
    no. 3: "Spring Song" 34, 49, 61
    no. 4: "Wouldn't That Be Queer" 36
op. 27: *Alleluia* 43
op. 28: *Trois Morceaux caractéristiques*
    no. 1: "Barcarolle" 141
    no. 2: "Menuet italien" 34-36, 47, 90
    no. 3: "Danse des fleurs" 35, 53
op. 29: *Four Songs*
    no. 1: "Within Thy Heart" 36
    no. 2: "The Wandering Knight" 158
    no. 3: "Sleep, Little Darling" 36
op. 30: *Rose of Avontown* 36, 43-44, 46-47, 49-50
op. 31: *Three Flower Songs* 43
op. 32: *Gaelic Symphony* 13, 37-43, 58-60, 76, 78-80, 82-83, 102, 109, 122-23, 139, 142, 155-56, 159
op. 34: *Sonata for Piano and Violin* 43-46, 49-50, 54-55, 72-74, 103, 109, 111, 117, 120-21, 138, 141, 155, 157-60
op. 39: *Three Shakespeare Songs* 43
op. 40: *Three Pieces for Violin and Piano*
    no. 1: "La Captive" 44, 111, 138
    no. 2: "Berceuse" 44, 111, 125, 153
    no. 3: "Mazurka" 51
op. 42: "Song of Welcome" 44, 53
op. 43: *Burns Songs* 47
    no. 1: "Dearie" 47
    no. 2: "Scottish Cradle Song" 47
    no. 3: "O Were My Love Yon Lilac Fair" 47
    no. 4: "Far Awa'" 47, 136, 141
    no. 5: "My Lassie" 57
op. 44: *Browning Songs* 54
    no. 1: "The Years at the Spring" 47, 55, 61-62, 66, 74-75, 79, 83, 93, 98, 112, 116, 122, 137, 140, 159
    no. 2: "Ah, Love, but a Day" 47, 75, 91, 93-94, 97, 125, 127, 139-40, 145, 150, 157-58
    no. 3: "I Send My Heart up to Thee" 47, 83
op. 45: Piano Concerto 47-49, 62, 65, 75-76, 79-82, 95, 159
op. 46: *Sylvania* 51, 55-58
op. 48: *Four Songs*
    no. 1: "Come, ah, Come" 52
    no. 2: "Good Morning" 51-52

no. 3: "Good Night" 51-52

no. 4: "Canzonetta" 52-53

op. 49: "Song of Liberty" 82-83

op. 51: *Four Songs*

no. 1: "Ich sagte nicht" 53

no. 2: "Wir Drei" 53

no. 3: "Juni" 53, 74-75, 100-01

op. 52: "A Prayer," arrangement of "America" ("Hymn of Freedom") 53, 163

op. 53: *La Fille de Jephte* 51

op. 54: *Two Piano Pieces*

no. 1: "Scottish Legend" 75, 83, 90, 99

no. 2: "Gavotte fantastique" 62, 90

op. 59: *Sea Fairies* 55, 116, 118, 122

op. 60: *Balkan Variations* 55-56, 62, 79, 121, 126, 141, 158-60

op. 61: "Give Me Not Love" 55

op. 62: "When Soul Is Joined to Soul" 55, 99

op. 63: *Service in A* 62, 90-91, 93, 102, 111, 115, 117, 123-24, 136, 140, 162

op. 64: "Eskimos," piano 63, 163

op. 65: *Les Rêves de Columbine* 62, 75

op. 66: *The Chambered Nautilus* 63-66, 80, 103, 111, 158

op. 67: Piano Quintet 34, 63-64, 75, 78-80, 94, 102-03, 109, 111-12, 115, 121, 125, 141, 155, 157, 159

op. 68: "After" 63, 142

op. 69: *Two Mother Songs*

no. 1: "Baby" 63

no. 2: "Hush, Baby Dear" 63

op. 71: *Three Songs*

no. 1: "A Prelude," arrangement of "America" 66

op. 75: *Four Children's Songs* 82

no. 1: "The Candy Lion" 80

no. 3: "Dolladine" 80

op. 76: *Two Songs*

no. 1: "Thou Knowest Lord" 66, 117, 124, 162

no. 2: "Lotus Isles" 101, 104

op. 77: *Two Songs*

no. 1: "I" 80

no. 2: "Wind o' the Westland" 80

op. 78: *Three Songs*

no. 1: "Meadowlarks" 80

no. 2: "Night Song at Amalfi" 80

no. 3: "In Blossom Time" 80

op. 78a: *Canticles*

no. 2: *Deus misereatus* 109, 115, 117, 123-24, 136, 140, 161-62

no. 3: *Cantate Domino* 94, 111-12, 123-24, 136, 140, 144

no. 4: *Benedic, anima mea* 96

op. 80: Variations for Flute and Strings 80, 102, 111, 121-22, 139, 155-59

op. 83: "From Blackbird Hills" 88, 125

op. 84: *Te Deum* 55, 88

op. 89: String Quartet 96, 138, 141, 158-59

op. 91: *Prelude on an Old Folk Tune* ("The Fair Hills of Eire, O!") 99

op. 92: *Thrush Songs* 88, 103, 138, 141, 144, 154

op. 95: "Constant Christmas" 88, 92, 115, 162

op. 97: *From Grandmother's Garden* 88

    no. 3: "Heartsease" 90

    no. 5: "Honeysuckle" 90

op. 100: *Two Songs*

    no. 1: "A Mirage" 158

    no. 2: *Stella viatoris* 125, 139, 158

op. 101: *Peter Pan* 88, 116

op. 103: *Two Sacred Choruses*

    no. 1: *Benedictus es, Domine* 88, 92-93, 101, 112, 114, 124, 129

    no. 2: *Benedictus* 88, 92-93, 96, 101, 109, 124, 126, 140-41, 161-62

op. 104: Suite for Two Pianos 66, 88, 94, 101, 116, 118, 139

op. 105: "Let This Mind Be in You" 88, 124, 140, 160-62

op. 106: "Old Chapel by Moonlight" 88, 90

op. 109: "Lord of the Worlds Above" 117, 124, 141

op. 120: "Rendezvous" 95, 158

op. 121: *Benedicite omnia opera Domini* 93-96, 124, 141

op. 122: *Communion Service* 94-95, 124, 141, 161-62

op. 123: *Canticle of the Sun* 89, 91, 95-96, 98, 102, 107-09, 111-12, 116-17, 124-25, 140-41, 144, 146, 161-62

op. 124: "Springtime" 91, 95

op. 125: *Two Sacred Songs*

    no. 1: "Shadows of the Evening Hour" 99-100, 141

    no. 2: "Spirit of Mercy" 100-01

op. 126: *Two Choruses*

    no. 1: "Sea Feaver" 90

    no. 2: "The Last Prayer" 99-100

op. 128: *Three Piano Pieces* 104

    no. 2: "Young Birches" 138

    no. 3: "Humming Bird" 90, 95

op. 129: "Drowsy Dream Town" 104-06, 122

op. 130: "Out of the Depths," Psalm 110 91, 116, 120

op. 131: "Dark Garden" 104, 109

op. 132: "Christ in the Universe" 103-04, 106, 111-12, 126

op. 133: Responses (Methodist) 104

op. 134: "God Is Our Stronghold" 106

op. 135: "To One I Love" 113

op. 136: "Fire and Flame" 113, 138

op. 139: "Hearken unto Me" 124, 126, 140, 162

op. 141: "O Lord, God of Israel" 126

op. 142: "I Sought the Lord" 141

op. 143: "I Shall Be Brave" 104

op. 145: *Pax vobiscum* (1943) 155, 158, 162-63

op. 146: "Lord of All Being" 140, 142, 162

op. 147: "I Will Give Thanks" 141, 161

op. 148: *Piano Improvisations* 137, 142

op. 149: *Cabildo*, opera 93, 113, 117, 160-61

op. 150: Piano Trio 138, 142, 150, 157-59

op. 151: *Pastorale*, quintet for winds 153

op. 152: "Though I Take the Wings of Morning" 153, 157-58

Names, Places, and Things

Abbey, Henry E. 10

Abbot Academy, Boston 37

Abram, Jacques 144

Adam, Miss 117

Adamowski, Timothie 7

Adams, Crosby 95

Adams, Mrs. Crosby 111

Adams, Katherine 104-05

Aeolian Hall, New York 78

Agnes Scott College, Decatur, GA 93, 160

Agosteo Concerts 96

Albany, NY 101

Albert, King of Belgium 120

Alexander, Mrs. George 103

Allen, Una 141

Allied Arts Salon, Boston 119

Alvarez, Louis 115

Alves, Mrs. Carl 26, 28-31, 33, 36, 141

Amateur Musicians Club, Chicago 33

American Academy, Rome 96

American Guild of Organists xi, 121, 141, 162-63

American Pen Women 90, 103, 109, 112-13, 121, 123, 127, 136-37

American Women's Association, New York 115, 117, 119, 127, 135, 152, 157-58

American Women's Club, Berlin, Germany 73-74

American Women's Club, New York 101, 106, 109, 111, 114

Amphion Club, Melrose, MA 57

Anderson, Dr. 128

Andover, MA 9, 12

Andrews, Jessie 88

Anniston, AL 95

Anthony, Susan B.   30
Apollo Club, Boston   51
Apollo Club, Chicago   31
Apollo Club, Cincinnati   33
Apthorp, William F.   50
Aristophanes   51
Arlington Chambers Hall, Arlington, MA   60
Armstrong, Suzanne   100
Arnold, Matthew   89
ASCAP   xiv, 103, 125, 147, 160
Asheville, NC   93, 95
Association Hall, Boston   43-44
Atlanta, GA   93, 95, 160
Attleboro, MA   81
Atwater Kent Radio Concert   97
Austin, Henry R.   100-02, 105, 125, 141
Austin, Mrs.   137
Avignon, France   90

Bach, Johann Christian   22
Bach, Johann Sebastian   7-8, 12, 23, 34, 53, 62-63, 74, 101, 120, 127, 144
Bachrach, photographer   143, 147
Baer, Frederic   108
Baermann, Carl   7, 10, 12, 21
Bailey, Francis   127
Baker, Dorothy   140
Baldwin, H. C.   19
Baltimore Symphony Orchestra   51
Bampton, Rose   108, 127
Bangs, Mrs.   33
Bargin, Leon   145
Barnstable, MA   99-100, 114
Barrett, Col.   35
Bartlett, Edwin Alonzo   97
Bartók, Béla   93
Bass, governor of New Hampshire   113
Bassler, Dr. Anthony   135, 150, 165-66
Bates, Esther   14, 19, 89, 94, 104, 113, 118, 129, 136, 139, 151, 154, 164, 167-68
Bath, ME   106
Battle of Bunker Hill   3
Bauer, Emilie Frances   78
Bauer, Harold   116
Bauer, Marion   78, 93, 103, 107, 113, 119, 127, 129, 138, 146, 154
Beach, Henry Harris Aubrey   12, 14-15, 19, 25, 35, 41, 58, 66-67, 71, 84-85, 149, 168-69
Beach Choral Society, East Stroudsburg, PA   47
Beach Club, Henniker, NH   147

Beach Club, Hillsboro, NH 92, 113-14
Beach Club, Providence, RI 136, 138
Beatrice Oliver Ensemble 122
Beaver, PA 93
Beel, Sigmund 50
Beethoven, Ludwig van 8-10, 12, 22-23, 26, 28-29, 34, 43, 52-53, 62,74, 84, 92, 96, 120, 127, 129
Beethoven Club 10, 127
Behr, John 42
Belgium 91, 120, 151
Beloit, WI 44
Bendix, Max 50
Bendix Quartet 50
Bennett, William Sterndale 144
Bennett Junior College xi
Benton Harbor, ME 83
Berezowski, Nicolai 163
Berg, Alban 109, 126
Berlin, Germany 45-46, 73, 76-77, 106
Berlin Philharmonic Orchestra 76, 78
Berlin Royal Opera 73
Berliner, Rudolph 44
Berlioz, Hector 22, 30, 91
Bernstein, Flora 119
Berrsche, Dr. 74
Bessie Tift School, Forsyth, GA 93
Bethlehem, PA 112
Biggs, E. Power 157
Birckenstock, John Adam 72
Bird, Henry 50
Birmingham, AL 46, 50
Bishop, Hattie 49
Blauvelt, Lillian 33, 52
Bliss, Eleanor 44
Bloch, Ernest 126
Bloodgood, Katherine 34, 36
Boardman, pianist 139
Bordeaux, France 90
Boret, Felix 32
Bori, Lucrezia 117
Boston Art Club 36
Boston Browning Society 47, 155
Boston Manuscript Society 122
Boston Music Hall 7, 10, 26, 33, 36, 48
Boston Opera Company 78
Boston Piano Teachers' Club 111, 120
Boston Pops 37

Boston Symphony Orchestra   12-13, 20, 22, 25-26, 35, 37, 39, 42, 48-49, 78, 81, 98, 100, 111, 118
Boston University   163
Boulanger, Nadia   145
Brackett, Dr.   135
Bradbury, Grace Lowell   57
Bradford, Harlan   119
Bradford, MA   9, 12
Bradley, Hattie   29
Brahms, Johannes   12, 22, 34, 46, 50, 52-53, 62-63, 74, 96, 109, 120, 127, 143, 145, 169
Brahms Club, Scarsdale, NY   112
Brahms Club, White Plains, NY   102, 128, 137
Brandeis, Louis   160
Branscombe, Gena   94, 101, 109, 112 122
Branson, Captain   122
Breslau, Germany   75
Brewer, John Hyatt   33-34
Bricker, John W.   153
Bridgewater, CT   103
Bridgewater State Normal School   103
Brigham, Amy (Mrs. Clifford)   71, 89, 98
Bristol, Mrs.   117
Broadrick, Alice   119
Brookline, MA   12
Brookline Society of Allied Arts   111
Brooklyn, NY   34, 40, 51, 80
Brooklyn Institute of Arts and Sciences   40, 52
Brooklyn Museum   121
Brooklyn Neighborhood Club   138
Brooks, Phillips   19, 25, 112, 150
Brown, Abbie Farwell   82
Brown, Ray C. B.   158-60
Brown, Rollo   99
Brown University, Providence, RI   xi
Browning, Robert   54-55, 61, 109, 155
Bruckner, Anton   92
Bryant, Annie   136
Buffalo, NY   33-34, 39, 44, 49
Bulau, Wolfgang   72
Bülow, Hans von   10, 22-23
Burleigh, Harry T.   138
Burlington, NC   93
Burnett, Dana   80
Burnett, Mary   158
Burns, Robert   25, 47
Busch, Carl   80
Busch String Quartet   118
Busch-Reisinger Museum, Cambridge, MA   157

Busch-Serkin Duo 118
Busoni, Ferruccio 62
Buxbaum, Lillian xiii, 54, 84, 94, 97, 99, 103, 105, 115, 137-38, 140-41, 143, 145, 151, 155
Byrd, Richard 91

Calcutt, Mr. 147
Calvary Episcopal Church, New York 115, 141, 162
Cambridge, MA 12, 15, 49, 97
Camp Edwards, MA 150
Campana, Rose 92
Campanini, Italo 26, 28
Campanoli, Mrs. 107-08
Canadian Club, New York 109, 116, 158
Cape Cod, MA 58, 67, 71, 84, 86, 91, 97, 99, 105, 123, 147, 151-52, 163, 165
Capen, C. L. 29, 44
Carl, William 121
Carllsmith, Lillian 29, 33
Carmer, Carl 129, 146
Carnegie Hall, New York 61, 78, 93, 126, 137, 142, 146
Carnegie Music Hall, Pittsburgh 58
Carpenter, Lillian 137, 153, 163
Carpenter, Marian 43
Carreño, Theresa 45-46, 48
Carroll, Otis 120
Cass, Mrs. 121
Castleton, VT xi
Cather, Willa 89
Cecil, Winifred 144
Cecilia Club, Buffalo 49
Cecilia Club, New York 64, 80, 93, 116, 158
Cecilia Club, Pittsfield, MA 49
Cecilia Society, Boston 29, 34, 43-44, 111
Cecilia Society, Brooklyn 34
Cecilia Society, Duluth, MN 47
Centerville, MA 54, 58, 66-67, 84, 91, 94-95, 97, 99, 106, 113-14, 123, 125, 127, 130, 135, 137, 141-42, 146-47, 149-51, 153-56, 160, 162-63, 165
Central Presbyterian Church, New York 162
Chadwick, George Whitefield 19, 23, 33, 35, 39, 44, 57-58, 82, 98, 104
Chadwick, Mrs. George W. 35
Chamber Music Society, San Francisco 80, 159
Chamberlain, aviator 90
Chaminade, Cécile 41, 47, 108, 164, 166
Chaminade Club, Yonkers, NY 118
Champlin, Gen. 35
Chandler, Lillian 34-35
Chapman, William 43

Chartres, France 90
Chautauqua, NY 98, 123
Chelsea, MA 7, 54
Cheney, Charles 3-4, 14, 19, 29, 35, 37
Cheney, John 3
Cheney, Mary 3
Cheney, Moses, Jr. 3-4
Cheney, Moses, Sr. 3
Cheney, Mrs. (maid) 165
Cherbourg, France 91
Chicago, IL 31-33, 36, 43-44, 54, 62, 80-82, 95, 112, 120-24, 128, 155
Chicago Opera Company 98
Chicago Symphony Orchestra 80, 96
Chicago Women's Symphony Orchestra 95, 122
Chickering Hall, Boston 9, 29, 34, 36, 52, 56
Chickering pianos 7, 20
Chidnoff, photographer 147
Children's Hospital, Boston 21-22
Chillicothe, OH 51
Chopin, Frederic 7-10, 12, 21-23, 26, 33-34, 52-53, 63, 65, 90, 93, 117-18, 120
Christ Church, Park Avenue, New York 124
Christian, Elisabet 75
Christian, Palmer 116
Christian Association Hall 22
Church of Our Savior, Brookline, MA 114
Church of Our Savior, Brooklyn 109
Church of St. Mary Virgin, Saratoga Springs, NY 116
Church of the Ascension, New York 117, 162
Church of the Epiphany, Washington, DC 112
Cincinnati, OH 33
Cincinnati Women's Club Chorus 88
Claremont, NH xi
Clarke, Caroline Gardner 57
Clement, Emma, Mrs. L. H. ("Auntie Franc") 5, 25, 65, 78, 83
Clement, Ethel 5, 65, 72, 78-80, 83
Cleugh, Mrs. Sophia 128-29
Cleveland, OH 82, 102
Cobb, Dr. 89, 123, 165
Cobb, Mr. & Mrs. Ferrar 35
Cole, Ulric 112
Colege, Mrs. B. S. 35
Coleman, Dr. 166
College Club, Boston 35
Colony Club 78
colors 5-7, 125
Colum, Padriac 99
Columbia, SC 93

Columbia University, New York   145
Columbian Exhibition = World's Fair   30-31
Columbus, OH   78
Column, Mary   89
Companini, Italio   26
Composer's Press   153, 162
Concord, MA   137
Concord, NH   3, 47, 97, 105, 109
Conservatory of Musical Art, New York   47
Contoocook River Valley, NH   3
Conus, Jules   72
Converse College, Spartanburg, SC   93
Coolbrith, Mrs. Ina   80
Coolidge, Mrs. Calvin   118
Copland, Aaron   xi, 111-12, 118, 126
Cornell University   122
Cornish, Miss   106
Corsica, Italy   90
Covenant First Presbyterian Church, Washington, DC   160
Covent Garden, London   135
Cowl, Jane   149
Craft, Marcella   78, 80, 97
Crafts, Rose Carter   23
Cratti, Marcella = Marcella Craft
Crawford, Marion   72
Crawford, Rebecca   78
Crisp, Dr.   135
Crist, Mr. and Mrs. Bainbridge   106
Crocker, Jeannie M.   32-33
Crooks, Richard   117
Crosby, Miss   106
Cutler, Dr.   89, 135
Cutler, E., Jr.   57
Cutter, Rebecca W.   57

Dalton, Gen.   35
Damrosch, Frank   31
Damrosch, Walter   30, 33
Daniels, Mabel   89, 99, 101, 105, 107, 111, 115-16
Dartmouth College, Hanover, NH   10
Darwin, Glen   161
Daughters of the American Revolution (D.A.R.)   100, 120, 147
Davenport, Warren   34, 36
Davidson, Mr. and Mrs.   44
Davis, Mrs. Shannon   35
Dean, Frederic   29-30

Dearborn, Godfrey 3

Dearborn, Gen. Henry 3

Debussy, Claude 63-64, 98

Decatur, GA 93

Defauw, Desirée 96

Dehmyer, L. E. 72

Deis, Carl 101

Dennee, Charles 33

Denver, CO 61

Derry, NH 87

De Tar, Vernon 115, 126, 141

Dessoff Choir 163

Detroit, MI 43, 47, 49, 51, 78, 83, 109

Detroit Madrigal Club 43

Dewey, Thomas 153

Dewitte, R. C. 56

Diamond, David 86

Dickens, Charles 5

Dillion, Fannie 130

Dillon, Eurica 78

Dirman, Rose 163

Doctor's Club, New York 112

Dole, Mrs. N. H. 35

Dole, Nathan Haskell 26, 35

Dougherty, Celius 100, 104

Dow, Howard M. 7

Downes, Olin 61, 95, 117

Downs, Margaret 140

Downs, S. C. 29

Dresden, Germany 72

Dresel, Otto 143-44

Drew Seminary (now Drew University), Madison, NJ 106, 133, 154, 158, 163

Duffield, Howard, Rev. 89

Duffield, Winifred 89

Duke, Mrs. Carrie Coleman 97

Duluth, MN 47

Dunham, George 111

Durham, NC 94, 126, 128

Durieux, W. 138, 145

Dutton, Jeannette 31

Dwight, John Sullivan 23, 144

Dwight, Marion 63

Eames, Emma 61

East Orange, NJ 116

East Stroudsburg, PA 47

Eastman School of Music, Rochester, NY   157
Easton-Maclennan, Florence   73-74
Eaton, Amy   97
Eaton, Elene   36
Edmands, Gertrude   44, 52
Edmunds, E. O.   82
Edward, King of England   136
Edwards, Clara   101
Elbogen, Julia   158, 160
Eliot, George   51
Elms School, Springfield, MA   31
Elson, Louis C.   7, 35, 48-50, 63
Emmanuel Episcopal Church, Boston   33, 66-67, 88, 92
Endicott, Mrs.   54
Engel, Carl   101
Erskine, John   128
Euterpeans, Milwaukee   49
Evanston, IL   49
Eversman, Alice   159
Exeter, England   3
Exeter, NH   3-4

Faelton, Carl   62, 65
Faelton Pianoforte School   55, 58, 62, 81, 92, 111
Fall River, MA   91
Fanning, Cecil   80
Farnham, Lynwood   101
Farrar, Geraldine   72
Fauré, Gabriel   9
Favor, Florence   83, 92
Fellows, Elise   35
Fennoilosa, Mr. & Mrs.   35
Ferrara Quartet   112
Fifth Avenue Presbyterian Church, New York   117
Finland   149
Firestone Hour   125
First Baptist Church, Boston   33, 43
First Church, Unitarian, Boston   33
First Congregational Church, Nashua, NH   29
First Presbyterian Church, New York   121-22
Fischer, Emil   26, 28
Fish, Helen   101
Fish, Prudence   121
Fisher, Edmund D.   53
Flagstad, Kirsten   144
Fletcher, John Gould   146, 149

Florence, Italy   55, 90
Foote, Arthur   23, 29, 33-34, 36, 47, 50, 143
Foote, Mrs. Arthur   35
Ford Sunday Evening Hour   139
Forest Hills Cemetery, Boston   37, 66-67, 168
Forsyth, Cecil   91
Forsyth, GA   93
France   150
Franck, César   63, 169
Franklin, Gertrude   9
Frederick the Great   51
Freeman, Mrs. Carrie Slone   80
Freie Volksbühne, Berlin   76
Frick, Mme. Karola   75, 78
Frick, Romeo   75
Friday Morning Music Club, Washington, DC   160
Friedel, Arthur   162-63
Fries, Wulf   9
Frost, Frances   113

Gabrilowitsch, Ossip   83, 118
Gadski, Johanna   61
Gage, Louise   47
Gallup, friend   162
Ganz, Rudolph   62
Garden, Mary   98
Garrison, Mr. & Mrs. Frank   35
Garrison, Mr. & Mrs. Wm. Lloyd   35
Garrison, Mrs. T. H.   29
Gaskill, Mrs.   146
Gates, Lucy   80
Genoa, Italy   90
George V, King of England   124
George VI, King of England   136
Gericke, Wilhelm   12-13, 20, 22, 56
German Lyceum Club, Berlin   72, 74
Gescheidt, Adelaide   144
Gevaert, François-Auguste   22
Gibson, Mrs., palm reader   116
Gieseking, Walter   117
Gilbert, Ella Lord, Mrs.   14, 87, 91, 119
Gilbert, Henry T.   89
Gilbert, Mr.   117
Glazounov, Alexander   98
Glen Ridge, NJ   119, 121
Glenn, Hope   7

Glenn, Mabelle   157
Godard, Benjamin   9
Godfrey, IL   81
Goetschius, Percy   39, 64-65, 139
Goetz, Margaret   36
Golden Hill Chorus   158
Goodbar, Mrs. Lafayette   78
Goodwin, Ms.   35
Goosens, Eugene   98
Gordon String Quartet   116
Gordon, Bernice Rickman   158
Gottschalk, Louis Moreau   65
Grace Church, New York   116, 141
Grainger, Florence   101
Grainger, Percy   93, 101, 116, 164
Granberry Pianoforte School, New York   78
Grand Rapids, MI   156
Grand Rapids Symphony Orchestra   156
Graun, Carl Heinrich   12, 23
Gray, publisher   106, 109, 155
Green, Vanderveer, Mrs.   36
Greenbush, MA   147
Greensboro, NC   93
Gridley, Dan   108
Grieg, Edvard   50
Grosser Saal der neuen Borse, Breslau   75
Guckenberg, Mrs.   46
Guffney, SC   49
Guglielmo, Mr.   113
Guild String Quartet   156
Gunn, Glenn Dillard   159-60
Gunn, Katherine   121

Hackett, Karleton   82
Hadley, Henry   102, 118, 137
Hagemann, Richard   79
Haggin, Mrs. Ban   78
Hail, Mrs. Mary K.   137
Hale, Irene   33, 105
Hale, Philip   29, 34, 38-39, 41, 44, 48, 50, 52, 56, 105
Halir, Carl   45-46
Halir Quartet   45
Hamburg, Germany   76
Hamlin, George   78
Handel, George Frideric   5, 9-10
Handel and Haydn Society, Boston   26-28, 122-23, 168

Hankins, Elsie Lovell 137
Hanson, Howard 126
Harlem Philharmonic Society 144
Harmony Guild, New York 137
Harris, Mr. and Mrs. Roy 138
Harris, Victor 64, 103, 111, 116, 158
Harrisburg, PA 156
Harrison, tenor 80
Hart, Bret 80
Harvard Medical School 15
Harvard University xi, 15, 34, 44, 50-51, 56-57, 145
Hastings-on-Hudson, NY 120
Haubiel, Charles 99, 104-05, 146, 156-58
Hecht, Elias 159
Heflebower, Mrs. Clara Keck 112
Hegermann-Lindencrone, Baroness de 33, 36
Heifetz, Benor 96
Heine, Florence 43
Hellen, Nora 145, 158
Hellman, Jack 80
Henders, Harriet 154
Henniker, NH 3-4, 10, 94, 97, 99, 105, 113-14, 119, 121, 125, 137, 139, 150
Henschel, George 8
Henschel, Mrs. George 8-9
Henselt, Adolf von 8-10
Hess, Myra 127
Heuhn, Julius 163
Heyward, Du Bose 89, 115, 165
Heyward, Mrs. Du Bose 89, 165
Hier, Ethel 93-94, 111, 113, 121, 149, 165-66
Hildach, Eugen 74
Hilgen, Elsa 102
Hill, Junius 22, 34
Hill, Mary Wood 94, 103
Hill, Mrs. 90-91
Hillsboro, NH 2, 83, 86, 88-89, 92, 94-95, 97-98, 100, 102-05, 112-15, 119, 121, 136-37, 150, 165, 167
Hillsboro Junior Beach Club 92, 95, 98, 103, 109-10, 119, 122
Hillyer, Raphael Silverman 146-47
Hindemith, Paul 96, 118
Hodgson, Hugh 160-61
Hoffman, Jacques 57
Hoffman, Richard 31
Hoffman Quartet 63, 78
Holland 151
Holmes, Oliver Wendell, Jr. 160
Holmes, Oliver Wendell, Sr. 15, 21, 142

Hood, Helen 33
Hoover, Herbert 115
Hoover, Mrs. Herbert 112
Hopekirk, Helen 49, 92
Horowitz, Vladimir 95-96
House in the Pines School, Norton, MA 111
Howe, Emma 33-34, 36
Howe, Julia Ward 26, 168
Howe, Mary (Mrs. Walter Bruce Howe) 94-95, 98, 104, 107, 113, 116, 140, 145
Hoyt, Phyllis Fergus 94, 112, 120
Hudson, Mrs. 138
Hudson Trio 157
Hughes, Bishop 124
Hughes, Edwin 93, 116
Hugo, Victor 32
Hull, Anne 94
Huss, Henry Holden 33
Hutcheson, Ernest 77, 98
Hyannis, MA 152, 163
Hyde, Arthur 64

Institute of Musical Art, New York 96
Isaacs, Lewis M. 100, 167
Italian Opera Company 10
Italy 54, 150

James, George Wharton 80
Jamestown, NY 120
Jefferson, Thomas 3
Jefferson Avenue Presbyterian Church, Detroit 43
Jeritza, Maria 93
Joachim, Joseph 12
John Church Company, publisher 88
Johns, Clayton 33
Johnson, Edward 126
Johnson, Mr. 151
Jones, Alton 93
Jones, Guy 94, 97, 99
Jones, Julia 94-95, 97, 100, 109, 113, 121
Jordan, Jules 7, 33
Jordan Hall, Boston 64, 98, 139
Juilliard School of Music, New York 96, 109, 115, 138, 140, 142, 163, 165
Juilliard String Quartet 146
Jungnickel, Ross 51
Juvenile Beach Club = Hillsboro Junior Beach Club

Kahn, Marianne Kneisel 156
Kansas City, MO 42-43, 78, 80, 104
Keach, Leon 9
Kellogg, Clara Louise 7
Kemper, Ruth 117, 120-21, 157
Kendall Hall, NH 145
Kent, Atwater 97
Kerr, Caroline 76
Khuner, Felix 96
Kileski-Bradbury, Mrs. 54, 64
Kindler, Hans 109, 116
King, Gilmer 157
King of Sweden 33
Kingsbury, I. F. 28
Kinney, Dr. 166
Kinscella, Hazel Gertrude 88
Kipnis, Igor 163
Kleiber, Erich 101
Klemperer, Otto 96
Kleuner, Baroness von 101
Kneisel, Franz 28, 34-35, 42, 44-45, 116, 156
Kneisel, Marianne = Marianne Kahn
Kneisel String Quartet 34, 43-44, 50, 80-81, 94, 103, 109, 115
Knopf, Alfred 105
Knox, Saida 150, 161
Kolisch, Rudolph 96
Koussevitsky, Serge 100-01, 109
Kraeuter, Phyllis 142
Kraft, Arthur 91
Kramer, A. Walter 83, 107-08
Krehbiel, Henry 40-41
Krehl, Stephen 45
Kreymborg, Alfred 129

Labrosa, Mario 96
Lakeman, Miss 125
Lakeside, CT 165
Lancaster, PA 81
Land, John 39
Lang, Benjamin J. 10, 26, 28, 43
Lang, Margaret Ruthven 10, 29, 33, 66-67
Lansing, MI 65
LaSalle String Quartet 102
Latchett, Austin 43
Lavallee, Calira 25

Lawrence, Margorie 127, 144
Lawrence, William, Rev. 67
Leach, William 158
League of American Pen Women = American Pen Women
Lehmann, Lotte 127
Lehner, Jenö 96
Leinsdorf, Eric 163
Leipzig, Germany 76-77
Leksin, Miss 165-66
Lenard, Olive Risley 22
Lenox Society Chorus 36
Lenox String Quartet 94
Lenz, opera singer 144
Lerch, Louise 107-08
Leslie, Grace 121
Lewis, Edward M. 94, 128
Lewis, Mrs. Edward 128
Library of Congress, Washington, DC 94, 103, 116, 118
Lichtenberg, Leopold 11
Limberg, Eugenie 129, 138, 142, 145, 158
Limestone College, Guffney, SC 49
Lincis, Miss 122
Lincoln, NE 88
Lindbergh, Charles 90
Linscott, Mr. 116
Lisbon, Portugal 90
List, Eugene 144
Liszt, Franz 8-10, 12, 21, 23, 30, 53, 62, 96, 169
Ljundberg, Göta 126
Loeffler, Charles Martin 8-9, 42
London, England 33, 36, 50, 133
Longwood, MA 34
Longy School of Music, Cambridge, MA 97
Loring, David W. 31
Los Angeles, CA 43, 79
Los Angeles Symphony Orchestra 79
Lothian, Mr. 34
Louisiana State University, Baton Rouge, LA xi
Louisville, KY 36, 49
Lourdes, France 90
Loveridge, George Y. 7
Lowell, James Russell 21
Lunde, Sigrud 33
Luxembourg 151
Lynes, Frank 33

MacDowell, Edward   23, 33, 41, 62, 84-86, 98, 120-21, 128, 144-46, 170
MacDowell, Marian (Mrs. Edward)   77-78, 84-86, 89, 92, 94, 98-99, 113, 121, 128, 130, 135, 145-46, 148-51, 154-55, 165-67, 170
MacDowell Club   51, 78, 93, 95-96, 101, 111, 115-16, 120, 124, 126, 128, 138, 142, 145, 158
MacDowell Colony   xii, xiii, 84-88, 91, 94, 98, 100-01, 104-05, 113-16, 118, 120, 125-26, 128, 130, 135, 141-42, 145-46, 149, 153-54, 162, 169
Maclennan, Florence = Easton-Maclennan
Maclennan, Francis   74
MacMahan Island, ME   106, 114
Madison Square Garden, New York   122
Madison, WI   44
Major, Amy   44
Malipiero, Gian Francesco   96
Manchester, NY   xi, 89, 119, 122, 139
Manchester Trio   137, 139
Mandell, Alice C.   14
Manhattan String Quartet   127
Manhattan Symphony Orchestra   102
Marble Collegiate Church, New York   141
Marcy, Chester   5
Marcy, Clara Imogene   3-5, 14-15, 19, 37, 67, 71, 101-02, 122
Marcy, Eliza Waterman   37
Marcy, John   3
Marcy, Nathaniel, Captain   3
Marcy, William   3
Marianne Kneisel Quartet   156
Marine Biological Laboratory, Boston, MA   23
Marlett, Earl   163
Marquand, John P.   15, 149
Marriner-Campbell, Mrs.   47
Marseilles, France   90
Marston, George W.   33
Martin, Josephine   64
Martinelli, Giovanni   97, 112, 139
Mascagni, Pietro   96
Masefield, John   99-100
Mason, William   12, 14
Massachusetts Federation of Women's Clubs   62
Massachusetts General Hospital, Boston, MA   15, 97-98
Massenet, Jules   98
Mattoli, Lino   10
Mayer, Jacques   75
Maynor, Dorothy   145
McAllaster, William R.   125, 139
McArthur, Mrs. Mildred   106, 151
McClosky, David Blair   109, 111
McCollin, Frances   167

McFarlane, Frances 137
McGreevy, Gertrude 138
McIntire, Ms. 35
McLeod, of First Baptist Church, Boston 33
Mead, Olive 52, 54
Melchert, Marsha C. 33
Melchior, Lauritz 144, 163
Melrose, MA 57
Mendelssohn, Felix 8, 10, 12, 21, 53, 129, 164
Mendelssohn Glee Club, New York 116
Mendelssohn Hall, New York 45
Menz, Lucius 161
Meter-Halmund 74
Methodist Church, Hillsboro, NH 114
Metropolitan Opera, New York 109, 117, 120, 126, 144, 163
Meyers, Gladys 162
Meynell, Alice 103-04, 106-09, 126
Michigan Madrigal Club, Port Huron 47
Middletown, CT 121
Milan, Italy 54
Miller, Clara Belle Taylor 83, 92, 165
Milligan, Harold Vincent 112, 141
Milstein, Nathan 145
Milton, MA 98
Milwaukee, WI 49, 81
Minneapolis, MN 43, 82
Minneapolis Symphony Orchestra 82
Mischka, Caroline 36
Mitchell, Ernest 116
Mix, Jennie Irene 58-60
Molinari, Bernardino 96
Monday Music Club, East Orange, NJ 116
Montclair, NJ 120
Moody, Anna 106, 113
Moore, Douglas 99, 116, 128, 145, 150
Moore, President of Skidmore College 116
Morgan, Anna 117
Morgan, Maude 36
Morris, Harold 109, 142
Morrison, Abraham 3
Morrison, Claire Felch 139
Morse, Charles H. 10
Morse, Frank 10
Morse, Mrs. Ira M. 35
Moscheles, Ignaz 7
Moszkowski, Moritz 23
Mozart, Wolfgang Amadeus 20, 22-23, 43, 72, 145

Mt. Carmel High School   137
Mt. Vernon Church, Boston   33
Mt. Vernon Methodist Episcopal Church, Washington, DC   112
Mu Phi Epsilon Sorority   95, 111, 118, 137, 154
Mulligan, Charlotte   39
Munger, Clara E.   10, 35-36
Munich, Germany   71-72, 74-75, 77, 97
Munich String Quartet   75
Museum of National History, New York   122
Music Teachers National Association   84, 95, 109, 116, 126
Musical Courier   153-54
Musicians Club, New York   80
Musicians' Orchestra   117

Nadeau, tenor   157
Naples, Italy   90, 96
Nashua, NH   23, 29, 135
National American Sufferage Association   30
National Association of American Composers and Conductors = Society of American
    Composers and Conductors
National Broadcasting Corporation (NBC), New York   115, 144, 157
National Federation of Music Clubs   84, 101
National Opera Association   112
National Opera Club, New York   101, 126, 139
National Symphony Orchestra, Washington, DC   xi, 109, 116, 145, 163
Neuman, Herman   125
Neundorff, Adolf   7
Nevins, Anna   99
Nevins, Marian = Mrs. Edward MacDowell
New Boston, NH   10, 151
New England Conservatory of Music   29, 44, 49, 58, 72, 122
New England Federated Music Clubs   113
New Hampshire Federation of Music Clubs   121
New Hampshire Federation of Women's Clubs   114, 119, 153
New Hampshire Music and Allied Arts Society   119
New Hampshire Music Teacher's Association   23, 29, 84
New Jersey Music Teachers Association   128
New Orleans, LA   xi
New York Civic Orchestra   122
New York Federation of Music Clubs   111
New York Glee Club   122
New York Manuscript Society   32, 34, 36
New York Music Teacher's Association   33
New York Philharmonic   101, 118, 129, 145, 147
New York Piano Teachers Association   118, 146
New York Symphony Society   29-30, 33

Newark, NJ   103, 115, 128
Newberry, MA   3
Newcomb College, New Orleans, LA   xi
Newell, Otis K.   19
Newport, RI   156
Newton, MA   91
Newton Highlands, MA   91, 114
Ney, Elly   103
Nice, France   90
Nikisch, Mr. and Mrs. Arthur   26
Nin-Cummel, Joaquin   145
Norden, Van   62
Nordica, Lillian   32-33, 49, 61-62
Northhampton, MA   151
Northwestern University, Evanston, IL   36
Norton, MA   92, 111
Norton, Rev.   158
Norway   144, 150
Norwood, Robert W.   102, 104-06, 113-15, 153
Notre Dame Cathedral, Paris   91
Novellis, A. de   37
Nungesser and Cole, aviators   90
Nursery for Blind Babies, Boston, MA   54

Ochsner, McCormick, Mrs.   95
Ohe, Adele aus der   72, 74
Old First Presbyterian Church, New York   89
Old South Church, Boston   43, 124
Oldfield, Harriet   143
Olive Mead Quartet   78
Ollendorf, Mrs.   111
Omaha, NE   44
Omaha Indians   88
Orr, Edith   89, 113
Osborne Club, New York   153, 163
Osborne Club, Stamford, CT   137
Ottawa, IL   120
ouija board   101, 129
Oxford, England   119
Oxner, Vera   125, 139
Oyster Bay High School   119-20

Paderewski, Ignaz Jan   78-79, 117-18, 144
Padua, Italy   90
Paeff, Bashka   139, 146-49, 160, 170

Paine, John Knowles   23, 34, 51, 56-57
Paine, Robert Treat   21
Palmengarten, Dresden, Germany   72
Palmer, Miss   165
Palmer, Mrs. Potter   30
Paris, France   49, 54, 88, 90
Parker, Caroline   153, 166
Parker, George J.   33, 54, 57
Parker, Horatio   54, 61, 64, 140, 167
Parker, Horatio, Mrs.   124, 130
Parker, James Cutler Dunn   25
Parker, Jessie   83, 89, 94, 100, 105, 109, 119
Parson, Barbara   137
Parten, Dr.   35
Pasadena, CA   43
Passaic, NJ   124
Paterson, NJ   106, 151
Patros, Greece   90
Pattee, John   3
Patterson, Frances   146
Patterson, Mrs.   112
Paur, Emil   34-35, 37-38, 40-42, 48, 58-60
Paur, Kurt   36
Paur, Mrs. Emil   35-36
Pawling School   137
Pease, Mrs. Marshall   49
Peck, A. P.   7, 10
Pennsylvania College for Women, Pittsburgh   93
Pennsylvania Symphony Orchestra   156
P.E.O. = Philanthropic Education Organization
People's Symphony Orchestra, Boston   92
Peoria, IL   43, 81
Perabo, Ernest   7, 95
Perry, Nora   10
Peterborough, NH   85-86, 92, 94, 98, 105, 109, 113, 121, 128, 135, 142, 150, 154
Petri, Egon   127
Peyser, Ethel   113
Phelps, E. C.   40
Philadelphia, PA   43, 50-51, 80, 83, 126
Philadelphia Opera Company   109
Philadelphia Orchestra   72, 78, 127, 144, 157
Philanthropic Education Organization (P.E.O.)   112, 119, 128, 137-38, 153, 155, 163
Phillips Academy, Exeter, NH   4
Phillips Memorial Gallery, Washington, DC   158, 160
Piano Trio Club, New York   31
Piastro, Michel   127
Pierce, Fannie   91, 97, 105, 114-15, 143

Pierce, Mabel   91, 97, 99, 105, 114-15, 143, 165
Pierce, President Franklin   3, 147
Pierné, Gabriel   107
Pines School, Norton, MA   111
Pittsburgh, PA   58-60, 80, 93
Pittsburgh Orchestra   58-60
Pittsfield, MA   49
Place, William, Jr.   108
Plotnikoff, Eugene   122
Plymouth Church, Minneapolis   43
Polk, President James   3
Pope, John   xi
Port Huron, MI   47
Porter, Frank Addison   33
Porter, Hugh   141
Portland, MA   78
Potter, Harrison   103
Potter Hall   63-64
Powell, John   107
Powell, Maud   31-32, 51
Pratt, Fernanda   80
Presser, Theodore, publisher   104
Prevost, Mr. and Mrs. Fitzhugh   90
Prince, Mrs.   145
Princeton, NJ   80, 125
Princeton University, Princeton, NJ   127
Pro Arte Quartet   111
Professional Women's Club, Boston   92, 103, 118
Prokofiev, Sergei   96, 98
Providence, RI   136-38
Pugno, Raoul   49

Quint, W. D.   49

Rachmaninoff, Sergei   93
Raff, Joseph Joachim   21, 40
Ralston, Marion   94
Ranck, Carty   113
Rapello, Italy   90
Rasely, John   120-21
Raudenbush, George King   156
Readville, MA   98
Regal, Mrs. Elizabeth C.   108
Reger, Max   64
Reiner, Fritz   144

Respighi, Ottorino 96, 112
Rettich, Richard 74
Reynard, Mr. and Mrs. Grant 115
Rheinberger, Josef 12
Rheinfeld, Marianne 74
Ricardo, Garcia 72
Richardson, Nina Maud 99, 151, 155
Richmond, VA 97
Ricker, Katherine M. 47
Riverside, CA 79-80
Riverside Church, New York 112, 124, 141, 162
Roberts, Emma 89
Robinson, Edward Arlington 86, 113, 129-30, 145, 147, 170
Roby, Luther 3
Rochester, NY 49
Rockford, IL 81
Rodin Studio, New York 120
Roerich Museum, New York 101, 103, 115-16, 137-38
Rogers, Clara Kathleen 33
Rolla, Kate 32
Rome, Italy 90, 96-97, 151
Roosevelt, Franklin Delano 149
Roosevelt, Mrs. Franklin Delano 121
Roosevelt, Mrs. Theodore 119-20
Ropartz, Guy 78
Rose, William 156
Rosenstein, Arthur 72
Ross, Hugh 126
Rourke, Agnes 99
Rowe, Mrs. Helen Barker 156
Roxbury, MA 3
Royal Opera, Berlin 73
Royal Opera Company, Munich 72
Rubinoff, Benno 98
Rubinstein, Anton 9-10, 12, 22
Rubinstein Club, New York 43, 112
Ruggles, Carl 162
Rundlett, Rebecca 3
Russell, Lillian 33
Ryan, Agnes 126

Sacco-Vinzetti case 91
St. Bartholomew's Episcopal Church, New York 90, 93-96, 101-02, 106, 111-12, 115, 117-18, 120-21, 123-24, 126, 129-30, 133, 135-36, 138, 140-41, 144-45, 158, 161-62, 164, 166-68
St. Cecilia Auditorium, Grand Rapids, MI 156
St. Francis of Assisi 89

St. George's Episcopal Church, New York 124
St. James, NY 124, 162
St. James' Episcopal Church, Chicago 124
St. John's School, New York 121
St. Louis, MO 81
St. Luigi's Church, Rome, Italy 90
St. Mary the Virgin Church, New York 93
St. Paul's Cathedral, London 133
St. Paul, MN 43, 62, 82
St. Thomas' Church, New York 141
Saint-Saëns, Camille 35, 40, 58-59, 62, 72
Salchi, S. 10
Salle Playel, Paris 49
Salmon, Felix 127
Salt Lake City, UT 80
Salter, friend 162
Samaroff, Olga 62, 72, 150
Samuel, Harold 98
San Diego, CA 80, 123
San Diego Exposition 79-80
San Francisco, CA 31, 43, 47, 61, 78-80, 98
San Francisco Quartet Club 80
Sanby, Herman 79
Sand, George 51
Sanders, Robert 96
Sanromá, Jesús María 98
Sargent, Dr. George P. T. 168
Sawyer, Mrs. Homer E. 33-35, 37, 54
Sayn, Elena de 103, 109, 111, 125, 158-60
Sayn String Quartet 158
Scandinavia 75
Scarboro, NY 153, 155
Scarlatti, Domenico 9-10, 22
Scarsdale, NY 128
Schaefer, Theodore 160
Schelling, Ernest 115, 128
Schiller, J. C. F. von 30
Schirmer, Gustav, Inc. 95, 101
Schlesinger, B. 33
Schmidt, Arthur P., publisher 33, 83, 97-98, 100-01, 117, 125, 141, 153, 163
Schoenberg, Arnold 118
Schofield, Gretchen 36
Schofield, Mrs. William 145
Schola Cantorum, New York 126-27
School, Fritz 43
Schorr, Friedrich 144
Schubert, Franz 53, 117

Schubert Club, Beloit, WI   44
Schumann, Robert   12, 34, 45, 50, 63, 117, 143
Schumann Club, San Francisco   31
Scituate, MA   147
Scott, Martha   149
Sears, Helen   89
Seattle, WA   88
Seidlowa, Miss   93
Sembrich, Marcella   10, 61, 65
Serafin, Tullio   126
Serkin, Rudolph   118
Sessions, Roger   96
Seward, Dr.   166
Sewickley, PA   80
Sgambati, Giovanni   72
Shaffner, Ruth   xiii, 84, 90, 93, 101-07, 109, 111-17, 119-24, 128, 130, 133-35, 137-38, 140-41,
     145, 147, 153, 155, 157-58, 163, 165-67
Shaffner, Tom   166-67
Sharlow, Myrna   78
Sheffield, George   78
Short Hills, NJ   98
Shub, Harry   102
Sigma Alpha Iota Sorority   146
Sill, E. R.   25
Silotti, Alexander   96
Simon, Chalie May   146
Simonson, Norma   160
Skidmore College, Saratoga Springs, NY   116
Smart, Clara   33
Smith, Albert   144
Smith, Carlton Sprague   139
Smith, Chard   99
Smith, Helen Rogers   65
Smith, Mildred   104
Smith, Wilson G.   33
Society for the Publication of American Music   93, 103
Society of American Composers and Conductors   102, 118, 137
Society of American Women Composers   94
Souther, Louise   98-99, 128
Sowerby, Leo   124, 163
Spalding, Albert   129
Spartanburg, NC   93
Speaks, Margaret   140, 157
Spencer, Allen   36
Spencer, Bishop   153, 157
Speyer, Leonora   104, 117
Spiering, Theodore   76, 78

Springfield, MA   31, 62
Stamford, CT   137
Stein, Gertrude   126
Steinert, Morris   45, 91, 96
Steinert Hall, Boston   33, 49-50, 62, 65
Steinertone piano   45, 48
Steinway, Theodore   92
Steinway Hall, New York   94, 111, 118, 139, 146
Steinway pianos   20, 32, 91-92
Stevens, Charles B.   43, 47, 49
Stevens, Henry Bailey   126
Stevens, Nan Bagby   93, 113, 115-16, 160
Stock, Frederick   78-80
Stockholm, Sweden   33, 36
Stockton, GA   80
Stoessel, Albert   98, 102, 107, 117, 123, 128, 142, 165
Stokowski, Leopold   62, 72, 79, 83, 109, 127
Stone, Elizabeth   75
Stone-Barton, Mme.   36
Story, Emma Eames   54
Strauss, Richard   51-53, 64, 98
Stravinsky, Igor   118, 126, 139
Strickland, Billy   163
Stringham, Edward   129, 146
Strong, pianist   139
Strong, E. B.   31
Strong, George Templeton   33
Students' Musical Club, Los Angeles, CA   33
Summit, NJ   117
Surman, John   49
Sutro Sisters (Ottilie and Rose)   88, 94, 101, 139
Swarthout, Gladys   126
Syracuse University, Syracuse, NY   121
Szigeti, Joseph   93

Taylor, Louise   138, 142
Tchaikovsky, Peter Ilyitch   96, 101
Teacher's College, New York   125, 146
Templeton, Alec   144
Terry, Frances   52, 103
Terry, Kenton F.   158
Thalben-Ball, George Thomas   135
Thiede, Alexander   139
Thomas, John Charles   144
Thomas, Theodore   13, 31, 43-44
Thompson, Oscar   101

Thomson, Agnes 33
Thomson, Virgil 126
Thorberg, Kerstin 163
Thornton, NH 3
Thursby, Emma 78
Thursday Morning Club, Boston 49, 64
Tibbett, Lawrence 125-26
Ticknor, Howard M. 22, 34-35, 49-50
Ticknor, Mrs. Howard M. 35
Toledo, OH 98
Tollefsen, Carl 138
Tonieri, Emil 89
Toronto, Ontario 81
Torrence, Miss 93
Torrey, Edith E. 36
Toscanini, Arturo 127
Tours, France 90
Town Hall, New York 78, 116, 145, 150-51, 153-54, 157-58
Trans-Mississippi Exposition, Omaha, NE 44
Traubel, Helen 127
Treble Clef Club, Birmingham, AL 46
Treble Clef Club, Boston 34
Treble Clef Club, Detroit 49
Tremont Temple, Boston 23
Trieste 90
Trinity Church, Denver 61
Trinity Episcopal Church, Boston 19, 25, 89
Tufts University, Medford, MA 63
Tulane University, New Orleans xi, xiii
Turner, Nancy Byrd 89, 99, 104, 113, 118, 135, 146
Tuthill, Bernard 149
Twain, Mark 80

Union Church, Hillsboro 147
United States Marine Band 122
University of Georgia, Athens 160-61
University of New Hampshire, Durham xi, xiii, xiv, 90, 94, 126, 128, 155, 170
University of South Carolina, Columbia 93
University of Washington, Seattle 88
Untermeyer, Jean Starr 170

Van de Wall, Dr. 125
Vaughan Williams, Ralph 115, 140
Venice, Italy 90
Vickers, Harold 100

Vienna, Austria 58
Viennese String Quartet 96
Vinton, Mr. & Mrs. 35

WAAB, Boston 111
WABC, New York 111, 138, 140
WEAF, Manchester, NH 115, 122
WEEI, Boston 103, 125
WHDH, Boston 139
WJZ, New York 93, 111
WMAL, New York 122
WNYC, New York 125, 140, 157
WOR, Newark 103
WPA = Works Project Administration
WQXR, New York 157
WQZR, New York 136
Wagenaar, Bernard 93
Wagner, Judge 89
Wagner, Richard 30, 48, 50, 61, 144, 163, 169
Wagner Club, Chicago 33
Wakefield, MA 103
Walker, Jennie Patrick 26, 28
Walker, Katherine Adams = Katherine Adams
Wallenstein Radio Hour 157
Walton, William 126-27
Ward, Rev. J. 35
Ware, Helen 101
Washington, DC 93-95, 103, 109, 111, 113, 116, 119, 121-22, 124-25, 130, 158-60
Washington, George 51
Washington State University, Pullman, WA 163
Waterman, Amy 5
Watkins, Morris 109, 150
Watter, Dr. 158
Waxman, Professor Samuel M. 147
Weber, Carl Maria von 10
Weinrich, Carl 127
Weirs, Lake Winnipesaukee, NH 23
Wellesley College, Wellesley, MA 10-11, 22, 34-36
West Barnstable, MA 97, 99, 105
West Newton, MA 81
West Yarmouth, MA 106
Westfield, NJ 117
Westminster Abbey, London 133
Westminster Choir School, Princeton, NJ 125
Wetzler, Miss 36

Wharton, Edith   168
Wheeler, Lillian   114
Wheeler, Margrette   114
White, Ernest   91
White, Priscilla   28, 33-37
White Plains, NY   102
Whitefield, NH   114
Whiting, Arthur   19, 93
Whitney, Mrs.   139
Whitney, W. F.   25
Wilder, Thorton   113, 145-47, 149, 164, 170
Willetts, Eliza   154
Williams, David McK.   84, 90, 93-95, 102-04, 106-07, 111-12, 117-18, 121, 123-24, 129-30, 136,
        138, 140-41, 145, 150, 153, 161-64, 168
Williamson, John Finley   125
Williamson, Mary   144
Willkie, Wendell   153
Wilson, Miss   33
Winston-Salem, NC   93
Wittgenstein, Mr.   157
Witzemann, violinist   79
Wolcott, Roger   35
Women's Republican Club   127
Women's Symphony Orchestra, Boston   139, 156
Wommer, John   157
Woodstock, CT   3
Woodworth, Elizabeth   106
Worcester, Rev. Elwood   66-67
Worcester, MA   44, 102, 107-09, 135-36
Works Projects Administration (WPA), Music Project   91, 119, 137-38, 140
Wylie, Elinor   87, 96, 145, 170

Yale University, New Haven, CT   54
Yarmouth, MA   106
Yonkers, NY   137
Ysaÿe, Eugène   36, 49

Zeisler, Fannie Bloomfield   31
Zerrahn, Carl   26, 28
Zethus Orchestra   36

About the Editor

Musicologist John H. Baron received his education at Harvard and Brandeis universities. He has taught at Tulane University—Newcomb College since 1969 and became chairman of the Department of Music there in 1993. His publications include studies of chamber music, baroque music, Spanish vocal music in the 17th century, and the music of New Orleans. Since his forebears have been professionally involved with American music for over a century, he inherited a keen interest in American music and has been a member of the Sonneck Society for American music since its inception. He and Walter Jenkins often discussed many aspects of music so that Baron was in a good position to prepare his late colleague's manuscript for publication.

April 25th 1935

Hotel Syracuse

Syracuse, N.Y.

FAY D. MARENESS, MANAGER

Dear Mr. Jenkins

I brought your letter here, to answer in a possible free moment, as there seemed to be none in New York! I am playing at the University here tonight, so am taking the morning for rest.

Here is a letter to Mrs. MacDowell (enclosed) and I hope that it is not too late for your name to be considered. She is probably at the Hotel Walcott, 31st St. near Fifth Ave. New York by this time, and you could reach her more directly there. Of course Peterborough always reaches her. You know she generally has about 500 applications, beginning to come in early in January, so do not be discouraged if she has already made up the quota which can only be about 50 or 60 for the entire season. I hope very much that you may have the